JESUS THE TEACHER WITHIN

JESUS THE TEACHER WITHIN

Laurence Freeman

A Medio Media Book
CONTINUUM
NEW YORK • LONDON

2000

The Continuum International Publishing Group Inc
370 Lexington Avenue, New York, NY 10017

The Continuum International Publishing Group Ltd
The Tower Building, 11 York Road, London SE1 7NX

Printed in the United States of America

Library of Congress Cataloging-in-Publication Data
Freeman, Laurence.
  Jesus the teacher within / Laurence Freeman.
    p. cm.
  Includes bibliographical references.
  ISBN 0-8264-1223-8
  1. Jesus Christ—Person and offices. I. Title.

BT202 .F695 2000
232—dc21   99-056233

For Rosie

'They are strangers in the world as I am.'
　　　　　　　　　　　　　　　　　　　　　　—Jesus (Jn 17:16)

Contents

Acknowledgements

In 1995 the World Community for Christian Meditation invited me to give the annual John Main Seminar entitled 'On Jesus'. This book took its first shape in those lectures at the University of San Diego. Since then many have helped and encouraged me and I celebrate them for helping me bring the book to its present form. I am particularly grateful for the help and encouragement of Professor Gerald O'Collins SJ for focusing me and for invaluable advice. Professor Robert Kiely, Fr. Brian Johnstone CSsR, Dr. Robin Daniels, Carla Cooper, Giovanni Felicioni, Doreen Romandini, Clem Sauvé, Teresa da Bertodano, Shirley du Boulay, John Little, and Dominic Schofield gave me the insights of their readings through several revisions. Polly and Mark Schofield helped generously with the notes and Susan Spence with the proofs. Dr Balfour Mount gave a final and most valuable review of the manuscript. My monastic community of the Monastery of Christ the King, Cockfosters, has enriched this book with its friendship, tolerance of my ways and much personal support. Meditators in the World Community have everywhere been my teachers and the love emerging from the silence of meditation with them has sustained and inspired this book on many occasions. His Holiness the Dalai Lama has, through the extraordinary dialogue of the past few years, asked illuminating questions that were more filled with consciousness of Jesus than answers often are. His love of truth and openness to what is different has often returned me to the gospels with new insight. To Doreen and those others who have died and also for those with whom the divisions of life have occurred I hope this book can be a sign both of gratitude and the healing of Christ that is unlimited by time or space.

Foreword

More than forty years ago, as a young man, I left my homeland as a refugee. Since then the sorrows that have befallen the Tibetan people have mounted up and the difficulties that I have faced as their leader have not diminished. However, there are often unexpected rewards to be found even in the darkest of times. And for me personally, one of the most fulfilling experiences of my life in exile has been the opportunity to make friends all over the world. From the many religious practitioners I have befriended I have learned the truth that it is not only the goal of all religions to help us to become better human beings, but that they are indeed capable of doing so. Moreover, it is my experience that when we overcome our doubts and suspicions and approach each other with respect, there is much that we can learn from one another.

However, I do not advocate attempting to unify our various traditions. I firmly believe that we need different religious traditions, because a single tradition cannot satisfy the needs and mental dispositions of the great variety of human beings. At the same time I do not believe that people should lightly change the religion of their birth. What we need to do is to develop an understanding of the differences in our various traditions and to recognise the value and potential of each of them. Indeed, I believe that one of the benefits of achieving an inner transformation in our own spiritual lives is that our experience helps us appreciate the value of other traditions, rather than the exclusive preciousness of our own.

Although I am no expert on Christian doctrine and its scriptures, my meetings with Christian brothers and sisters have reinforced my conviction that many common strands can be found in our spiritual endeavours. I am therefore honoured to have been invited by my good friend Father Laurence Freeman to contribute a few words of introduction to this book.

As a Buddhist monk I am filled with admiration for the deep Christian sense of community and social responsibility. It is an inspiration to see practical expression of this in the dedicated work that so many Christian monks and nuns perform in the fields of education, health care, alleviation of poverty and so forth. This aspect of compassion in action is something I continue to encourage within the monastic bodies of Tibetan Buddhism.

Meanwhile, many of my Christian brothers and sisters, led notably by such figures as Thomas Merton and John Main, have taken up the practice of meditation in their daily lives. This is very important, for I believe that if we combine prayer, meditation and contemplation in our daily practice, it will be very effective. Focussing less on building great temples to religion on the outside, in favour of constructing temples to goodness within ourselves, is true to the real intention of spiritual practice, which is to help individuals bring about inner transformation. If we meditate, it is possible for the undisciplined, scattered mind to become disciplined, focused and matured with insight.

Some Christians for whom the practice seems unfamiliar might ask how meditation can help us in our spiritual pursuit. The spiritual traditions that have evolved in India, for example, where meditation is accorded great respect, employ one method of focussing meditation to bring calm and focus to the mind and another, more analytical method, to improve understanding. Christian teachings lay great emphasis on love. In meditating on this you might take the example of Jesus Christ himself and reflect on how he conducted his life, how he worked to help other people, how he lived a life of compassion, generosity, patience, tolerance and forgiveness. Once your contemplation gives rise to a certain depth of understanding, you can focus your mind on it in a calm and concentrated way. This is how you develop deep familiarity with the quality of the object you have chosen.

Meditation, therefore, is a means to develop positive qualities that I believe come naturally to us. Christian teachings speak of all human beings sharing the same divine nature. I believe that our basic human nature is intrinsically disposed towards compassion, affection and creativity. Our true nature is gentle, not aggressive or violent, and it is this fundamental nature and its qualities that are revealed or awakened through meditation.

The Christian tradition has been a source of inspiration and solace to millions of people throughout the world for two thousand years. An important factor here, as in Buddhism, is the way the lives of the founding masters, Jesus Christ and Buddha, exemplify and embody the teachings they gave. The story of Jesus' life repeatedly shows his profound love and compassion, his generosity, patience and forgiveness, the very qualities that he encourages his followers to cultivate. Perhaps just as important, we can see from his example too that spiritual growth requires dedication and commitment, an ability to withstand hardship and to hold to your principles.

Father Laurence has written this book, *Jesus the Teacher Within* in full Christian faith, explaining from his own experience how relating to Jesus Christ and his teaching, combined with meditation, can illuminate the spiritual life. He has given deep thought to all these issues, as well as being an active participant in several interreligious meetings such as the Good Heart and Way of Peace seminars. I am particularly grateful to him for the initiative he has taken in this direction, because there is enormous potential for mutual enrichment in the dialogue between Buddhist and Christian traditions, especially with regard to ethics and spiritual practice, such as the practices of love, compassion, meditation and patience. I feel sure that readers of this book, especially those who seek personal transformation and inner peace, will find much here to ponder and apply in their own daily practice.

The Dalai Lama
June 15, 2000

Introduction

Faith and Experience. Faith *or* Experience? For many today the tension between the two has led to an unhappy polarisation of their spiritual journey. There is a great interest in spirituality but also great confusion about what it means. Polls show that increasingly we prefer to call ourselves spiritual rather than religious. Is this because spiritual means experience and religious means faith? And so we feel that as experience has the higher claim to be authentic, it is better to be spiritual than religious.

There is a lot to support this point of view. Firstly, the founders of the major religions do not seem to have thought of themselves as that, although they were all both deeply religious and spiritual. Secondly, religious leaders today, with some notable exceptions such as the Pope and the Dalai Lama, seem unable to inspire. And thirdly, the perennial tendency of organised religions to merge entirely with a culture and to fight with others is singularly unedifying in a world where globalisation and tolerance are valued so highly.

The problem is that faith and experience cannot be polarised so easily. Faith means more than belief, the dogma or tenets of religious systems. Experience means more than the good or bad vibes I get when I do this or that: it means the lifelong journey of becoming fully who we *can* be, who we *really* are. And religion is not so easily dispensed with either. We cannot be truly spiritual without encountering others on the same path and relating, with them, to those who went before us. Tradition is also a form both of faith and experience.

Jesus is an indispensable force in the achievement of any authentic spirituality. Even though most people have problems with the church—as do most church-goers themselves—the person of Jesus is one of the constant beacons guiding humanity beyond egotism and the violence of despair towards the higher goals it continuously sets for itself of kindness and serenity. As East and West meet and explore each other's spiritual heritages in a friendship new to human culture, we are all encouraged to requestion the essential meaning, purpose and identity of our religious traditions. Perhaps this will help ease the conflict in people's minds between faith and experience as we rediscover the essential unity and simplicity at the heart of our founders' teachings.

For Christians the requestioning of their tradition has an obvious starting-point. It is the central question of the gospel around which the identity of a Christian disciple pivots: Jesus' own question, 'Who do you say I am?' This book is really a play of variations on that theme. It is a *lectio*, a spiritual reading, of this question before some of the big issues of religious understanding: the historical reality of Jesus, the experiential and faith-meaning of reading the scriptures, personal conversion and naming one's religious identity, the inner journey. And, running through it all, is the universal understanding that we cannot know anything, let alone God, without knowing ourselves.

This question I would suggest, is important not only for Christians. Those who follow another tradition but have their roots in Christianity can often carry negative baggage, misunderstanding and even guilt which this question can relieve them of. The response to Jesus' question by a sincere practitioner of another religion, as the Dalai Lama's response shows, can be highly illuminating for all, as well as helping to develop the dialogue that is so essential to the third millennium. For many Christians, too, this is a question they have never really listened to seriously or taken personally. Doing so will have a profound effect on their self-understanding as well as their sense of who *he* is. It awakens us to the need for silence and attention as the prerequisites for all listening. And it makes us appreciate better the noble attempts of the past—sometimes called orthodoxy—to respond to a question that can only be fully answered in a faith-filled experience of the Spirit.

However objective one tries to be about it, thinking of Jesus is inescapably personal. I should therefore, by way of example, express something of the personal experience of faith that has led to my writing this book. The first may seem more 'experiential', a one-off event; the other more of a process of faith, a long twisting journey. The point, it seems to me, is that they both express the same personal reality of unfathomed richness called Jesus.

Shortly after I became a monk, I was agonising over what I was doing with my life, who on earth or in heaven Jesus was or is, whether the church and all its baggage was only a massive collective self-deception, whether Christian faith gave sufficient backing to my odd and perplexing decision to be a monk. My questioning was not curious but desperate. I was not depressed but I was in great pain. Whether I was wasting or investing my life was what was at stake.

One evening as I was reading the gospel and had put the book down to think and pray I was suddenly filled with the only experience I could to that point really call *praise*. Suddenly and for no obvious reason I felt myself caught up in an orgy of praise and *saw* that it was both directed to but also *through* the person of Jesus. I knew that this was happening at the heart of the world—or at least of everything I was capable of understanding as the world. It was an ecstatic praise not a formal one, more like a rock concert than a church service. Yet its ecstasy was of the most deeply satisfying order and harmony imaginable. The words of the New Testament to him be all glory, honour and praise which had seemed exceedingly grey to me before now expressed a participation in the risen Christ 'in glory' in which every sentient being shares. Although for me Jesus was the hinge on which all this swung, the overwhelming conviction was that everyone and everything was involved. A great party is somewhere in full swing which no one is turned away from and where the fizz will never run out. Finding where this is happening and how to get there as soon as possible seems a good way of spending one's life. This individual, to me 'memorable', experience has passed away in time. I don't think of it much now. But I sense—maybe this is an aspect of faith—that what it exposed is always present, undiminished, and even always deepening.

A second, different kind of experience of Jesus came through a third person. My teacher John Main was a powerful personality. He never used his power to control others' beliefs or behaviour. But to be near him was certainly to be influenced by what he believed and how he acted. When I first started to train with him my aim was not specifically to know better who Jesus was. That might have been a long-term goal but in the short term I had to begin to iron out my own problems and grow in self-knowledge. Gradually I came to see how deeply central Jesus was to John Main, not just as a religious symbol. I came to see how Jesus lived in John Main's own person as a living presence, in a personal relationship that was hidden (mysterious) but not secretive. Perhaps this is why to hear John Main read and comment on the scriptures aloud so refined one's faith. The words rang with the authority of his own experience. He was not always talking to or thinking about Jesus of course. For some religious people

John Main was in fact a little too irreverent and worldly. But, from time to time, I would glimpse with awe the depth, intimacy and reality of his faith-filled experience. These insights accumulated and focussed my attention over these formative years. Perhaps this is essentially how all faith is transmitted. I did not at first know what to make of it. I did not seem to feel it experientially myself. But I was not sure. While I was wondering what to do I put the subject of how real Jesus is on hold.

John Main died at fifty-six. The future of his work of teaching Christian meditation, through the small community he had formed, seemed highly precarious. I was at a loss to know what to do except to continue meditating. I was prepared to see everything he had worked for collapse in ruins. What in fact happened reflected the Resurrection experience of the early Christians. The expansion of the meditation community over the following years seemed like a Pentecostal event, the burst of new life in the primitive church. It was often very turbulent too, but palpably a work beyond the power of the individuals concerned. This is not to say that the development of the meditation community was the creation of a new church. In fact the reverse was true. It was rather about the renewal of the existing church. I came to see that after every death there is resurrection. Within every resurrection there is something universal. Individual experience is part of a greater reality. So, the growth of a world-wide community of meditators became for me another seeing and feeling of the elusive but inescapable mystery of Jesus. It was not restricted to particular *experiences* but was more like the *unfolding* of a greater single experience. It was personal but in a sense that exposed the illusion of the individual as an isolated, autonomous existence. It grew partly from that relationship with Jesus that I had felt and in some way shared in with John Main.

Over the years the growth of the work he left behind has transformed my sense of the relationship between the living and the dead. For anyone interested in wondering who Jesus is, this question of our relationship with the dead is an important bridge to cross. The fledgeling Christian meditation community became a way to understand Jesus' promise to his heartbroken disciples that his death did not mean he was abandoning them as they first felt. He would be 'with them till the end of time'. I began also to understand that what enriches the heart of a person is not exclusive. It can and should be shared.

Through others who shared their spiritual journey with me, including their questions, doubts, insights and fidelity, there came the incomparable gift of feeling the life of Jesus working in them, guiding and teaching them with compassionate personal precision. Usually it has been through the lives of others, rather than by focussing on my own experience, that I have seen the truth that he never leaves us.

Human beings will never cease telling stories. Our lives are understood when we narrate them. Similarly we first meet the question of Jesus through the stories we call the gospels. I am grateful for having grown up with them: the wonder of these stories is precisely that they speak to the child and the man. Coming to love them prevented the dogmatic approach to faith from becoming too dry. The Jesus in the stories always seemed more alive than the catechism. This book then is simply another way of telling an old story. It is one that belongs to humanity and so becomes fresher with every telling. The story's effect on us, not an interpretation we are told to believe, constitutes its deepest meaning. But the story is now also embedded in a tradition of its own making.

In writing this book I found it helpful to refer to a small but highly charged element of my personal history: a small island in Bantry Bay, on the south-west coast of Ireland, where my foremothers came from. The relevance of this to my attempt to understand Jesus in the light of contemporary spirituality and its problem with faith and experience will, I hope, become clear. I hope it makes the book more readable. It should clarify the subtle relationship between imagination and reality, story and truth, past and present.

Mummy, what was Bere Island really like? My questions about it brought it alive and my mother and aunts (my uncles rarely got a word in) had plenty of answers. There were multiple answers to my question and they were nourished by memories kept alive by the art of retelling them. My questions about Jesus seldom met with the same depth and liveliness. It was not in catechisms but in people who seemed to me to genuinely know Jesus that I felt my questions about him could be answered. Gradually I learned to listen to his question for myself.

Reality, like the meaning of good stories, never stops expanding. No answer is final. This itself spells the pain of loss as a condition for growth. When I eventually went to Bere Island I had to disown the fairy-tale image I had formed earlier. There were family stories I heard later which undermined some of the prettier versions I had been given as a child. But in visiting it as an adult the enticing, magical beauty of Bere Island—like faith itself—has not been lost but developed. In a strangely similar way, through all of my life the mystery of Jesus continues its silent expansion.

The Key Question

*T*he Lost Continent of Atlantis or Shangri-La, Treasure Island or the world of Sherlock Holmes, were not more magical to my childhood than Bere Island in Bantry Bay in the County of Cork. I had not much sense of its geography or of the life really lived there but it burned as one of the most luminous centres of my imagination.

My mother was born on the West End of Bere Island in 1916. She left for England at the age of eighteen, married an Englishman and did not return to her place of birth for half a century when I took her back shortly before her death. Yet the relatively small proportion of her life that she and her ten brothers and sisters lived on Bere Island had an enormous and enduring influence. It coloured their imaginations and shaped their characters. It was the womb, or cauldron, of the myths, legends, histories and symbols which helped them, and later their children, articulate the meaning of their lives. I was proud to learn I was related to the kings of Ireland until I later discovered how many kings there were. The stories and legends of the island, of Irish history and particularly of the O'Sullivan Bere clan enlivened our family gatherings on five continents.

Personally, I constructed a wonderful fantasy about Bere Island and about Ireland in general as I grew up in London. It became a personal myth that did not need facts or even much sense of history. I longed to go there and at the age of eleven made a disastrous visit. My first disillusionment was to see electric light on the streets of Dublin as the plane landed. I had expected gaslight and horse-drawn carriages. The problem with Bere Island, when I got there a few days later, was different. It was too primitive and I felt a very self-conscious and adolescent Englishman.

Years later, in my thirties and as a monk, I was drawn back there again for periods of prayer and solitude. Its meaning had changed for me. Seeing Bere Island more clearly was not easy with so many layers of cultural myth and personal fantasy to clear away. But asking what Bere Island was for me helped me in the long hard work of self-knowledge. Valuing the power of my roots there, but learning to grow up in my relation to it and to shed my fantasies and false expectations changed me too.

⟨○•○•○⟩

'And you, who do *you* say I am?'[1]

Who *is* he? This simple, timeless question rolls down the centuries. The answer is simple, too, but not easy. If we choose to listen and to respond to this question of Jesus, the way we live, think and feel is transformed. The transformation happens because the question brings us to self-knowledge and self-knowledge changes us. We can answer such a question only when *we* have been simplified by long and deep listening.

Every culture has its own images of Jesus and so no response can ever be the final answer. In a fourth-century Roman villa in Dorset there is a beautiful mosaic showing what seems at first glance to be a typical portrait of the young god Apollo. When you look closer you notice the chi-ro Christian symbol[2] which identifies it as one of the earliest pictures of Jesus. For many British empire-builders of the nineteenth-century God, and therefore His Son, were quintessentially British. Baptism and British citizenship were closely related. In 1988 the American Senate was debating a proposal to spend more money on teaching foreign languages in state schools. A senator opposed it. The whole world was learning English now, he said, so why should Americans waste time learning other languages? To clinch his case he concluded, 'If English was good enough for Jesus Christ, he said, it's good enough for me.'[3] Our thinking about Jesus, the way we respond to his question, is culturally conditioned.

We can only *imagine* Jesus with the means provided by our cultural and personal imagination. Most of us are not scholars with in depth knowledge of the cultural norms of the ancient Middle East two millennia ago. And even if we were, we would still be constricted by our personal and cultural point of view. Once we have pictured Jesus in our imagination, it is tempting to enrol him in support of our opinions and prejudices. The Jesus Christ we call to life in our imagination today, in our post-Christian and post-modern world, is a very different reality from the Galilean Jew of humble origins who was born when the emperor Augustus ruled in Rome and who was crucified by order of Pontius Pilate on a small hill near an abandoned quarry outside

[1] Mt 16:15.
[2] The Greek letters X (chi) and P (rho) are the first two of the word *Christos*. Superimposed, they form a monogram which was a widespread symbol in early Christian art.
[3] Quoted in the *Guardian*, 30 April 1988.

the walls of Jerusalem. Innumerable images through the history of Christianity, the world's largest and materially most successful religion, have been developed to describe who Jesus is and what he means.[4] Because of the distance between the historical and the imagined Jesus, Christians often seem more concerned about promoting *their* Jesus in support of their moral or social opinions than in discovering who he really is.

Who he really is is far more than who he historically was.

⟨◦⟩◦⟨◦⟩

According to the author of the Letter to the Hebrews, Jesus Christ is the same yesterday, today and tomorrow.[5]

How can this timeless identity be described? From the gospels it is clear that Jesus avoided titles that defined himself too narrowly. When he called himself *Son of Man* he was sometimes saying only 'I, a man' as when he remarked that the 'Son of Man has nowhere to lay his head.'[6] But even this single title has a wide range of meanings: from a circumlocution for the first person pronoun to the One who will come in glory to judge all people. On other occasions, the 'Son of Man' is associated with the authority that bestows forgiveness of sin and power over the sabbath.[7] This simple title sounds many chords. It evokes the figure of the prophet of Ezechiel, the fragile humanity of all the prophets and the vision of Daniel where one like a (or the) Son of Man appeared as a figure in celestial glory. In the passion and resurrection predictions in Mark's gospel (Chapters eight-ten) this ancient title is used to show just how directly and compassionately Jesus relates to his fellow human beings. It also explains why he suffered the prophet's fate. But neither 'Son of Man' nor the many other titles by which Jesus has been known can adequately express the response that his simple question invites.

Jesus clearly seems to have wanted people to think about who he was: not merely in received biblical or theological terms but in terms of their personal relationship to him. To ask who Jesus is implies who is he for me, to me, in relation to me? This is true, of course, of all human relationships. How else can *I* say who *you* are except in relation

---

[4] See Jaroslav Pelikan, *Jesus Through the Centuries: His Place in History and Culture.*
[5] Heb 13:8.
[6] Mt 8:20.
[7] Gerald O'Collins, *Christology: A Biblical, Historical and Systematic Study of Jesus Christ*, p. 62.

to me? Who am I in your eyes except in relation to you and who you see yourself to be?

When Jesus says he is the Son of Man he is stressing the simply but profoundly human way that he relates to us and we to him. This one expression, drawn from the idiom of his time and region, also shows how anyone listening to his question must first see him in his cultural context if we are to read the gospels intelligently. Christians, too, need this informed intelligence for their faith to grow. Their understanding of Jesus leads them to a deeper understanding of God precisely because their relationship to Jesus is grounded in his humanness. To emphasise the human nature of this relationship is not to say it is mundane or superficial. It leads to an extraordinary discovery of the full meaning of humanness. One consequence of this is that when we ask who he is we will always be led to ask who we are as well. It is always a specific person who knows Jesus. He can no more be reduced to an abstract definition than any human being. It is primarily as a human being that Jesus wants to be known by other human beings.

This is how Jesus puts the question in the gospel of Luke:

> One day when he was praying alone in the presence of his disciples, he asked them, 'Who do the people say I am?' They answered, 'Some say John the Baptist, others Elijah, others that one of the prophets has come back to life. And you, he said, 'who do you say I am?' Peter answered, 'God's Messiah'.[8]

Before leaping in with an answer, as Peter did, using a term charged with meaning for him, we might wish to stay silent a moment. In that silence we could reflect on the nature—and the power—of the question Jesus poses, just as a question. We should make sure we have truly heard the question before trying to get the answer right.

·◇··◇··◇·

Important questions create silence.

Early in his first book on meditation, *Word into Silence*, John Main[9] stresses the importance of the right question rather than the right

---

[8] Lk 9:18.

[9] John Main (1926-1982) was a Benedictine monk whose rediscovery and description of the Christian practice of meditation from the tradition of the early church has led to the formation of a world-wide community of Christian lay contemplatives.

answer. Get the question right before getting confused or intoxicated by the variety of answers. First of all, to hear the question demands that we pause, pay attention and repeat the question. John Main uses the myth of the Fisher King in the Arthurian cycle of stories to describe the power of a question to transform the world.[10]

Parsifal, a knight of the Round Table, meets Anfortas, the Fisher King, who has been wounded by a lance through both thighs. The king is restricted to lying down and fishing from the bank of a river. Around him his kingdom languishes, a wasteland of freezing mists. On his first meeting with the Fisher King, during which he actually sees the Holy Grail, Parsifal does not ask any question of the king. This is a mistake whose impact he soon experiences. His failure to ask a question threatens the very existence of the Round Table, the symbol of global order. Realizing his sin of omission, Parsifal swears never to spend more than two nights in the same place until he has found his way back to the King and discovered the meaning of the Grail.

After five gruelling years he finds Anfortas's castle again. Going straight up to the king, who is still lying prone with pain, Parsifal poses his question: 'Who serves the Grail?' Immediately the Grail appears before them. Parsifal falls to his knees and prays that the king's suffering may be ended. Then he turns again to Anfortas and puts his second question, 'What ails you?' Instantly Anfortas rises healed. With the king's newfound wholeness, the whole land is restored to life and fertility. Trees flower; streams flow; animals breed. Parsifal had simply asked his *questions*: one about the meaning of life, the other conveying compassion. The story is not preoccupied with the right answers to these questions but simply the caring, mindful way in which they are asked. Questions that can work such wonders just by being sincerely asked are redemptive questions. They must be heard and attended to. Then they change and renew the world.

By retelling this myth John Main addresses the dilemma of a Western culture which has for so many people today become a disabling and barren wasteland: a polluted environment and increasingly unstable ecological system, a sense of psychological isolation and social alienation in urban life, chronic levels of anxiety and increasingly dysfunctional families, shamefully widening gaps between rich and poor, addictive lifestyles and demeaning entertainment, unsupported institutions of democracy and manipulative media, a sense of powerless-

[10] John Main, *Word into Silence*, p. 25.

ness and abandonment among the young, confusion between personal and social morality, the loss of religious authority and the dangers of shallow syncretism. The malaise of the modern soul can be redemptively touched by those timeless myths that remind us of the eternal questions. These are the questions we must return to, not with easy answers but with new reverence. We have reached the point, John Main believes, where we do not need more answers, instant diagnoses and solutions. We need to relearn how to listen, humbly and profoundly, to the redemptive questions.

⋰⟡⋰⟡⋰⟡⋰

This does not imply that redemptive questions are in themselves magic solutions. They initiate a process of redemption. This means a conscious process of healing and of liberation from all that blocks joy, compassion and creativity. They liberate us, for example, from the grip of illusion and prejudice, from obsessiveness and fanaticism, from the fear of strangers and the prison of hatred. A redemptive question is not like other mundane questions. It does not expect an ordinary, rational, correct answer. Instead, it opens up a deeper level for experiencing the truth. The well-timed question in psychotherapy can cut the psychological chains of many years—*and why do you think you said that?* Or simply, *what does that mean to you?* Such open questions also operate at the root of the spiritual quest and trigger definitive awakenings.

Unlike answers, questions attract and hold our attention. They are irresistible, like a half-open door. Answers, especially wrapped in dogmatic certainty or claiming to be right in this form for all time, soon come either to bore or oppress us. Even the best answers can be as unwelcoming as a door banged in our face when they exclude alternative responses. Rather than giving answers and making rules Jesus called people to experiential knowledge. By asking questions or telling stories he invited his hearers to a personal discovery of truth, a redemptive recognition of reality. Throughout the gospels it is his questions which magnetize and capture our attention. Often they also deftly turn the attacks of his hostile critics back on themselves.[11] It is by questions that he leads his disciples into a deeper understanding

---

[11] E.g., Lk 10:36; 15:4; 20:16; 7:42; Mt 18:12, 21:2.

of who we are and who he is. These are the inseparable twin insights of his gift to humanity.[12]

Often, however, answers can be fatally attractive. They make us feel we can bottle the truth in a slogan, a dogmatic definition or scientific formula. 'How many floors does the Empire State Building have?' has an, easy, once-for-all answer. To deeper questions than this our responses require continuous and deep listening. Philosophy makes no progress but keeps returning to the basic questions asked by the first thinkers. This does not mean that truth is merely a subjective judgement or that there are no simple truths about right and wrong (do not kill, do not tell lies, help the poor). It means that the ways we formulate responses to these questions are constantly changing. Cardinal Newman (1801-90), one of the greatest of Christian theologians, wrote *The Development of Christian Doctrine* to show that one of the tests of a true answer is precisely that its way of expression evolves over time.

When we stop questioning we die. We only stop asking questions when we have despaired of life or when delusion or pride have mastered us. All the same, we hardly ever give up dreaming that a single definitive formula could solve all life's problems. The temptation is very strong to cheat on the challenge of the mystery of life by reducing it to the status of a problem. So, people go on demanding absolute *answers* even to the redemptive questions. It is precisely these kinds of questions, though, that frustrate the ego's attempt to control the mystery. The right questions constantly refresh our awareness that life is not fundamentally a secular problem but a sacred mystery. Mysteries are not solved. They are entered upon and they embrace us. Responding to Jesus' question about himself and us involves not a discussion but a way of life. His disciples were first called 'followers of the way'.

Every spiritual tradition treasures the power of the question. In Zen practice a *koan* is a question thrown to the rational mind which arrests the ego's attempt to control reality. Like a key the koan opens consciousness beyond reason to truth as unfiltered experience, pure knowing. Receiving the koan from the teacher, the student's rational mind may recoil in anger and frustration as it futilely tries one clever solution after another. And the ego's need for control appears to be endless, even for some would-be Zen practitioners. In a bookshop I

---

[12] Mt 21:23; Jn 1:38.

once saw a paperback enticingly called *A Hundred Zen Koans—and their Answers!*

Answers are most dangerous when we egotistically fight to defend them against a broader vision of the truth. Visiting Bere Island in my thirties made me rework some of the answers I had received as a child to questions about my family history. This involved me in both emotional and intellectual change. Ideologically or theologically we can also cling to familiar answers until they seem to be the *only* answers. Then they can be used to justify the condemnation and rejection of others. Even the most tolerant people cling tenaciously to their views. Listen in to any conversation and you see how quickly people defend their own answers by attacking others. Then, hopefully, we recognise how we are no different! Set answers breed conflict and prejudice. Wisdom and tolerance are found by listening to the important questions, keeping them open, pausing in silence to listen again and again.

Over the past two thousand years there has been no lack of answers to that searching question which Jesus put to his close disciples one day in the village of Bethsaida: 'Who do you say I am?' Peter, the impetuous leader of the disciples was characteristically quick to reply. It is the first recorded answer to a question around which two millennia of Christian life has formed. It was brief: 'God's Messiah', he answered. Many church councils subsequently wrestled with the right way of expressing a longer response. In AD 381 the Nicene Creed, as expanded at the First Council of Constantinople, clarified the Christian perception of the divine identity of Jesus. This is the grounding insight of faith embedded in the Creed most universally recited by Sunday congregations around the world to this day. Bathed in biblical language the Nicene Creed can be used as a beautiful meditation on the mystery of who Jesus is in relation to biblical revelation:

> We believe in one God, the Father, the Almighty, maker of heaven and earth, of all that is, seen and unseen. We believe in one Lord, Jesus Christ, the only Son of God, eternal begotten of the Father, God from God, Light from Light, true God from true God, begotten not made, of one being with the Father. Through him all things were made. For us and for our salvation he came down from heaven: by the power of the Holy Spirit he became incarnate from the Virgin Mary, and was made man. For our sake he was crucified under Pontius Pilate; he suffered death and was buried. On the third day he rose again in accordance with the scriptures; he ascended into heaven and is seated at the right hand of the

Father. He will come again in glory to judge the living and the dead, and his Kingdom will have no end. We believe in the Holy Spirit, the Lord, the Giver of Life, who proceeds from the Father and the Son. With the Father and the Son he is worshipped and glorified. He has spoken through the prophets. We believe in one holy, catholic and apostolic church. We acknowledge one baptism for the forgiveness of sins. We look for the resurrection of the dead, and the life of the world to come. Amen

What does this mean and how do we experience its meaning? It can be read and pondered sitting in a library but a quite new dimension of meaning is discovered when this creed is sung by a community of worshippers at the Eucharist. The power of its meaning is then understood to be more than cerebral. It is felt to be reaching deep into the intelligence of the heart.

There have been many other attempts to answer the question of Jesus. In AD 451 the Council of Chalcedon,[13] in over three hundred carefully technical words, defined *its* answer through the dogma of the two natures in the one (divine) person of Jesus: two unseparated but not confused natures. The seminal Councils of Nicea and Chalcedon, and the subsequent centuries of Christological debate have reverently, and sometimes irreverently, attempted to settle the question of who we say Jesus is once and for all. Often in the heat of polemic the debators have forgotten the essentially personal tone and the dimension of mutuality in the actual question Jesus asked. Not just 'who am I?' but 'who do *you* say?'

In response to Peter's answer Jesus 'gave them strict orders not to tell this to anyone.' He did not reject Peter's confession of faith. His reason for strictly instructing them to keep silent becomes clear in what follows immediately in the next section of the gospel. Jesus links his question to the personal cost of discipleship. The cost is nothing less than everything: to leave self behind and to imitate the self-transcendence of his Cross and Resurrection. By binding his disciples to silence about the answer to his question he was doing what he did when he ordered them not to publicise his miracles. His messiah-ship, like his powers, could easily divert people from the real challenge he was presenting. Everything else was a side-show beside the central

[13] In its early history the thought and theology of Christianity was debated at formal gatherings of bishops and theologians from the global church. These great Councils formed what came to be Christian orthodoxy.

challenge of listening to his question with a depth of attention that would awaken self-knowledge. His question summons a response from a silent depth within the heart itself.

Silence harmonizes the many different answers that are possible and will test their authenticity. We can only validly say who he is when we know who we are. Silence is the source of both insight and tolerance. For example, in Matthew's account of the scene Peter's answer is more elaborate and is commended by Jesus. But the same injunction to silence follows:

> Simon Peter answered: 'You are the Messiah, the Son of the living God' Then Jesus said: 'Simon son of Jonah, you are favoured indeed! You did not learn that from mortal man; it was revealed to you by my heavenly Father. And I say this to you: You are Peter, the Rock; and on this rock I will build my church, and the powers of death shall never conquer it.' He then gave his disciples strict orders not to tell anyone that he was the Messiah.[14]

Some scholars think that Jesus' response to Peter's answer suggests a later addition to an original text or story. For his readership Matthew wanted to emphasise Peter's preeminence among the apostles. Luke's version does not mean we should never give a thoughtfully worded answer to the question. Matthew's account does not say there is only one possible formula. These differences between the two gospels illustrate how all the gospels must be read, not that they are contradicting each other. Matthew and Luke both show Jesus emphasising silence. He did not seem to believe that his mission would be helped by his being popularly acclaimed as the 'messiah'. The same injunction to silence is found in the 'secrecy motif' of Mark's gospel, the earliest of the four gospels, concerning miracles. Mark also reports Peter's response but without Jesus' comment.

The identity of Jesus can be validly expressed in diverse and even divergent ways. The most eloquent and universal expressions are at home in silence. The main purpose of this book is to stress the often neglected value of silence in responding to the question of Jesus that, more than any other question, defines our relationship to him. It is the indefinable silence at the heart of the mystery of Jesus which ultimately communicates his true identity to those who encounter it. And it is a universal identity. He belongs to the Jewish tradition mes-

---

[14]Mt 16:13-20.

sianically. But he has come to belong no less to the rest of humanity. Every religious tradition will employ its own terms to describe him. If there is a unity in all these responses it will not be linguistic or theological but a mystical unity beyond words, concepts and images. We know the highest truth by love not thought: the Christian mystical tradition, together with its sister traditions, is sure of this. The silence of love, not logic, is the sharing of one's self-knowledge with another.

Jesus' question welled up from the silence of his own self-knowledge. He posed it while he was 'praying alone in the presence of his disciples'. This context of prayer is all-important for understanding his question. It is the context of discipleship and spiritual awakening: community, friendship and shared consciousness. Let us look at what this context of prayer, in which the defining question of Christian identity is first raised, means for us today. By understanding prayer we learn how to read the gospels, the essential texts of Christian faith. We also learn what discipleship means and how to see prayer as a journey of the soul into the boundlessness of God.

◦◦◦

Who do you say I am? The answer *is* to listen.

Jesus is not there in history just to be looked at, examined, and judged. He is not here only to be observed, to be seen with the eyes of the body or the mind. He is to be *known* in relationship—known with the eye of the heart. When he is seen just as an object of scholarship or historical analysis, the perceptive faculty of faith is lost. Faith is the bonding-power of all relationships because it allows inter-subjective knowledge to develop. It disintegrates and degenerates into scepticism as soon as the person we relate to becomes an object. When we coldly objectify Jesus we miss our appointment with him. His power as spiritual teacher, liberator, healer and redeemer, the same today, yesterday and tomorrow, passes us by. *He could work no miracles there because of their lack of faith.*[15]

Of course, historical and critical faculties should be employed in reading the gospel and in investigating Jesus as a historical figure. To repress this kind of inquiry merely blocks the deeper understanding that resists rational analysis. We need to ask who the historical Jesus was and what he actually said. And what people said he was and what they say he said. But the 'pursuit of the historical Jesus' is

---

[15] Mk 6:5-6.

the beginning not the end of the quest we embark on by listening to his question.

It all depends on how deeply we listen, how much time and attention we give to it. The quality of our attention enhances the way we ask all questions about him. It affects the way we encounter him as a personal reality because it moves the place of meeting from the mind to the heart. By heart I do not mean an emotional or physical centre. Heart is a universal term used by spiritual traditions to designate that centre of integrated consciousness where all ways of knowing are focussed. It is where sense becomes spiritual, where imagination may become insight. It is the centre and the wholeness of the human person. In the heart my self-knowledge and my knowledge of God are in harmony, the peace found beyond ego consciousness.

Discovering Jesus' identity for us is not achieved through intellectual or historical enquiry. It happens in the process of opening to our intuitive depths, to deeper and more subtle ways of knowing and seeing than we are accustomed to. This is prayer and the experience quickly makes it clear that prayer is more than thought. It is an entry into an inner space of silence, where we are content to be without answers, judgements and images. Later in this book I will turn to meditation[16] as a way, time-honoured and universal, of entering this inner space of the heart and developing the state of silence. For many, meditation, a way of faith-filled silence, has transformed religious belief, whether Christian or non-Christian from arid theory to vital personal experience. The silence of prayer that is deeper than thought and image enhances our knowledge of Jesus because it leads into the reality of pure presence. Our response to the redemptive question is not, however, a matter of either intellectual or spiritual techniques. Meditation is not a trick for answering the question of who Jesus is. It is, in my experience, a way of listening to the question more deeply and clearly.

The redemptive question requires selfless attention. To listen is to be truly 'obedient' as the Latin root (ob-audire, to listen) suggests. To grasp for an answer is symptomatic of distraction. The sign of scattered, superficial or intermittent attention during meditation, for ex-

---

[16] By meditation I mean wordless and imageless prayer rather than the discursive mental prayer that employs memory and imagination.

ample, reflects our repeated tendency to get lost in thought and fantasy. Similarly, a sign that we have stopped paying attention to his question or have filtered it through our own preconceptions is that we do not even answer the actual question he put. Overconfident answers usually address the question that no one has asked. Or they are the answers we were taught years before but which have remained untested in the light of experience. A further danger signal is when the redemptive question becomes boring. This is often the result of having lost respect for the religious authority associated with the question. The answer to this question is not a solution but an insight. Through the struggle of faith, and with the balm of grace, insight dawns. As science, art and religion can all testify, the actual source of insight remains forever mysterious.

Jesus asks Who do you say I am, not What am I or even Who do you think I say I am? It is an intimately personal question. If we do not feel its intimacy as disturbing—even intrusive—we have not listened to it. It is not twisting our arm however. Its authority is not violent but vulnerable, not forceful but humble. To ask a person who they really think you are is a declaration of love.

Redemptive questions illustrate what redemption means. This is important for all humanity, not just for Christians. If we can understand what Jesus, as one of humanity's great teachers, is getting at in his question, we will see where he is trying to get *us* to. We will be the wiser for it. And wisdom is the principal value that human beings need to develop today. According to the Book of Wisdom, the 'hope for the salvation of the world lies in the greatest number of wise people'.[17]

◦◦◦◦◦

The meaning of any question depends on its context. 'Are they off?' means something different when you are at a racetrack, ordering in a fish and chip shop, or smelling a bag of old fruit.

Considering the context of Jesus' question leads us to look at the gospels themselves and their tradition. We are alerted about *how* to read the gospels prayerfully. For the early Christians reading and interpreting the gospels was not an essentially academic and certainly not a journalistic undertaking. It was a means of entering contempla-

[17] Wis 6:24.

tion and an integral element of salvation and enlightenment.[18] It was both prayer and a preparation for deeper prayer.

As described in Luke's gospel Jesus was 'praying alone in the presence of his disciples' when he put his disturbing question to them. The apparent contradiction is illuminating: how can one be alone *and* in the presence of others? We can be alone on a crowded subway train or at a party where everyone is a stranger. This is loneliness, knowing no one and feeling known by no one. But there is another kind of aloneness which is solitude. For example, when we meditate or engage in creative work we are solitary but not isolated. Alone, not lonely. All spiritual growth leads from loneliness into solitude. The recognition and acceptance of our eternal uniqueness is solitude. At first it can be more terrifying than loneliness because it dissolves the crowd around us and reveals instead the mutual presence of other solitudes, other unique persons. Solitude is the basis of all relationship. In solitude we run the supreme risk of paying attention to a reality other than our own. Whoever wants to find his life must lose it.

Jesus poses his most intimate question from his vast solitude. He turns to his disciples, his friends and companions, from the self-knowledge in which he has recognized and accepted himself in prayer. He is baptized in self-knowledge. He knows where he comes from and where he is going. The self-knowledge of Jesus, like all human self-appropriation, arises from the creativity of prayer. Prayer means growing in self-knowledge rather than merely performing or mouthing a set ritual. It is about paying attention rather than listing needs, making statements, articulating our intentions or even obsequiously saying please and thank you to God. Prayer underpins religion more essentially than religion legislates about prayer.

> *You are here to kneel*
> *Where prayer has been valid.*
> *And prayer is more*
> *Than an order of words, the conscious occupation*
> *Of the praying mind, or the sound of the voice praying.*[19]

Jesus' piercing question highlights the intimacy which is discovered by sharing a spiritual path. This intimacy is the community of the True Self in which the many know they are one. Prayer is the expan-

---

[18] See *The Gnostic Scriptures*, trans. B. Layton (Garden City, New York: Doubleday, 1987), p. 367.

[19] T. S. Eliot, *Four Quartets*, Little Gidding I (London: Faber & Faber, 1983).

sion of consciousness within this communion of self-knowledge. It is light years beyond what our individual egos know about ourselves. When Jesus uses the first person pronoun (who *I* am) he claims the rare right to say *I* authentically. It is no longer the little *me* of the ego at which most of us are stuck.

All relationship is to some degree about sharing in self-knowledge. This does not mean merely what we know *about* ourselves and what can be verbalised or conceptualised. It is pure consciousness, simplified of self-reflection and free of anxiety. Childlikeness rather than philo-sophical cleverness comes closer to showing us what this means. 'Un-less you become like a little child...,' Jesus teaches. His question expresses his desire to share his self-knowledge. Behind this desire is divine 'love—longing'—as the Upanishads call it.[20] It is found deep in Jesus, in God and in the human being, and it unites God and humanity in their common thirst for each other. Behind the question of Jesus is the longing to be loved by those he loves. The selfless passion at work is the consuming longing to transmit the whole of one's self to another. This is the 'eros' aspect of all love. But when this longing expands to embrace all others it has become 'agape'. The meaning of the universal, selfless agape of the Trinity is that this passion for self-communication is at the very heart of reality. In the minutest atomic force, in the expansion of the universe and in every human relation-ship. Behind his question, therefore, is his personal insight into the nature of God as a communion of love.

The authority of Jesus, which his contemporaries felt both posi-tively and negatively, flows from the well of his self-knowledge. He knows his life's source and destination.[21] Self-knowledge of this depth consists of more than information about ourselves. It is richer than the most perceptive psychological insight. To know who one is and where one has come from is a knowledge which can only be enjoyed in the 'community of the True Self', that is, in the knowledge of God which is love. It is known not by trying to possess it but by self-transcendence.

Self-knowledge is also humility. By putting his question in the way he does Jesus humbles himself and proves the authenticity of his authority. What authenticates it is partly the fact that it can be so easily misinterpreted. True humility is easily mistaken for pride. Some

[20] *Upanishads*, trans. Juan Mascaro (London: Penguin, 1965).
[21] Jn 8:14, 42.

religious people are particularly skilled at masking pride as humility. When they encounter real humility they mistake it for an exceptionally good mask and enviously want to expose it. It is not so surprising that to many of his contemporaries Jesus appeared as a manifest egomaniac claiming, as they said, to be equal to God.

◦⊷◯⊷◯◦

Perhaps this is why Jesus said the first will be last and the last first. His humility is the authority which turns the tables of the ego's power.

It is never those hungering for power who recognise him. Humility of this intensity is revolutionary and dangerous. It upsets the balance of power constructed by egotism. The ego plays its power-game at every level: individual, relational, social and political. It *must* find the question of Jesus disconcerting because the question threatens to expose the ego's need for total control. Jesus was playing with fire when he provoked the ego's reaction to the true self. We can see it in ourselves daily. Hearing his question the ego rushes to dismiss both question and questioner. This simple question has all the revolutionary humility of a *guru*, a teacher, a rabbi and a prophet. Whoever truly knows himself can help others to know themselves simply by asking them who they think he is. There is no playacting in this. He communicates himself simply by being himself. Such humility allows the community of the true self to unfold towards us and to enfold us.

Redemption is knowing with our whole being who we are and where we have come from. It is the grace of the spiritual guide or *guru* to awaken this knowledge. By communicating himself through a gentle question Jesus invites our attention. This has the potential to become a relationship with him as our teacher.

The word *guru* is not a common term in Christian vocabulary. But that does not mean Christianity lacks a rich tradition of spiritual friendship and union with the guides we need for the inner journey— from the *didaskaloi*—, or teachers of the New Testament, to the monastic *abbas* and *ammas* of the Desert Tradition to the *staretz* of Eastern Christianity or the *anamkara*, the soul-friend of Celtic Christianity. The modern idea of a spiritual director can be a somewhat psychologised version of this ancient wisdom of spiritual friendship. In the gospels Jesus is called *rabbi*, or teacher, more often than by any other title. Yet it can seem strange to Christians to think of themselves as his students or disciples. This could only happen because they have been diverted by answers and stopped listening to the question—the skilled question by which any teacher awakens knowledge.

⟨∘⟩⟨∘⟩⟨∘⟩

A Christian is essentially a disciple of Jesus. And *he* is their guru. Good disciples do not feel their guru is in competition with other gurus.

Tolerance, dialogue and collaboration are the challenges facing Christian disciples today. For the first time since the fourth century institutional Christianity is not bolstered up by a secular power that supports religious exclusivism. Christians are being invited to see themselves as disciples of Jesus in a new relationship to the disciples of masters in other traditions. Realising that Jesus is their personal *guru* is decisive for freeing Christians from engrained attitudes of imperialism and historical intolerance. They are then freed for dialogue and spiritual partnership with other faiths. The question by which Jesus relates to his disciples therefore also connects him to the spiritual search that is common to humanity.

Jesus is not seeking disciples to enhance his self-esteem. In fact the gospels tell how he let many opportunities for guru stardom pass him by.[22] He saw many of his followers turn away from him because his teaching threatened them by its sheer personal authority. For this or other reasons it may not suit us to think of Jesus as our guru. We may not want a guru at all or we may feel called to another. Jesus does not condemn that decision. But even if this is how we feel about him we can still listen to the silence from which his question arises and touches everyone.

The word disciple derives from *discere*, to learn. A disciple is one who acknowledges that he has got something to learn and that his teacher, at least for the present, knows more. There is a paradox involved in acknowledging this. It implies a separation from the person in union with whom we are to learn how to transcend duality. Beyond duality lies the full participatory being of love. So in fact discipleship does transcend itself. The disciple goes beyond the teacher because the teacher goes beyond himself. This paradox—is the essence of the identity of Jesus. It is good for you, Jesus told his companions, that I am going away. *Discipline* is the way the disciple learns to enter this

---

[22] E.g., Lk 13:31.

paradox—the discipline of listening, of silence, of reading with the heart, of meditating without desire.

When we are unaware of the stages by which relationship unfolds, we risk premature failure in every relationship we make. The first phase of romantic attachment seems like the end of everything. In learning to relate to Jesus, we begin by listening to his question, sitting at his feet. But as we hear his silence we find that we are inside his question, compassionately known by his self-knowledge. The mystical truth of the New Testament is that we are in a union with Jesus that takes us beyond every kind of ego-centred relationship with him. Christian fundamentalism, like all forms of fundamentalism, is arrested development—relationship that gets blocked at an early stage. In union with Jesus the disciple's individuality, though not destroyed, is transformed. What else does love or death mean? As a second-century Christian writer put it:

> For you in me and I in you, together we are one undivided person.[23]

Deep prayer guides us beyond dualism into union, beyond ideas and images into reality. From the gospels it is clear that Jesus did not want hangers-on or devotees but full disciples or friends. Insight—into our being 'in Christ' and of his being 'in us', of our sharing the same God and Father with him[24]—dawns when egotism has given way to self-knowledge nurtured by the grace of relationship with him. We need duality in order to transcend duality. In other words we must work with the ego to transcend the ego. Similarly we need the historical Jesus to reach the Cosmic Christ. And yet we encounter the Jesus of ancient Palestine not as he was then but as he is now. Meeting him now we encounter everything he has ever been and all he will yet be.

In listening to the question which Jesus puts to humanity we are also hearing a call to self-discovery. Listening *to* him leads to listening *with* him to the mystery of existence at its source. This process is what makes the question and person of Jesus so relevant for the modern spiritual seeker. If we are to see Jesus as he is, and not just as our ego imagines him to be, we must learn to listen to his question in the very silence from which he asks it.

---

[23] *An Ancient Homily for Holy Saturday*, Roman Breviary, Holy Saturday.
[24] Jn 20:17.

~ 2 ~

'And Who Do You Say I Am?'

Because of its position at the entrance to Bantry Bay, one of the world's great natural harbours, Bere Island once enjoyed great strategic military importance. Churchill even had to be dissuaded from reoccupying it with British troops during the Second World War with the reminder that Ireland was now a sovereign state.

To reach Bere Island, you take a little ferry that leaves at the discretion of its owner from the dock in Castletownbere about a mile away. On my first visit there since childhood, I arrived direct from London. It was a day of driving rain and gale-force winds. The pub, however, not the weather, was delaying our brave captain. So I took dry refuge in the tiny cabin to anticipate stepping ashore again on my magic island. I was startled to see a young woman sitting silently in a corner by the steering wheel. She said nothing as I entered and returned my greeting with a fleeting glance and nod. Despite being English it seemed to me too absurd to sit there saying nothing so I attempted a conversation. After trying the weather I asked if she lived on the island. She shot me a frightened look as if I was probing her most intimate secrets. After mumbling an incoherent answer she looked resolutely out of the window. Wondering if she was just shy I launched on a number of friendly questions which I soon realised were merely compounding my error, whatever that was. The psychological temperature fell lower than the weather. Eventually we retreated into a neutral silence until the melancholic captain tottered on board. The crossing took fifteen minutes. As we climbed off the boat onto the island my fellow passenger turned suddenly to me and with a softly knowing smile, as if we had been chatting easily all along, asked if the weather was as bad as this in London. Had she read my mind, looked into my soul with psychic powers? I had given her no information about myself. I guessed that the island grapevine had informed her that one of the O'Sullivan Bere's girls' children was coming from England to visit his cousins. She probably knew before I did.

I had learned an important lesson about island silence and privacy. The truth is a sensitive creature around which you have to tread very gently. Too many questions scare the truth away. When we want to find out about others too directly we often forget that we ourselves are also known.

◈◈◈

What are we trying to find out about Jesus by listening to his question?

Luke tells us that the people considered Jesus to be a kind of reincarnation of John the Baptist, a second coming of Elijah or one of the other prophets.

> ... he asked them, 'Who do the people say I am?' They answered, 'Some say John the Baptist, others Elijah, others that one of the old prophets has come back to life.'[1]

This was what the people were saying about him[2]. Neither Jesus nor the gospel writers discuss these as literal answers, although Jesus once indicated that John the Baptist was the Elijah who was expected to be the forerunner of the messiah.

The New Testament uses about one hundred and thirty titles to describe Jesus: Christ, Lord, King, Lamb of God, rabbi, Son of Man, Son of David, Son of God, being the most frequent. 'Teacher' is used about 50 times in the gospels ('Rabbi' is found only in John's gospel, and there nine times.) 'Son of David' is found about seventeen times and so less often than 'King' or 'Lamb of God'. The characteristic title 'Son of Man' is found eighty-five times and has a rich fabric of meanings which Jesus found useful. The prophet Ezekiel uses the title often to mean a weak or mortal human being (the prophet himself). The book of Daniel (Chapter seven) uses the phrase in a heavenly sense and it is found in some psalms where it means, simply, a human being. Jesus thus knew the title from scripture and used it of himself. The uses of ambiguity in the phrase are revelatory. It does not only mean 'an ordinary human being' because it is the Son of Man who will come to judge the world, a work associated with God. And the Son of Man, like God, forgives sins. Sometimes, indeed, Son of Man is a circumlocution for Jesus the speaker as, for example, when he says the Son of Man has nowhere to lay his head. The interpenetration of divine and human connotations of identity in this simple phrase is highly subtle.[3]

In addition to 'Son of Man' the New Testament uses 'Christ' over 500 times, 'Lord' 485 times, 'Son of God' seventy-five times, 'Son of David' seventeen times. These titles were attributed to a man who, to

---

[1] Lk 9:18-20.
[2] '... they wanted to arrest him, but they were afraid of the people, who looked on Jesus as a prophet,' Mt 21:46.
[3] Gerald O'Collins, *Christology*.

all appearances a politician and religious failure, had died the most shameful death possible under the Roman Empire as a common criminal.

In the encounter with his disciples which is our starting-point here, Jesus neither approves nor rejects what people were saying about him. Instead he speaks about the suffering that lies ahead both for himself and his disciples. Soon after his public ministry began, Jesus probably guessed that he would become a victim of a power-play by the authorities. He was too popular to be ignored and he had no power base of his own to protect him. His family and friends were deeply frightened for his safety[4]. The gospels agree that he was well aware of the ordeals lying ahead. His socially radical, religiously revolutionary teaching and his preference for silence over self-definition all point to a deep sense of his destiny.

He exposes the high cost by which self-knowledge is achieved. As a teacher more than as a political radical he describes the path by which his disciples will come to know him and themselves. He does not trivialise the cost of discipleship. To know oneself requires unknowing one's self. Finding involves loss. Seeds grow only through death. To find the light of the true Self there is no way except through the dark tunnel of the way of the cross. Finding demands losing. Life is gained only through death: sometimes even physical death but every day demands the death of the ego's old illusions, habits, values and beliefs.

> And to all he said, 'If anyone wishes to be a follower of mine, he must leave self behind; day after day he must take up his cross and come with me. Whoever cares for his own safety is lost; but if a man will let himself be lost for my sake, that man is safe. What will a man gain, by winning the whole world at the cost of his true self?'[5]

To listen is not mere passivity. To listen is to turn towards another, to leave self behind; and that is to love. St. Augustine said that whoever loves Jesus believes in Jesus. The question Jesus asks, and which is so central to Christian faith and identity, does not throw up denominational barriers between Christians and non-Christians as answers can do. Indeed by leading to the universal question, *who am I?*, his

---

[4] 'Rabbi,' his disciples said, 'it is not long since the Jews were wanting to stone you. Are you going there again?' Jn 11:8.
[5] Lk 9:23-25.

question positions him as one of the universal teachers of humanity
and therefore as one in whom human beings can best find their unity
with each other.

‹❍‹❍‹❍›

All religions, it has been said, share three basic elements: a liberating
experience of truth, enlightenment or awakening; a tradition that interprets this formative experience; and a set of rituals or systematic
symbolism that derive from this.

Christianity like all religions can be understood in this way. But
behind and before (and within) Christianity is Jesus. And at the heart
of Jesus' encounter with our humanity is his relational question. Jesus
asks us who *we* say he is. What he tells us about himself does not
replace the relationship opened up by the humility of his question. It
is essential to Christian faith that we listen to Jesus with such unclouded attention that we lose ourselves. His question, if we listen to
it, rather than only answering it, hooks our mind like a *koan*—a thought
that stops thought. It is thus that he becomes, as he called himself,
a 'door' that leads to self-knowledge.

The gospel of John says that the words of Jesus are 'spirit and
they are life'. His question bears a primal power to awaken the dormant, unrealised part of us and to guide it towards the knowledge of
the Self. Through contact with the power of his self-knowledge his
question persuades us to ask 'Who am I?' Immediately it alerts us to
who we are *not* and who we cannot possibly be. Asking *Who am I?*
demands that we face the uneasy question of *Who I am not?*

I am not my moods and thoughts, my beliefs or my social roles
and status. All of these are powerful aspects of myself. They possess
a temporary, partial reality. But they are too arbitrary, too conditioned
and too ephemeral to constitute Selfhood. Nor can I identify myself
with my sensations, my desires, my fears, my pleasures and my pains.
Passing emotional states, however intense, are uncertain foundations
for a true sense of identity. This simple truth is the universal truth in
the Buddha's assertion of *anatta*: the no-selfhood of all things, including
the human thing. I may say I am victim, ruler, lover, judge, hunter,
artist, priest, father, mother, child, clown or trickster—there are many
archetypal roles and combinations. But they don't answer the important question. Until knowledge of the Self has dawned their impermanence will always lead me back to the same question *Who am I?*—
the essentially religious question.

Self-knowledge, as we will see in Chapter Six, characterises the state of what Jesus calls the Kingdom of God. We make sense of the process of discovering the Self with the help of the great religious traditions, their themes and archetypes. Any one person's journey, of course, may not be restricted to just one religious institution. Many religious themes and symbols span different traditions, uniting them and enriching their dedicated practitioners. Often today, too, these themes and archetypes have a life outside overtly religious contexts. This need not lead to syncretism or confusion. It offers us today a new kind of recognition of the fundamental unity of all paths of human growth and self-transcendence. It expresses the unity of humanity itself, our common origin and destiny. For all our crises, humanity seems to be growing into a new corporate self-awareness today. What seemed recently to be irreconcilable differences and divisions are now, through dialogue, often recognized as parallel paths. It may well be that, at least for some people, the mutual enrichment of differing traditions will be necessary in order to fully understand the subtler stages of the path to true Selfhood.[6]

One of the stages of self-knowledge which all traditions recognise, although by different terms, is repentance. This is a pre-condition for any spirituality and it involves the purification of one's way of life. Jesus began his preaching with the call to repentance. Some more negative styles of Christian spirituality in the past interpreted this as a call to fixate upon one's personal sinfulness and then develop an abiding sense of guilt. The guiltier you felt the more repentant you were. Nothing could be more inconsistent with Jesus' meaning here. If anything, his call to repentance is a release from the psychological disorder of guilt. He urges repentance, not to instil a fear of punishment but because the kingdom of heaven is imminent. Time is short and we have to get ourselves ready for a long journey. Guilt wastes time, even a lifetime. If it lingers for more than a few seconds it becomes unhealthy. Repentance is nothing to do with guilt. It is all to do with seeing ourselves unclouded by self-deception.

Listening to his question about self-knowledge clarifies the need for repentance precisely because it confronts us with our own emptiness and impermanence. It leads to an open space of the spirit that is uncluttered by institutional and psychological props. Poverty of

---

[6] Huston Smith, *The World Religions: Our Great Traditions* (San Francisco: Harper Collins, 1991).

spirit is another term for it. This naked self-awareness is the stage in us in which the great biblical theme of repentance is enacted.

> After John had been arrested, Jesus came into Galilee proclaiming the Gospel of God: The time has arrived: the Kingdom of God is upon you. Repent and believe the Gospel.[7]

Repentance is both more serious and more joyful than fundamentalists and prophets of doom suggest. It drives us to seek a more interior and demanding spiritual practice. It lightens the burden of the past and breaks the shackles of sin. It sets us free for our life's work. By the light of meditation and the guiding question of Jesus we can see repentance as a liberating, redemptive insight into what we are *not*. If this experience of emptiness seems at first to be destructive or nihilistic, it is not for long. In fact, it precedes the discovery and full affirmation of who we are.

With repentance there ensues a process of detachment, one by one, from all the interwoven false identities to which we cling with such passion and fearful desperation. Each interweaving is a knot we must untie, a death to die. Quite naturally, we dread the poverty that brings self-knowledge. It seems horrible to imagine we might discover a void of nonbeing, an eternal anonymity at the core of our being. So we cling to anything, however superficial, which seems to give substance to the claim 'I am this or I am that'. Our fear of emptiness and our evasion of repentance can be so intense that it blocks us from hearing any redemptive question in our life at all. Or the question is rejected because it is felt as a threat to our integrity. This fear of nonexistence, the fear of death, costs us many opportunities. The desperate need for identity can be so great that mere self-expression or an egocentric search for self-fulfilment can get enshrined as the ruling value of life. The emotional exploitation of others quickly replaces compassion and love. We drop others when they no longer seem to fulfil us. Without the clarity of repentance, in other words, we try to make the ego fit the Self. We are deluded by self-ignorance, the selfishness which is sin.

·◦❖◦·

We cannot understand grace without understanding sin. Sin is what is actually not but what we *think* is.

[7] Mk 1:14-15.

It is the nonreality that the East calls *maya*, the cycle of addictive desire and disappointment called *samsara*. The great teachers of Christian life, like the desert Fathers of the Egyptian Desert in the fourth century, have also explored with deep psychological perception this human affliction that robs us of happiness. The *abbas* of the desert described the operation of the 'seven deadly sins' just as Buddhist teachers expanded on the 'afflictive emotions'. The Christian understanding also places sin in the context of personal freedom that is an aspect of our being images of God, and so of our personal relationship to a loving God. But they do not say that sin is only what we choose to do. It arises from ignorance, our fallen state. It is a further state of disharmony and suffering that we fall into when we miss the target.[8] We should be aiming at or when our attention fails and we get lost in fantasy. Sin is the consequence of unwise, irresponsible choice, not only the act of choice itself. It has consequences for ourselves as for the universe to which we are responsible. Personal freedom explains why we each must listen for ourselves to the redemptive questions that bring us to self-knowledge by dispelling illusion. This is why we must repent personally. No group, church or sangha, not the best of gurus even, can do it for us without our willing consent.

Sin includes all attempts to avoid the truth of emptiness. It evades the repentance from which all authentic spiritual practice derives. The badness of sin lies not in the fact we are breaking rules, failing to conform as we should, but that it creates suffering for ourselves and for others. All suffering arises from the sinful, false identification of the ego with the true Self. We fall into this trap time after time when we forget that the Self we seek to know is not different from the person who is seeking to know it. The true Self is not something anyone can objectify in mental concepts or contain in ritual actions. Self-knowledge is really the state of *self-knowing* rather than the possession of knowledge *about* something. The *Self*, according to Sankara, the Indian philosopher eight centuries before Jesus, is the 'inner light'. It is self-evident and it does not become an object of perception.

When the Pharisees asked Jesus when the kingdom would come he responded with a similar comment, reminding them how its interiority could never be objectified:

[8]The Greek word *hamartia* translated as sin means literally missing the mark.

You cannot tell by observation when the kingdom of God comes
... for, in fact, the kingdom of God is within you.[9]

Seeing how repentance, the kingdom of heaven and the true Self are
related is an integral insight for Christian faith. These are interdependent aspects of the human spiritual journey. They become clarified
and embodied in that form of relationship with Jesus that is discipleship. Thus, through discipleship, as all traditions affirm, we learn saving truths. We learn that the Kingdom is the experience of God in the
nonduality of the Spirit. No one can know God except by sharing in
God's own self-knowledge, as St Irenaeus said in the third century. We
learn that there is no way to the true Self except the narrow way of
renouncing all the false selves of the ego-system. What is left when I
have let go everything that I am not *is* who I truly am. It is who I
have been all along but without recognising it. At that point the duality
of discipleship itself dissolves. Master and disciple are experienced as
one in the Friendship of the Self.

May they all be one; as you, Father are in me, and I in you, so
also may they be in us, that the world may believe that you sent
me.[10]

Illusion breeds disunity and the excessive individualism of our modern
culture. Ignorance and self-deception are aspects of sin that need to
give way to truth before the light of the Self can shine. There is
nothing less abstract than this. A favourite story of the East is often
told to show how simple and down-to-earth it is. A man returns to
his home at night and sees a large snake coiled up in front of his
door. Terrified to move he stays frozen to the spot all night. As the
light of dawn breaks he finally sees that the snake is in fact a coiled
piece of rope. The false identification of the snake had to be abandoned
before the truth could be known. Nothing new is created but what is
there is finally, clearly seen. Ultimately only the light of truth can
dispel falsehood. The mystery is where the light comes from. It takes
time for the light of dawn to grow strong enough for us to see clearly.
St Peter uses the same image of dawning light when he says that the
clearing of mental obscurity requires the work of attention—a work in
which the reading of Scripture is a powerful spiritual tool:

[9] Lk 17:20.
[10] Jn 17:21.

All this confirms for us the message of the prophets, to which you will do well to attend; it will go on shining like a lamp in a murky place, until day breaks and the morning star rises to illuminate your minds.[11]

⟨◦◦◦⟩

The quest for self-knowledge entails the shedding of false personas. Listening to Jesus' question leaves us in the end with no image of him at all, only real presence. All the false messiahs in our imagination, forms of projection, must be exposed and toppled before the truth of the messiah can be recognized. The Zen practitioner is told that if he meets the Buddha on the road he should kill him. When two disciples met Jesus on the road to Emmaus, after the Resurrection, they failed to recognise him until he broke bread with them. Then, in the Eucharist, their eyes were opened and they recognised him. So, meeting Jesus, the Christian disciple does not kill him. He has already been killed. Perhaps the equivalent to the Buddhist practice is to eat him. In any case, for the original to be recognised all images must go. St. Gregory of Nyssa in the fifth century warned that every image and concept of God becomes an idol.

Of course there are different kinds of recognition. All religions recognise Jesus as a universal teacher. Not everyone follows him as their personal guru. His greatness as a teacher, even for a Buddhist or a Hindu, is not only in his moral or religious wisdom but in his power to awaken in others the experience of reality. The East especially knows that a guru is more than an exemplar of moral or religious truth. A guru is one who has himself or herself become a bridge for the disciple to cross over from the land of illusion to the reality of the kingdom, of the Self.

For many people today of all traditions a particular Indian guru of modern times exemplifies this. He is one who has reminded many Christians of the directly human quality of their relationship with Jesus.

⟨◦◦◦⟩

Ramana Maharshi, the sage of Arunachala in southern India, is one of the great spiritual teachers of the modern world. His influence is still

[11] 2 Pet 1:19.

felt fifty years after his death.[12] Yet for most of his life he dwelt in silence and it was from silence that he radiated the experience of nonduality that dwelt in him.

When asked about the role of the guru, Ramana Maharshi would always insist on the absolute nonduality subsisting between the teacher and the disciple.

> The guru is both 'external' and 'internal'. From the 'exterior' he gives a push to the mind to turn inward: from the 'interior' he pulls the mind toward the Self and helps in the quieting of the mind ... There is no difference between God, Guru and the Self.[13]

This is a language and understanding very different from traditional Western ideas about God, human teachers and disciples. Some Christians react to it as threateningly pantheistic (God *is* everything). Without seeing the option of *panentheism* (God is *in* everything), they are scared of sliding into the gnostic heresies (the word *heresy* literally means *choice*) that confronted the early church. Furthermore, as Westerners they balk at the apparent loss of personal identity suggested by Ramana's words. But as Christians they might also recall those sayings of Jesus where he spoke—shockingly, too, for many of his listeners—of the oneness between himself and the Father: 'My Father and your Father'; 'to have seen me is to have seen the Father.' Or of St Paul's personal confession that he lived no longer but that Christ dwelt in him.

> I have been crucified with Christ: the life I now live is not my life, but the life which Christ lives in me; and my present mortal life is lived by faith in the Son of God who loved me and gave himself up for me.[14]

Ramana expressed his experience of the Self, the immanent and transcendent presence of the Divine Guru, in his own terms conditioned by his Hindu context. He constantly returns to the unity of nonduality (*advaita*) just as St Paul does to the indwelling Christ,

> The guru never sees any difference between himself and others and is quite free of the idea that he is enlightened and those around him are not.

[12] Ramana Maharshi, *The Spiritual Teaching of Ramana Maharshi*.
[13] Ibid., Response to questions, and following quotations.
[14] Gal 2:20.

Seeing Jesus as *guru* serves to understand the New Testament titles used most frequently of Jesus, *teacher* and *rabbi*. The signs of a true guru, as described by Ramana, are abundantly evident in the gospel picture of Jesus as a human being in communion with God (whom he called 'Father'). But we see him also as a person of his own time and place with the natural limitations this implies. Ramana says a guru possesses the following qualities:

> a steady abidance in the Self, looking at all with an equal eye,
> unshakable courage at all times, in all places and situations.

If Jesus is *guru* we are invited to see ourselves as disciples. Our ego may find that unacceptable or impossible. 'I'll listen, but I'm not bowing to anyone.' But dedicated spiritual practice eventually makes disciples of us all. It is interesting then to know what Ramana saw as the qualities of a true disciple:

> an intense longing for the removal of sorrow and the attainment
> of joy and an intense aversion for all kinds of mundane pleasure.

Perhaps the reason that our spiritual practice seems to 'take so long', as people often complain, might simply be that we do not intensely enough long for what we protest we want immediately!

The role of the guru in his exterior manifestation is to push the disciple inwards to the quest for the Self. When Ramana Maharshi was asked what method or discipline was best to follow he did not offer an array of meditation techniques. He pointed people to Self-inquiry. The constant thought 'Who am I', he said, destroys all other thoughts. Like the stick used for stirring the burning pyre, it will itself in the end be destroyed. Then Self-realization naturally arises.

> Of all the thoughts that arise in the mind the I-thought is the
> first. It is only after the rise of this that the other thoughts arise.
> It is after the appearance of the first personal pronoun that the
> second and third personal pronouns appear.

·◇··◇··◇·

According to Ramana the aim of all spiritual practice is to lead the mind to stillness. When the I-thought has been traced all the way back to its origin, it disappears in its ultimate source of all things, the Self. The radical simplicity of Sri Ramana's teaching is the expression of a compassionate, decisive but noncondemnatory personality. This is reminiscent of the way Jesus himself treated sinners and outcasts. Ramana remarked to a Hindu visitor discouraged by his inveterate sinfulness:

> Even if one be a great sinner one should not worry and weep, 'O, I am a sinner how can I be saved!' One should completely renounce the thought 'I am a sinner' and concentrate keenly on meditation on the Self. Then one will surely succeed.

Compare this with the parable of the Prodigal Son who returns home to his father's unconditional, impartial forgiveness;[15] or the story of the sinner and the religious official praying in the Temple and the way the former's simple humility finds God's favour rather than the Pharisee's complacency.[16] When he met with sinners and outcasts, Jesus loved. His anger was reserved for the rigidity of religious authority, the sin that denies that it is sin and even claims to be from God. It was not directed against ordinary sinners. His power was felt not in punishment but in the reintegration of the sinner both to himself and to society. He called them to repentance and a new life: 'go and do not sin again' as he told the woman he saved from being stoned to death.[17] He convinced people that they were forgiven and he empowered them to take advantage of the invitation to live more fully that is intrinsic to that discovery. Jesus' compassionate response to sin emphasises both the person's *will* to transcend the habit of sin and the *action* necessary to fulfil that intention. People did not leave his presence fixated on their sinfulness. They left in liberty to live differently. The energy of this newfound freedom is related to the joy felt in his presence. He was one in whose presence, as a contemporary theologian wrote, it was impossible to feel sad.

Ramana Maharshi's question 'Who am I?' leads beyond all the false identities that constitute the ego. It leads to a tranquillity of mind which evokes the 'stillness' of Psalm 46 which Ramana liked to quote: 'be still and know that I am God'. For those who listen to it, the self-inquiring question of Jesus, 'Who do you say I am?', discloses just this power of inner stillness. 'The false perception of the world and of our self,' Sri Ramana taught, 'will disappear when the mind becomes still.'

Seeing Jesus as a guru who teaches by means of question and presence, rather than as a moralist and rule-giver, may be a challenge for many Western Christians. Yet full Christian faith recognises Jesus

[15] Lk 15:11-32.
[16] Lk 18:9-14.
[17] Jn 8:11.

as the incarnate manifestation of the essential quest and question of the human journey to God: the incarnational form of the 'Who am I?' which makes us human. Jesus, as the Word of God, like a mantra, draws our attention from its scattered state of egotism, unifies it and awakens us to the truth he identified with life itself. 'I have come,' he said, 'so that you may have life, and may have it in all its fullness.'[18]

Jesus does not have this effect by magic or through psychic powers. According to the gospel we come to know and understand Jesus by 'faith'. Listening to his question is the beginning of an un-mapped expedition of faith. As we tread the narrow path of his ques-tion we discover how much more than *belief* faith means. The intellectual mind (*manas* in Indian philosophy) believes; but faith is our capacity for insight (*buddhi*, or spiritual intelligence). Faith is the 'vision of things unseen'.[19]

◦◦◦◦◦◦

In a "Peanuts" cartoon Lucy once told Charlie Brown that she had a new philosophy: 'All will be well.' 'That's nice', he replied. 'Only thing . . . ' she added. 'What's that', he asked? 'I don't know what it means.'

Faith is not the dream but the felt conviction that things *will* eventually work out for the best. Without denying the reality of evil or innocent suffering faith knows that the broken can be repaired, the meaningless can be understood, the wounded can be healed, and even that what is dead in us can be raised to new life. Faith knows that despite all signs to the contrary, and there are many, life has construc-tive meaning and beneficial purpose. The mystery of life is that even its tragedies and setbacks, its disappointments and failures can serve to awaken and deepen faith.

Why should we trouble ourselves to listen to the question Jesus raises concerning himself and how we see him? Because faith is born in the listening. By discovering what we are listening to we find mean-ing, authentic consolation, joy and fulfilment, in ways which no an-swers can bestow. How does this transforming, healing and revelatory energy of faith arise through the stilling of the mind? How does the Self shine forth?

It happens through every action of life performed faithfully as a disciple. This means when they are not done selfishly or even for *my*

[18] Jn 10:10.
[19] Heb 11:1.

own spiritual benefit. These practices are not necessarily overtly religious. They cover everything in a normal human life: the love of family, friends and enemies; the finding of our duty and the doing of our work; psychological integration and the development of our personal talents; care for the body and harmony with the material world; mental truthfulness and the study of sacred teaching. Upholding all these activities and converting them into spiritual practices is the work of meditation. Faith leads to discipleship and then, whatever our lifestyle, leads into the contemplative life.

The question of Jesus is significant because it touches the heart and wholeness of human experience, all our aspirations and deepest concerns. Listening to it can make us fully human. It simplifies us without the loss of human dignity.

⊙⋯⊙⋯⊙

His question rises out of silence, the still consciousness of his prayer. It stills the mind and awakens the human capacity for faith which is the door to knowledge of the Self. Stillness is not rigidity as when we become fixated on ourselves. Stillness is the condition of unselfcentered attention. It is inherently compassionate and .agile. Whatever is still is also silent, therefore, because it communicates directly and not through the medium of any language. We make a serious mistake by thinking that this state does no good for others. Sri Ramana indeed said that silence is the most potent form of work.

> However vast and emphatic the scriptures may be, they fail in their effect. The Guru is quiet and grace prevails in all. This silence is more vast and more emphatic than all the scriptures put together.

Today we listen to the question of Jesus in a culture that can make little sense and gives even less time for silence. Technological society is infatuated with the audio-visual and the tangible. It confuses the transfer of information with true communication. It tries to reduce consciousness to mechanics, prayer to positive thinking. It no longer allows the human mind and heart to be expanded by faith that sees what is ordinarily (to sense or thought alone) unseeable. Only faith understands the productivity of silence and the efficiency of stillness. To listen, to be silent, to have faith does not come cheap as the call of Jesus makes crystal clear. Modern spiritual practitioners or disciples may seem to conform to the values of their society but, as we will see in Chapter Eight, they will have to embrace the detachment of an outsider. Discipleship, too, does not come cheap. And if you think the first step is not easy, the demand does not let up.

Jesus' question and its orientation to silence put us into touch with ancient wisdom. The great spiritual cultures of the world, which materialistic technology so easily discounts, treasured the knowledge that silence is a truly great and beneficial human work.

> I will teach thee the truth of pure work, and this truth will make you free.
> And know also of a work that is silence: mysterious is the path of work.
> The person who in his work finds silence, and who sees that silence is work sees the Light and in all his works finds peace.[20]

The question of Jesus is all-important for contemporary culture precisely because it recalls us to silence. He does not shout this at us. His silence says it:

> Indeed it is better to keep quiet and be than to make fluent professions and not be. No doubt it is a fine thing to instruct others, but only if the speaker practices what he preaches. One such teacher there is: 'he who spoke the word and it was done'; and what he achieved even by his silences was well worthy of the Father. A person who has truly mastered the utterances of Jesus will also be able to apprehend his silence and thus reach full spiritual maturity, so that his own words have the force of actions and his silences the significance of speech.[21]

Jesus speaks by silence throughout the gospel: the preverbal silence of the newborn child; the look he passed into peoples' souls to set them free from fear or ignorance; the stillness when Pilate was questioning him and he declined to be enticed into the word games that might have saved his life; the post-verbal silence of the crucifixion. So too in any life today that is guided by the gospel we meet his silence in thought, word, deed and prayer in the Spirit of truth he sent to be humanity's guide.

We are silent whenever we pay attention. We pay attention when there is no 'I' thought, no self-reflective consciousness, no thought that we are the observer. This attention is the essence of prayer. Whenever

---

[20] *Bhagavad Gita*, 4:16-17.
[21] Ignatius of Antioch, *Letter to the Ephesians* Nn 13-18, 1.

we are in this state we are in prayer whether we are in church or supermarket, bedroom or boardroom, making love or making money. The dimension of our being that is addressed by the question of Jesus is perpetually in this state. When we pray, we return to prayer. When we listen, we return to silence.

⊸⊸⊸

All images echo some original reality. The original always has a silent presence which purifies and energises those who meet it. To encounter the *original* Jesus, however, means more than contacting the historical Jesus. The original Jesus manifests when we allow the countless *images* which religion and culture have accumulated to slip aside and be, at least momentarily, silent. A clear reading of the gospels and the work of silence in meditation prepare us for this.

∽ 3 ∾
Self-Knowledge and Friendship

*I*t was one of the long golden summer evenings on Bere Island that made one forget the usual wind and drizzle. I was spending some weeks of solitude there. I had come down from my simple one-cold-tap cottage to give my cousin John a hand with putting a new roof on his barn. Though by nature, as I thought, more genuinely solitary than myself he had asked for some unskilled assistance in moving the timber beams. He was a couple of years older than me, healthy looking and handsome, extremely silent and reserved. Like his father he never stopped working. He had an Irish temper which could flash from his quiet depths like storms on the Sea of Galilee but he loved his chirpy ever-sociable wife and two boisterous little boys who all seemed to know how to handle his moods.

We were working on the roof and in my leisure moments I contemplated the slow gorgeous sunset over the sea. Evening was dying peacefully into night. I was gazing contentedly at the merging of the lines of sky and sea. Suddenly I realised John was calling me to help move some wood and I turned towards him. Our eyes met and there was an affectionate, amused look on his face as he caught my absent-mindedness. It was a fleeting personal connection but, for me at least, a moment of immense depth. As our two attentions met each other I saw our family likeness with a shocking, strange and impersonal kind of clarity. For a second I felt the presence of the bubbling soup of DNA that we all splash around in and from which our treasured individuality arises. It was quite different from any conceptual knowledge that could have been expressed as 'he is my mother's brother's son' or 'there is the O'Sullivan look in us both'. The self-awareness was sharp and sudden; different from the way my self-absorbed ego usually tells me what I am feeling and what others think of me. It was not an emotional moment, not sentimental anyway, but it was painfully tender. It reassured me for an instant with a taste of the kind of human friendship that is deeper than we make merely as individuals. It takes longer to describe than it did to feel. It passed instantly and John pointed silently to the end of the piece of wood I was supposed to pick up and withdrew again into his hard-working solitude.

St Irenaeus and many others in the Christian tradition have said that
'God became human in order that humans may become divine.'

Does nonduality and union mean that Jesus is really after all just
me, my 'true Self', whatever that may be? Am I *his* true Self and is
everything blurred into one like the sky and the sea at dusk?

Christian faith does not claim this. It is not the experience a person has of the risen Jesus. Yet non-duality was at the heart of his
teaching and it is what he shares with us now. From the beginning
Christian thinkers have reflected on the meaning of Jesus' sayings
about his union with the Father and their union with us. They have
thought hard about the experience of faith which allows us to know
him in his risen form. The great thinkers have seen how self-
knowledge and the knowledge of God go hand in hand and dovetail
in our knowledge of Jesus.

> I am the good shepherd; I know my own sheep and my sheep
> know me—as the Father knows me and I know the Father—and I
> lay down my life for the sheep.[1]

St Augustine was fascinated by the question of self-knowledge, aware
no doubt of how hard he had worked to gain it himself:

> A person must first be restored to himself, that making of himself
> as it were a stepping-stone, he may rise thence to God.[2]

In his *Confessions* St Augustine was the first Western writer to define
the sense of personal identity as intimately interior, self-conversing,
seeking and anxious. He initiated the autobiographical narrative style
that we take for granted as the way we think and talk about ourselves.
Describing his search for himself as a search for God was not a mere
literary device. His self-concern was given meaning because it pointed
towards an ultimate self-transcendence. By self-analysis and writing he
advanced towards self-knowledge in the telling (and invention) of his
story and by the sharing of his hidden personality. This seems all
quite familiar to us today, in the culture of the television chat show,
as a means of understanding who we are. Yet there is a difference in
motivation. However self-centred his autobiographical self-awareness

[1] Jn 10:14-15.
[2] Augustine, *Retractiones* I (viii)3 (Migne PLXXXII).

might appear at times, it was led by a consuming passion to know God. This was the God he said was closer to him than he was to himself and who knew him better than he could know himself. He could therefore pray that he would come to know himself so that he could know God. It was a sublime kind of egotism waiting for an ecstatic release from the ego.

Augustine's self-description is a particular example of a universal Christian theme. Throughout its tradition Christian mysticism has acknowledged the connection between self-knowledge, pointing towards self-transcendence, and the knowledge of God. It has been the consistent testimony of the great masters. For St Bernard self-knowledge is a process that begins by discovering how difficult it is to be human:

> When someone first discovers that he is in difficulty, he will cry out to the Lord who will hear him and say 'I will deliver you and you shall glorify me.' In this way your self-knowledge will be a step to the knowledge of God; God will become visible to you according as God's image is being restored within you ...[3]

St Catherine of Siena in the fourteenth century stubbornly remained outside the cloister but cajoled popes and emperors with an authority born of her self-knowledge in God. Her 'cell', she claimed, was self-knowledge. In the beautiful flowering of the English mystical tradition in the turbulent fourteenth century, *The Cloud of Unknowing* stresses self-knowledge as the necessary pre-condition for all spiritual progress. It is the true meaning of humility, the *Cloud* says, distinguishing it from the many counterfeit forms which religious people are adept at confecting. Meister Eckhart in the same century preached on self-knowledge as the means for experiencing the divine likeness of the human person that is the truest reality of Selfhood.

Augustine, Catherine, the author of the *Cloud*, Eckhart are among the Christian teachers who affirm the spiritual significance of knowing oneself. Each person knows himself uniquely and so uniquely expresses his insight into the nondual, simple, nature of God and the Self. Union transfigures but does not destroy personal identity. A transformation of what we think we are, which at times however does feel like total annihilation, must take place in what St John of the Cross calls a dark night.

[3] Bernard of Clairvaux, *Sermon on the Song of Songs*, trans. L. Braceland (Kalamazoo: Cistercian Publications, 1978-79), 36, 6.

> It is as if God is saying: You will never become humble while
> you are wearing your ornaments. When you see yourself naked
> you will learn who you are . . . Now that the soul is dressed in
> working clothes—dryness and the abandonment of human de-
> sires—and now that its previous enlightenment is dimmed into
> darkness, it has better lights in the form of self-knowledge. . . .
> From this arid type of clothing comes not only the source of self-
> knowledge, which we have already described, but also all the
> benefits which we shall now describe . . .[4]

It is this same insight gained in self-knowledge that illuminates the
way we listen to his question and know Jesus. Self-knowledge introduces us into that quality of spiritual consciousness where knower
and known are known (by whom?) to be one. By self-knowledge and
in the Spirit, Jesus and we meet and know each other. We are changed
by the meeting. And, while becoming more and more uniquely ourselves, we also become increasingly like him as this process unfolds.

> What we shall be has not yet been disclosed, but we know that
> when it is disclosed we shall be like him, because we shall see
> him as he is.[5]

People in close relationship often grow to resemble each other, in the
way they speak, their idiosyncrasies and mannerisms and attitudes,
even in physical appearance. Just by living together union perceptibly
happens even though it may be resisted and denied. In marriage or
religious communities it can be amusing, mysterious, inspiring, sometimes slightly scary to see the signs of union at the level of personality.
Spouses sometimes panic at the idea that they have merged or are
losing their identity in marriage. All this simply shows that every
healthy relationship entails a death of the ego. Co-dependence, domination or absorption by a stronger personality have quite different
signs. What unites people is faithful love growing ever stronger
through the recurrent deaths of the ego. Then human communion
evolves into the vision of God. Two people can become one while each
remains who they are as individuals. Perhaps this helps to understand
the theology that describes the human and divine natures: united and
yet distinct in Jesus. Light, quantum physics tells us, is neither wave
nor particle but both. It depends how you look at it. Similarly, it

[4] St John of the Cross, Collected Works, *Dark Night of the Soul*, Book I. Ch. 12.
[5] I Jn 3:2.

depends how we look at Jesus. Who he is and who we are become, for the disciple, two intertwining experiences of self-knowledge. They are intertwined in time, the medium in which human relationship achieves full awareness. We can measure time. But there is also the dimension of spirit, the immeasurable medium in which time is transcended. The best way to see this in relation to Jesus is to situate it in the context of what happened in the early morning on the first day of the week after Jesus had been executed.

<O><O><O>

A lot happened on Easter Sunday.

As the day is described in the gospels, it seems more than could possibly have happened on one day. If the question of Jesus reveals the connection between self-knowledge and the knowledge of God, his Resurrection awakens us to the relationship of time and eternity. How long did Easter Sunday last? One day or all the days that have ever happened, before and since? In what way is the Jesus who died on the Cross the same person we encounter in the abyss of our self-knowledge today? What happened, the gospel suggests, is an absorption of space-time and matter into spirit. Historians, theologians and scripture scholars will not end their research and polemics about the Resurrection before we discover what that means. The attempt to understand it has value, however, because it sends us back to reread the gospel story and so to listen to the question the gospels contextualise for us.

Mary of Magdala had no doubts about the Resurrection she experienced. For her it was a reality in which she knew herself known:

> So the disciples went home again; but Mary stood at the tomb outside, weeping. As she wept, she peered into the tomb; and she saw two angels in white sitting there, one at the head, and one at the feet, where the body of Jesus had lain. They said to her, 'Why are you weeping?' She answered. 'They have taken my Lord away, and I do not know where they have laid him.' With these words, she turned round and saw Jesus standing there, but did not recognise him. Jesus said to her, 'Why are you weeping? Who is it you are looking for?' Thinking it was the gardener, she said, 'If it is you, sir, who removed him, tell me where you have laid him, and I will take him away.' Jesus said, 'Mary!' She turned to him and said 'Rabbuni!' (which is Hebrew for 'My Master'). Jesus said, 'Do not cling to me, for I have not yet ascended to the

Father. But go to my brothers, and tell them that I am now ascending to my Father and your Father, to my God and your God.' Mary of Magdala went to the disciples with her news: 'I have seen the Lord!' she said, and gave them his message.[6]

These words are so densely charged with meaning they constitute a supreme example, perhaps the greatest, of the form of poetry we call sacred scripture. Its level of reality can hardly be compared with the language of newspaper prose or scientific journals. Mary's experience of the risen Jesus has the certain feel of reality but of reality *undergone* rather than *observed*, reality seen in and by its own light. 'In your light I see light', as the psalm puts it. The gospels and St Paul sometimes use the Greek verb *ophthe* ('appeared to' or 'was revealed to') to describe the encounters with Jesus that individuals and groups experienced after his death. St Paul, who never met the historical Jesus, said 'He appeared to me.'[7] Yet Mary's experience of vision was also clear and personal. Afterwards she said simply 'I have seen the Lord.'[8]

The Resurrection appearances do not conform to the usual sort of biblical 'visions'. They are not associated with sleep and do not occur at night. They are sensory but different from sensual. The gospel accounts of these historical events do not aim at cinematic or scientific reality. (Cinematic realism is the result of high artifice.) They are events in which the usual constraints on the full experience of reality have been thrown off. Reality has been fully thrown open. It is disclosing itself in a dimension where there are no detached observers. At the same time it is wholly and literally down to earth.

Mary's experience on Easter Sunday morning illustrates the role of self-knowledge in understanding who Jesus really is. She shows how we do not recognise him without knowing ourselves. She is brought to self-knowledge by the simple means of being known by another. He knew her and called her by name. Self-knowledge does not just mean knowing more about ourselves. It is generated by relationship. In such a relationship we feel ourselves known and loved. But the center of consciousness also unhooks from its usual egotistical moorings and relocates in the other. Mary suffered her way through total grief to self-realisation in her Resurrection experience.

[6] Jn 20:10-18.
[7] 1 Cor 15:8.
[8] Compare the language of disclosing in Jn 21, the appearance of Jesus to his disciples by the Sea of Tiberias.

Maybe later, through the years in which that fresh morning's experience was being understood and absorbed, she recalled how Jesus had warned them of his approaching death. Perhaps she then understood why he had taught that to discover the true Self they would, like him, have to suffer the loss of their old selves. She would have understood why she had not recognised him; why, in some sense, we must become unrecognisable to ourselves in order to see who he really is.

Overwhelmed by grief at losing him Mary is in search of his body, the familiar form of his presence. She suffers the human agony of bereavement and the desolation of irreversible absence. So absorbed is she in her stricken memory of Jesus that she fails to recognise him when he meets her in his spiritual body, his new way of being present to her. The nonrecognition, however, validates the experience. It is an element on every occasion that the disciples first saw him. If Resurrection meant only the resuscitation of a corpse or if it was no more than a subjective 'psychological' event, then those to whom he 'appeared' in those Easter days would have had no difficulty recognising him. They would have been seeing what they wanted to see. They would not have been surprised—as reality always surprises us.

In a small monastic cell in San Marco in Florence Fra Angelico painted a fresco of this scene which gives a commentary where words fail. On the far left of the painting is the black rectangle of the empty tomb contrasting almost eerily with the lush green of the Resurrection garden. Jesus, translucent and weightless, bearing the wounds of his death on his hands and feet, and carrying the gardener's hoe turns towards Mary in the instant of her awakening. She, dressed in the red of this world is bathed in his light, her robes changing colour as she gazes in pure wonder at the beauty of his new form. They reach towards each other, never closer in spirit, but do not touch in the world of sense.

He is not invisible; not an insubstantial ghost or just a disembodied voice. If he were one of these, he would have been less complete in the Resurrection than he had been 'in life'. He would have been less alive. His new body however is more alive; he is even more real. His new freedom to reach into human beings beyond the barriers imposed by the mind or senses testifies to this. He is real enough to Mary's senses (she hears and sees him) but she just doesn't recognise him. Even questioned by him, talking to him, obsessed with him, she cannot *see*. She mistakes him for the gardener, just like someone cutting the grass you might pass as you walk down the avenue of a cemetery, or someone you brush past in the street or stand beside on the subway. Would she ever have recognised him unless he had first revealed himself to her by showing her that *he* recognised *her*?

Once again he communicates this through a question, similar to the compassionate question by which the Fisher King is healed and freed. The process of healing and self-recognition is begun. Awakening starts when he speaks her name. Knowing that she is known, her self-knowledge clears the veil of illusion which had hidden him from her. Spontaneously she addresses him as her guru: *rabbuni*, teacher. He is the same teacher who started her journey to self-knowledge and taught her through their friendship over the years. Now he speaks to her from deep within herself. It is a new degree of friendship, a level of intimacy where the usual dualities of inner and outer, even of the visible and invisible, strangely seems to be suspended. What has happened to her now explains and authenticates everything he taught her. Being known and knowing that we are loved, is how human identity comes into its own. We fully exist only in relationship. Outside relationship (or thinking we are outside it) we are illusory beings, no more than impermanent individuals. As individuals we are sentenced to death. But knowing we are loved, boundlessly and uniquely, raises us to a new degree of life as risen persons capable of truly loving. What Mary now experiences she 'sees'. What she sees is what she shares in.

There are three significant turnings in this scene after her encounter with the angels who also ask her why she is weeping. First she turns round and sees Jesus but does not recognise him. Then when he speaks her name she turns to him again. Had she turned away from him after asking him to take her to the body? Or is it an interior turn, a revolution of perception which has changed everything? The third turn is implicit in her leaving him. She lets go of the particular experience of this appearance and goes to the disciples with her news, 'I have seen the Lord.' He had told her not to cling to him because his return to the Father was not yet complete. There is no sense that she felt spurned. It had not been a passing experience. She knew he was with her. So, as the first Christian missionary, she ran to the disciples with nothing less than sheer joy. Mary's third turn is towards others.

The new kind of life made possible by the Resurrection does not rely upon the forensic evidence of the empty tomb or even the circumstantial evidence of the apparitions. The evidence is found in daily living. In fact Mary is told not to cling to the experience. Faith in the Resurrection is not crazy but it rests on a particular kind of sense and rationality. Ideas of what constitutes reason are historically variable. Like love, faith in the Resurrection has its own reasonableness and cannot be argued away by logic alone. Its truth is attested in a new quality of being, a heightened degree of wholeness that is caught rather than taught. Experiences, even Resurrection appearances, come and go. They become memories. We, however, know the Resurrection, in what the early disciples called the 'Day of Christ'. It is the present moment illuminated with faith's ability to see the invisible, to recognise the too obvious. As Simone Weil wrote,

> He comes to us hidden and salvation consists in our recognizing him.[9]

◦◦◦◦◦

The question that Jesus asks is the *rabbuni's* gift to us: its very asking bestows the 'grace of the guru'.

In every era his question is the gift waiting to be received. Its power simply, subtly to awaken Self-knowledge in our own experience of the Resurrection is perennial. St Thomas uses the present tense when he speaks of the Resurrection. He can be understood to be saying that the Resurrection by the divine power transcends all categories of space and time. In a similar way icons of the Resurrection in the Orthodox tradition suggest the same transcendence and show that the power that raised Jesus is presently and continuously active.[10]

The essential work of a spiritual teacher is just this: not to tell us what to *do* but to help us see who we *are*. The Self we come to know through its grace is not a separate, isolated little ego-self clinging to its memories, desires and fears. It is a field of consciousness similar to and indivisible from the Consciousness that is the God of cosmic and biblical revelation alike: the one great 'I AM'.

Jesus of Nazareth knew who he was within the limits of his mortal humanity. The risen Jesus is the Jesus of the Cosmos whose love of life was stronger than death and who knows himself in the bound- lessness of the Spirit. This knowledge, not miraculous powers or su-

---

[9] Simone Weil, *Waiting on God.*
[10] *Summa Theologica* III, q. 56, a. 2. resp. I am grateful to Fr Brian Johnstone of the Gregorian University in Rome for this and other perspectives on the Resurrec- tion.

pernatural experiences, is what he shares of himself liberally with humanity. This is what it was his nature and destiny to do:

> My task is to bear witness to the truth. For this I was born; for this I came into the world.[11]

His self-knowledge is the catalyst necessary to awaken his disciples' self-knowledge. Self-knowledge is the fundamental therapy, that healing of the soul which is the meaning of salvation. Carl Jung said that the crucial element in the relationship between analyst and patient is the therapist's own self-knowledge. This is a continuously evolving consciousness which derives much of its life from the therapist's interaction with the patient. We benefit ('receive grace') from the self-knowledge of Jesus in a way analogous to any deep human relationship. Because it is human and therefore reciprocal, we can even say that Jesus benefits from his relationship with us. Through us, with us and in us, he also comes to fulfilment. In St Paul's letters Jesus now lives in the 'Body of Christ' which is the whole of humanity and even co-extensive with the material universe. And so all individual human development, as in the growth of a community, contributes substantially to the building up, the completion of his Body.

God's 'need' for humanity can be glimpsed in Christ's love for us. It has been one of the great insights of Christian mystics down the centuries that if love is mutual, the love flowing between God and humanity somehow shares in the pain and joy, longing and fulfilment of the human condition. The more pedestrian theologians of the day were outraged by Meister Eckhart's witty exploration of this insight. Playing with words and paradox best conveys it. Julian of Norwich has this same mystical sense of humour and lightness of thought. She shares the same sense of the profound delicacy of divine love. She speaks of God's thirst for human well-being and the 'courteous' and joyful way that that thirst expressed itself in the suffering and resurrection of Jesus. It is 'inevitable', she says, that we will sin 'because of our weakness and stupidity'[12] yet there can never be any anger in God towards us. She conveys the entirely unconditional nature of God's love by describing God as Mother. She applies this to Jesus as well. As much as any mother 'our Mother Jesus' needs to feel loved by his children. In her great work, *Revelations of Divine Love*, Mother Julian drew

[11] Jn 18:37.
[12] Julian of Norwich, *Revelations of Divine Love*, Ch. 77.

her response to his question and her experience of his continued life. Because of it she cheerfully accepted the sufferings of life.

> Thus he is our Mother in nature, working by his grace in our lower part, for the sake of the higher. It is his will that we should know this, for he wants all our love to be fastened on himself . . . And this blessed love Christ himself produces in us.[13]

Everyone must work hard at coming to the self-knowledge necessary to know who Jesus is. The harder we work the more we are helped. Then our personal growth in turn builds up his Body. Individual spiritual practice is thus saved from the danger of spiritual egotism. It is never for the individual alone but through the greater Body of Christ that spiritual practice benefits the whole of humanity. Mother Julian knew that when she risked describing her experience and said that it had been given her for the cheering of others.

⋅◇⋅◇⋅◇⋅

Self-knowledge, which can hurt like hell at times, is nevertheless essentially joyful. And it always has the element of surprise. It is never predictable because it is never *going* to happen. It is always here. To realise that it is, and has always been here, is like finding that the glasses you have been looking for everywhere have never left the top of your head. We are surprised at finding them and maybe feel a little foolish. But we laugh with others, in joy and relief, because it is so clear we were never really separated from them.

Self-knowledge is also like freedom. It cannot be forced or cajoled. Being complacent and denying problems do not facilitate it. Forgiveness and love, on the other hand, can make it flourish. Repressive power structures, social or psychological, slow down the process. True spiritual practice, like good art, enhances human freedom. It develops the taste for freedom and a passion to let others enjoy it. So eventually it overturns every egotistically driven power-structure whether internalised within us and institutionalised around us. The spiritual path will therefore cause conflict, or bring it to light, within and outside us; but it also resolves conflict and accelerates growth. The process of self-knowledge develops discipline, perseverance, patience, all of which are necessary for freedom and justice. Because it is a process rather than an event, we may not know the dates and times of our awakening

---

[13] Ibid., Ch. 60.

any more than we know when we will die. But we can see it happening within us and we can see its influence on the world we inhabit.

We also learn soon enough how impatience slows us down. As soon as you begin to practice a serious spiritual path, to listen to the silence, you meet inner resistance. To continue to meditate is then to struggle with all the innumerable conditioned habits and patterns of the ego, our individual and collective narcissism. The East calls them the countless *vasanas*. Soon after the first turn on the spiritual journey, one that can be accompanied by feelings of bliss and many sweet consolations, it all seems to get blocked. It feels as if some inner negative force is complicating and spoiling what had felt so simple and delightful. A demonic curve seems to be thrown into the divine directness. This is where the grace of the teacher is indispensable.

And be assured, I am with you always, to the end of time.[14]

Even with the *rabbuni* so close—closer to us than we are to ourselves according to St Augustine—the power of self-deception and illusion can be overwhelming. Often the path disappears beneath us as we struggle with the demons of anger, fear, pride, greed and ignorance.

At times we may even glimpse embarrassingly the absurd envy of the ego towards the guru. Being jealous of Jesus is the Judas-reflex in the human psyche, the dark side of the luminous night of faith. It has shown itself in many powerful minds like Nietsche. The ego only slowly learns, like a difficult child, that there is no need to compete with Jesus. It is eventually stopped in its tracks when it discovers that there *is* no competition anyway. You cannot argue for long with someone who is silent when you expect them to retaliate. You cannot fight forever with someone who turns the other cheek. You cannot push someone over who gives way. Every predictable power-structure which the ego seeks to defend is overturned by the humility of the true Self. As our own experience of the Self awakens we see how we do not have to prove ourselves equal to Jesus. He has already renounced his superiority. He has called us his friends.

I call you servants no longer; a servant does not know what his master is about. I have called you friends, because I have disclosed to you everything that I heard from my Father.[15]

[14] Mt 28:20.
[15] Jn 15:15.

⟨◦⟩◦⟨◦⟩

Friendship is perhaps the most evocative way of describing our relationship with Jesus.

Pilate asked Jesus if he was a king and Jesus did not deny it. But made it clear it was a different kind of kingship from any that Pilate had in mind. Every friend is a king in the sense Jesus used: a benevolent ruler, protector and educator in the life of the one befriended. Friendship expresses itself in precise acts of love, concern, and intimate thoughtfulness. Jesus performed one of these before the last meal that he was to share with his friends. He washed their feet. Peter, who thought he knew who Jesus was, recoiled at this offer of menial, humiliating service. Jesus insisted. And when he had finished the ritual he asked them if they had understood what he had done for them. Clearly they had not. History went on to show how often his later disciples would also miss the point.

> You call me Master and Lord, and rightly so for that is what I am. Then if I, your Lord and Master, have washed your feet, you also ought to wash one another's feet. I have set you an example: you are to do as I have done for you.[16]

Later during the meal, the first Eucharist, Jesus opened their minds further to the meaning of what he had done, of who he was for them. He told them they were not his servants, his devotees or acolytes, but his friends. Friendship needs to be expressed and grows through its signs. His sign of friendship was that he had disclosed to them everything he had heard from his Father. By word and deed. He had come to know who he was through his listening to the silence of the Father. It was this knowledge he shared with them. His friends are those who allow him to wash their feet with his self-knowledge. A profound new symbol of God entered humanity's history at that moment. It is one we have still not fully understood because it so surprisingly confounds all earlier images of God. His friendship with humanity opens new depths of consciousness that reach into the abyss of the Creator's love.

Outside the divine friendship all other knowledge of God is tainted by the ego's sense of separation. Without friendship the spiritual path is distorted by the religious roles we play: fear, formal reverence, self-conscious submission, bargaining, flattery, guilt, forced praise. All of

[16] Jn 13:12-15.

these are substitutes for true ways to the knowledge of God. Sometimes, of course, as AA members know, you have to 'fake it to make
it'. But when we fail to see God in the light of friendship it is because
our own role-playing deceives us. These roles give the ego a stage for
self-exhibition, to dress up in religious garb as saint, sinner, priest or
martyr, philosopher or mystic. The friendless part of us clings to these
identities in compensation for its loneliness. We even begin to enjoy
it. Friendship, however, permits no pretence or deception. Nothing
more is needed in friendship than fidelity. Even self-justification is
irrelevant because no one knows us better than a true friend. If we
fool a friend we fool ourselves. And without being known by a friend
who can come to self-knowledge? By this high standard we can see
how few real friends we make in a lifetime. How many are the mis-
judgements of friends we call betrayals. And yet, when we do find
God in the gift of friendship and glimpse God's friendship towards
humanity, we have reached the highest goal, the 'end of love-longing'.

Friendship has been devalued in our culture. In other times however it was recognised as the noblest expression of relationship. A life
without a friend was less than human. One of the essential goals of
life for a civilised person was to find and cultivate a person suitable
to be a true friend, 'another one's self' as Plato called it. Friendship
was understood to develop in the sharing of self-knowledge. You cannot be friends without knowing it and knowing it means you know
you are known. This rich classical tradition of friendship entered into
Christian thought and one of its greatest exponents was a twelfth-
century English monk, Aelred of Rievaulx. He wrote the only complete
treatise on friendship in medieval Christian literature, *Amicitia Spirituale*.
It is a psychological and spiritual masterpiece combining both passion
and prudence. In his work he drew into Christian thought the main
classical themes: the dignity of friendship and its ennobling effect, the
different types of friendship, from the utilitarian to the most selfless
and the need to balance emotion and reason by not forcing the pace
of growth in the friendship. His unique Christian contribution however
was the insight that all human friendships are born and grow to fulfilment in Christ. When two friends truly love one another as Jesus
instructed, they would experience the wonder of recognising him as
being present with them.

And thus a friend praying to Christ on behalf of his friend and
for his friend's sake desiring to be heard by Christ, directs his

attention with love and longing to Christ: then it sometimes happens that quickly and imperceptibly the one love passes over into the other and coming as it were into contact with the sweetness of Christ himself, the friend begins to taste his sweetness and to experience his charm...Thus ascending from that holy love with which he embraces a friend to that with which he embraces Christ, he will joyfully partake in abundance of the spiritual fruit of friendship, awaiting the fullness of all things in the life to come. Then with the dispelling of all anxiety by reason of which we now fear and are solicitous for one another, with the removal of all anxiety which it now behooves us to bear for one another, and above all, with the destruction of the sting of death together with death itself, whose pangs now often trouble us and force us to grieve for one another, with salvation secured, we shall rejoice in the eternal possession of Supreme Goodness; and this friendship, to which here we admit but few, will be outpoured upon all and by all outpoured upon God, and God shall be all in all.[17]

'Eternal life'—life free of all constraints—becomes humanly accessible in this great incarnational vision of God.

As with any human relationship, friendship with Jesus proceeds by stages. One of the first things we do when a relationship begins to deepen is to remember the history of the friendship from the moment of first meeting. It becomes one of the irreplaceable stories within the story of our life. It is inconceivable that we could be friends with someone without wanting and needing to know the basic facts about their life and origins. Their past in some way needs to be appropriated into the shared story the friendship is creating. This is why it is natural to want to know what Jesus of Nazareth was like, what influences formed him, what he really taught and did. A lot of time has passed and his contemporaries had different ideas about biography from ours. There is a lot we will never know about him but the gospels give all we need to know.

---

[17] Aelred of Rievaulx, *On Spiritual Friendship*, 3:133-34.

∽ 4 ∽

What Are the Gospels?

*E*arly one glorious evening when the sun seemed determined not to set I
stopped in at my cousin's house and found his two young boys glued to the
television. It was rare to find them indoors when the weather was so good unless
it was to watch Ireland play football. I wondered what programme had proved
stronger than their irrepressible instinct to have real adventures outdoors. They
were watching Baywatch, a series set on the beaches of southern California with
huge ratings and a low budget for the cast's wardrobe. How these Bere Island
boys would compare the fantasy world of southern California with the cold pebbly
beaches of West Cork where any bathers attracted admiration more for their
physical courage in undressing than for their defined physiques, I discussed later
with my cousin. He looked pensive.

In the old days, he said, before twenty-four hour TV, people entertained each
other with the recital of their family histories. Every evening, even in the worst
weather, they would do the tour of each other's houses to sit by the peat fire with
a glass of the real stuff in reach and recount again the epic stories of each
household. The same stories would be repeated continuously, often re-interpreting
familiar facts. There would be frequent updates with news about those who had
gone to America or Australia or England. Personalities, deaths and births, feuds
and reconciliations. Powerful feelings tempered by time or the instincts of justice.
Storytelling was a liturgy of the island community. It was also a way of entertainment, a characteristic Irish delight in the use of imagination and words for
their own sake. But it was serious too: a way of making meaning of the close-
knit world of Bere Island and its now dwindling population.

Privacy and the low whisper were important values among this community
that constantly communicated itself to itself. People lived so closely to each other
that mistakes were hard to undo. What was said in anger or bitterness today
might take years to stop hurting. But nothing went unnoticed or uncared for.
Privacy did not mean isolation. And in the perspective of history all events
belonged to the community not only to the individual or the family. After the
invasion of television people no longer braved the winter cold, the devil that
prowled abroad to chase late-night card-players on their way home or the spirits
that were older even than the church's angels and devils. People no longer did

the rounds of their neighbours to talk their own stories into the larger stories of the island. Now they stay indoors and watch soaps made in Hollywood for a global market. The ancient stories were dying for lack of telling, as friendships or plants die when they are not given the time needed to tend them. To forget is the unforgiveable sin.

The gospels were written only after they had long been talked. Even today their stories need to be spoken aloud and can only be properly read within the oral as well as a bookish tradition. Word of mouth is still their essential means of transmission. And the old wisdom of the islanders applies to this story-telling as well: to tell a story you have got to believe it, to put yourself and all that is important to you, into it.

◦❯◦❯◦❯◦

To read the gospels through is to see that, to understand who Jesus is, we must start by seeing him at the least as a teacher. Everyone agrees that Jesus is a teacher.

His way of teaching was both private and public: to an inner group of disciples and to the crowds. But it was not esoteric in a secretive sense. He told his judges at his trial that he had taught openly and not in secret.[1] He did not have a schoolhouse or Academy in the style of Greek philosophers. Instead he walked the roads of Palestine. He spoke in the open air, by the side of lakes, hillsides, in fields and also in synagogues, at meals in private homes and in the courts of the Temple in Jerusalem. He taught by parable and aphorism. His language was simple and graphic showing a preference for natural symbolism and the kind of stories which a people in touch with the life of nature and of a local community would have enjoyed. It avoided intellectual analysis and legalistic hair-splitting. He drew on well-known stories and daily images familiar to his listeners.

We know his teaching almost entirely from the four gospels. In a sense the gospels are the notes taken by others of the living words of a teacher who, like Socrates and the Buddha, did not himself write books. Only once is he shown writing when he bends to write unknown words in the dust.[2] He communicated his message orally, in the interactive process of teaching people who sat listening to his words, some spellbound, some thinking of dinner, everyone watching his facial expressions and gestures. It is a living teaching of 'one who

[1] Jn 18:21.
[2] Jn 8:8.

taught with authority' waiting for us in these inspired notebooks. That is why it is so important to consider how we should read them.

First of all, there are four gospels not one. Like all notebooks they remind us that everyone takes different notes of the same talk and in the later oral report further elaborations are made. An industry of scholarship today explores the theories of how the gospels were written, by whom, for whom and how they influenced each other. There will probably never be universal agreement. The major goal however is not to explain how they were written but how to read them well. To try merely to reduce the four perspectives to one 'historical' reality behind them is to seriously misread them.

We make the same misreading when we dissect the gospels in search of the 'real historical Jesus'. The problem, to paraphrase Pontius Pilate, is to know 'What is real?' We have become so conditioned to the prose of science and sociology as the language of reality that we have lost an ear for the other tones in which human experience expresses itself and what is beyond itself. We dismiss them as 'unhistorical' or 'mythical' and try to translate them reductively back into the language of 'factual truth'. This attempt betrays the text. It fails to see how other methods can communicate truths that the scientific method will never grasp. To deny the many-layered texture of reality that calls for different methods of expression is like claiming that the mystery of human consciousness can be reductively explained away as electro-chemical processes in the brain.

We can never know for sure, 'in fact', who wrote the gospels attributed to Matthew, Mark, Luke and John. As texts they grew within both oral and written traditions but were further refined by personal prayer and communal discussion. People walked from place to place thinking of the stories and sayings that later coalesced in the texts we know. As in the first moments after the Big Bang, the bits and pieces of the cosmos of the gospel were still in a disconnected and chaotic state in the early days of the Christian movement. By being told and retold they fell into shape and eventually into the form of the written texts we know. Each textual problem illustrates how a text represents the mind of a whole community for whom the individual is a channel. Such rich texts enshrine many levels of meaning of which the literal-historical is only one.

The gospels make explicit what was already implicit in the several oral traditions that developed in the first Christian generation. Although they are based on historical events they are not investigative journalism. How can we ever neatly separate different levels of meaning or draw a sharply defined line between the symbolic and the historical? Partly, at least, by not worrying about the inconsistencies between the four books. The gospels have a unity but they are not uniform nor were they intended to be. Their various strands cannot be unraveled without losing the whole pattern. Early modern scholars, like Strauss, Renan and Schweitzer, attempted to do just this. Their failure nevertheless helps to define our way of approaching the historical Jesus and the way the gospels were composed. Bultmann, the German biblical scholar, came to the conclusion, one largely accepted today, that a normal historical biography of Jesus cannot be conceived because historical or psychological biography was not what the gospel writers were about. Some modern scholars do claim that by the standards of their time the gospel writers were writing biographies. Nevertheless, for us, the great silent gaps in the early life of Jesus, the loss of the original contexts in which Jesus' sayings were uttered and even of a sure chronology of events, all mean that we should not expect to read the gospels as normal biography.

A new book about Tolstoy means a reinterpretation of well-attested facts or the revelation of new facts or documents. Any book on Jesus adopts or adapts a position of faith not just an interpretation. The historical facts about Jesus that we can be sure of are important but they are principally interesting with regard to *who we say he is*. The insight into his identity is the first and foremost meaning of the gospels not just 'what really happened' in a journalistic or legalistic sense. What really happened in a spiritual sense, as in the case of the Resurrection precisely reveals who he really is. This means that we cannot talk about the identity of Jesus without in some way asserting or rejecting faith. The method of modern investigative reductionism is a rejection of faith. It leads to a profound misreading of texts which themselves are expressions of faith. If this sounds like saying that you can only *fully* understand what the gospels are and mean if you share their faith, that is what I am saying. How we respond to the redemptive question of Jesus determines how we read the gospels—and vice versa.

In 63 BC the Roman general Pompey strode sacrilegiously into the Holy of Holies in the Temple of Jerusalem to find out what was at the heart of the Jewish religion that was causing him so much trouble. He expected to find a statue or cult object, some kind of visible mystery. He found nothing at all, merely a small empty room and left

astounded and contemptuous. To invade the gospels with that kind of
insensitivity will breed the same kind of insensitivity. To read them
well we must also understand what we should *not* be looking for.
Otherwise we will not see what is there, waiting silently for us to find.

⌒⊙⌒⊙⌒⊙

Reading the gospels means more than studying and analysing them or
performing textual surgery. But it also means more than making a cult
object out of them and reading them with daft literalism. Another
kind of reading is required: a *prayerful* reading. The monastic tradition
called this method *lectio divina*.

One of the most ancient Christian ideas is based on this: *lex orandi
est lex credendi*, the structure of prayer is the structure of belief. The
way we believe is the way we pray. The quality and depth of prayer
determines the quality and depth of our beliefs and therefore also of
our way of living. For so many Christians the gospels, like prayer itself,
have got stuck at a superficial cerebral level—the level of merely thinking about and speaking to God. Cerebral here does not mean highly
intellectual. Getting stuck here encourages fantasy just as much as
rational thought. As the experiential wellsprings of faith remained un-
opened in the training of most Christians, it is no wonder that their
spiritual maturity is often so shallow. Even Christians trained in their
religion from childhood have seldom read the gospels right through
on their own. And few are encouraged, in school or parish, to pray in
more than the way they learned as children, checking in with heaven
from time to time to ask for favours or to assuage guilt. Without deeper
spiritual development earlier, it is hardly surprising when the storms
of adult life shake such faith to its roots.

Whether and how we *read* the gospels shapes how we believe, not
only about Jesus but also about ourselves. Our way of reading the
gospels is itself trained through a regular contemplative practice of
prayer. If most Christians have to learn how to read their scriptures,
most also have to discover that prayer is more than telling God what
we want and flattering or bargaining with Him to get it. Like reading
the gospels, to pray is a continuous education and training in faith.
Prayer and *lectio* are not scientific methods or techniques but spiritual
arts. Neither is an art that one perfects in a lifetime. They require
regular practice and perseverance. They are delightful and challenging
in themselves. But both demand the generous commitment needed for
all learning: attention, discipline, detachment from preconceptions and

prejudices, and openness. What are these gospels that we must learn to read prayerfully and that also teach us to pray?

⋅◇⋅◇⋅◇⋅

There are four official versions of the life and teaching of Jesus. But we could as well have had six, ten or twenty gospels rather than four.

St Luke remarks at the opening of his gospel that there were many other accounts in circulation in the first century after the Resurrection 'following the traditions handed down to us by the original eyewitnesses and servants of the gospel'.[3] The four standard or canonical gospels (Matthew, Mark, Luke and John) were written for people living outside Palestine two or three generations after the events they describe. Probably none of the four evangelists was an eyewitness of the events he describes. Luke's reference to many other accounts would not have included the gospel of Peter or the gospel of Thomas which date from the second century, later even than John who is thought to have been the last of the great four evangelists. We no longer possess the sources which Luke knew about.

Mark, a disciple of St Peter, wrote in Rome and portrays Jesus especially in terms of a healer and the awaited but concealed messiah, but is also focussed upon his identity as 'Son of God'. *Matthew*, popularly identified with the tax-collector who left everything and followed Jesus,[4] was writing for Jewish Christians in Greece and Syria and sees Jesus as the new Moses and the fulfilment of Jewish prophecy. *Luke*, a disciple of St Paul, a physician and the most literary evangelist, portrays Jesus as the defender of the poor and the outcast and gives special recognition to the women disciples. For *John*, traditionally identified with the 'beloved disciple' of Jesus' core group of twelve, and author of perhaps the last of the gospels, Jesus was the Christ of faith, the Incarnation of the divine Logos. And yet in John's account Jesus also appears at his most human: we see Jesus weep; we see him tired on a hot afternoon's journey; we see him grieving for the death of a friend; we learn that he had a favourite disciple. From its own unique perspective each gospel sees the details of Jesus' life and teaching charged with symbolic significance. Nothing lacks meaning.

Apart from many apocryphal gospels, there is also the fifth evangelical wheel, the gospel of *Paul*, who claimed to be no less of an

[3] Lk 1:2.
[4] Mt 9:9.

apostle than those who had walked with the Cosmic Christ, the New Man, the Second Adam.

The gospels are different windows looking into the same reality. Two thousand years of reading have not exhausted the views they give of a public life that lasted no more than three years and the extraordinary, disastrous culmination of that life. The diversity of interpretations they offer reinforces a fundamental unity of faith. The idea that there once existed only a single, monolithic Christian orthodoxy which was later fragmented or diluted is not supported by the richness and diversity of the perspectives found in the gospels. In them we find a broad spectrum of views and responses to the question of who Jesus is. Some of these views were already distinct enough to create conflict in the early church.[5]

Christianity seems to many commentators to be an exhausted institution today. It can also be seen as undergoing yet another of the periodic renewals which its many vocabularies and theologies have generated from its inception. Its renewals are driven by experience rather than theory, by personal insight and conversion. Behind this is an experience of faith radicalised by the rereading of the gospels in the light of a contemplative experience of prayer. From this perspective Christianity appears as a relatively young religion on the world stage standing today on new thresholds of self-knowledge and preparing to evolve into its next phase through contemplative renewal and dialogue and with other religions. Through all its cycles of change the central question of the gospels, the defining question of Christian discipleship, remains constant. It is still *who do you say I am?* We listen to it today as did the first hearers of the gospels, with minds opened by prayer and nourished by the art of spiritual reading—and by visiting each others 'homes to tell the same stories and talk about them'.

◦•◦•◦•

Long before the gospels were written down the Eucharistic meal was celebrated in Christian homes.

The presence of Jesus was tasted and enjoyed in the friendship, the *koinonia* as the New Testament calls it, of the Eucharistic fellowship. This is expressed in a sacramental ritual which both nourishes and is nourished by a reading of the gospels. Reading aloud a passage

---

[5] James D. G. Dunn, *Unity and Diversity in the New Testament: An Inquiry into the Character of Early Christianity.*

of the gospels selected in thoughtful relationship to other biblical readings is a pivotal moment in the celebration of the Eucharist. A spiritual teaching inspired by the readings follows and should stimulate some shared reflection among the participants. There is not an audience. In the Eucharistic friendship clearer insight into the gospel, not always so easy to achieve in personal *lectio*, frequently comes to light. When this is shared it is felt as a sense of Jesus' own presence.

According to St Gregory the Great the scriptures are waters where lambs may walk and elephants swim.[6] They suit a variety of temperaments and moods. At least up to the twelfth century Christian spirituality and its mystical tradition were rooted in *lectio divina*, the subtle reading of the gospel. This kind of reading is in itself neither scholarly nor polemical. You don't read in this way to prove a point or win an argument. *Lectio* is a 'breaking of the word'. It is as real a form of presence as the Eucharistic breaking of bread. Early Christian teachers said that the crumbs of meaning which fall when the Word is broken should be treated as reverentially as the crumbs of the consecrated bread.

The desert monks are an early inspiration both for *lectio* and for the contemplative prayer with which it is so closely related. The monks had a profound love for scripture, but not for books. First they performed immense feats of biblical memorisation regarding the gospels and the psalms as the minimum requirement for their life in the desert. The books they then gave away. Their minds were thus continuously saturated and nourished by the words they had interiorised. The Word of God itself, they felt, entered into their flesh, deepening their inner life and strengthening their emotional responses to the tests and ordeals of their outer life.

St Bernard inherited this ancient monastic practice of the interiorisation and of what he called the 'inverbation' of Scripture. He describes this 'tasting' of the Word in strikingly sensory terms:

> As food is sweet to the palate, so does a psalm delight the heart. But the soul that is sincere and wise will not fail to chew the psalm with her teeth, as it were, of the mind. Because if she swallows it in a lump without proper mastication her palate will be cheated of the delicious flavour, sweeter even than honey that drips from the comb... With what sweetness he suffused my nostrils and my ears when he breathed forth and sang of the oil

---

[6] *Moralia sive Expositio in Iob*, dedication, iv.

of gladness ... What is more fragrant than the breath of John who makes sweet for me the eternal generation and divinity of the Word? What shall I say of Paul's breathings, how they have filled the world with sweetness? Now the sweet savour of Christ is everywhere.[7]

The practical advice of the teachers of *lectio* is to chew the words of scripture in small doses. You chew the Word as a cow chews the cud. By continuous rumination the finer flavours and nutrients are released to delight and enlighten the mind and heart. If you are not living in the fourth-century Egyptian desert or on Bere Island the practice can be adapted to any life style: Choose a time and a quiet place to sit or walk with a short passage of the gospels. It could be a parable, a healing story or some words of Jesus. Modern editions of the gospel arrange the texts in short sections very suitable for *lectio*. The aim is not to read a lot. The discipline is to stay within the passage selected but with a sense of deepening freedom and openness. Read and reread the passage or parts of it, even aloud when you feel like it. After several rereadings you will probably find a particular word, a detail or phrase standing out and asking for closer attention. Zoom in on it not like a jet attacking a target but like a birdwatcher following a rare specimen. The art is to listen with the heart. To taste the truth of an experience with the spiritual senses.

Interpretations will present themselves in the course of *lectio* according to your temperament, your mood of the moment and the circumstances of your life at that time. These readings of the gospel will thus also become a way of reading your life.

⋅◌⋅◌⋅◌⋅

For centuries people who have wondered who Jesus is have explored the truth about him through this kind of spiritual reading. An experience of truth results from it because we both read the gospels and we are *read by* them. This relationship with the Word allows the text of the gospel to become a pathway from the head to the heart. The same path connects a contemplative state of imageless inner silence to the conversations and decisions of active life. The Word has this power to bridge and harmonise both dimensions of reality.

[7] John R. Sommerfeldt, *The Spiritual Teachings of St. Bernard of Clairvaux*, p. 76.

We may practise *lectio* alone or in community but the art is a solitary one. Yet it is also performed within a tradition. Study and spiritual training help us to become at home with it and even to contribute to its further development. A tradition is born and grows through all the ways people enter the truth and teach each other. All these are attempts that fall short but, held as they are in the lore of the community, even failures and misreadings have meaning. Because of this we learn how to read the gospels better by seeing how others misread them.

Thomas Jefferson[8] for example read the gospels carefully with a quick, eighteenth-century rational mind. He liked a lot of what he found—'many passages of fine imagination, correct morality, and of the most lovely benevolence'. These passed the test of his criteria of reason. However there were other passages, such as the 'hard sayings of Jesus' or the attack on the Pharisees, which he dismissed as so 'ignorant and absurd' that they could only be explained as interpolations by later Christian authors. So Jefferson, like many other readers in history and today, rewrote the gospels to his liking. He composed a little book called *The Life and Morals of Jesus of Nazareth* in which he drew an eighteenth-century Americanised portrait of Jesus. Leo Tolstoy made a similar selective reading of the gospels. He allowed them to convert him to the teaching of Jesus—but not to the teacher. He rejected everything he considered 'supernatural' which included the miracles, the doctrine of grace and the Resurrection.

Fundamentalists misread the texts also when they allow no interpretation or rather when their literalism is imposed as the only possible interpretation. A similar retailoring of the gospels happens when religious syncretists mismatch scriptures from different traditions and try to force equivalency onto them. Of course, parallels between different scriptures are at the core of interreligious dialogue, the challenge of which is the great project of our time. But, as the Dalai Lama said at the 1994 John Main Seminar where he performed a Buddhist *lectio* on the gospels, when you draw parallels you must also recognise that the differences are as important as the similarities. To focus only on the parallels, he said, twists the truth. The Dalai Lama believes that dialogue should not aim to create an amorphous 'universal religion'.

---

[8] Thomas Jefferson, *The Life and Morals of Jesus of Nazareth* (Princeton, NJ: Princeton University Press, 1983).

In searching for unity, he said smiling, we must not create an unnatural religious hybrid: 'You cannot put a yak's head on a sheep's body!'

We listen to the teaching of Jesus from our own point of view but our point of view is contained in a tradition. We can risk making mistakes because the friendly wisdom of orthodoxy (literally, 'right teaching') is there, not to condemn, but to catch us if we fall. But only by being in our own place can his redemptive question reach us personally. It sounds in every passage of the gospel. Reading his teaching or his healing miracles, his passion and death gives us the uplifting sense that comes from being close to a great teacher. However we have not just been touched by his words and actions but also by the wisdom of the Word itself, the universal Logos, that sounds through them. In *lectio* we break through language and go beyond thought into *insight*. We *see* Jesus more clearly than before. We see our world and ourselves more clearly in this light of the Self. As St Paul put it, we are now seeing with the 'mind of Christ' and not merely with our own.

Reading the gospels is a key, therefore, into the true nature of the Self. This knowledge is tasted through experiential insight not merely through thought or active imagination. Insight is the intuitive perception of truth beyond the hundred thousand operations of mind. The light by which we read is the Resurrection-faith in which they were written. It is in the time-free, egoless consciousness of the Resurrection that we meet the historical Jesus in the fullness of his story as he is now. In that place without boundaries his words *dwell in us and bear fruit in plenty.*[9]

> You have already been cleansed by the word that I spoke to you. Dwell in me as I in you.[10]

> And the word you hear is not mine: it is the word of the Father who sent me . . . I am not myself the source of the words I speak to you.[11]

◦◦◦◦◦◦◦

Origen who taught in Alexandria in the third century was the first great Christian thinker to describe systematically how the mind's encounter with the scriptures lifts the mind above itself.

[9] Jn 15:7.
[10] Jn 15:3.
[11] Jn 14:24, 10.

He saw the reading of the Bible as a way of deepening conscious-ness. Many levels of understanding are therefore involved: literal, meta-phorical, moral and mystical. Later St Bernard described it as like extracting the fruit of meaning that lies beneath the rind of the letter.[12] The process, as Origen understood it, begins with the literal meaning of the text, a meaning that requires both knowledge of history and grammar. The letter killeth however when it is taken no further than the literal: fundamentalism misreads the text precisely because it is so superficial. Seeing the stories and characters of scripture as 'types' or symbols opens the second level of *lectio*. These teach us divine truth by analogy with our present life-situations. Then, Origen said, the level of 'allegorical' or mystical meaning awaits us when we are lifted above ourselves and absorbed into the Logos itself. Understanding the mir-acles of Jesus, for example, benefits from this more subtle approach. The miracles can pose great problems of credibility when they are read only at the literal level. This does not mean they did not really happen but the literal interpretation is not the only and may not be the most rewarding one.

Origen applied his method to the whole Bible. Of the Old Testa-ment he said:

> You must not think that all these things happened only in earlier times ... in fact all these things come true in *you* in a mystical way.[13]

The goal of reading the Bible is not less than to ascend where Jesus has ascended. Then, as Origen said, in reading the gospels we come 'to gallop through the vast spaces of mystic and spiritual understanding'.[14]

St Bernard spoke of scripture as a window or lattice through which we look into the divine reality. In reading scripture we pursue the timeless Word of God back to its source. St Bernard called it an 'endless following of the Word'. On the way we experience *inverbation*—by which the Word becomes actually part of us and we of it.

Reading the gospels is an awakening of mystical intelligence. The time given to reading them strengthens spiritual understanding which when awakened benefits the whole of life. Dante called it the *intelli-*

[12] Sommerfeldt, *The Spiritual Teachings of St Bernard of Clairvaux*, p. 77.
[13] Origen, *Commentary on St Paul's Epistle to the Romans*, trans. W. S. Plummer (Grand Rapids, MI: Kregel Publications, 1993).
[14] Ibid., 7.11.

gence of love that begins spontaneously to operate in all our activities and in every situation. It comes to regulate how we deal with the inner weather of moods and feelings as well as their outer environment of life. Like the training of attention in the use of a mandala, like gazing into the great rose window of a medieval cathedral, contemplating and ingesting the words of the gospels stills the seeking mind.

⊸⊙⊶⊙⊶

Reading the gospels therefore requires selfless attention.

More of a personal commitment of effort is asked in reading them in this way than in the superstitious way in which many of the ancient systems of divination are used today. *Lectio* is not white magic. The work of *lectio* requires an *interaction* with the text and with all its levels and dimensions of meaning. It is faith and intelligence, reason and imagination, word and silence harmonising together. We are not *passive* before the Word. Listening to it energises us to hear it from an even greater stillness and so prepares us both for selfless action and contemplation.

When a person in therapy wants the therapist to do all the work they lose their own authority. A therapist who does not understand his own ego can encourage this and thereby feed a dependency that traps the patient in an infantile state. The Spirit however, who is the guide in the therapeutic act of *lectio*, as of all prayer, teaches the reader how to do the work and to stick with it through dry and difficult periods. Stillness of attention is then necessary to respond to the redemptive question that permeates every word of the gospel. Through attention faith grows, nourished by the two sources of all spiritual authority: personal insight and tradition.

The wisdom we are seeking in reading the gospels is not magically located in any mechanical process. Wisdom is found to reside in the person who is seeking it through the spiritual practice to which they are devoted. By interacting with the accumulated wisdom of the tradition that supports the personal reading, the Spirit is released, realised and recognised within and by the reader.

We develop mystical intelligence by reading the gospels in this way. Progressively this intelligence illuminates and enriches ordinary life. This is quite different from attributing magical power to the literal meaning: a misreading which disrupts rather than enhances ordinary life. A fundamentalist reader of the Bible once appealed to his well-thumbed book for instant guidance in a moral dilemma. He flicked the pages and placed his finger blindly on a verse. It read 'and Judas went and hanged himself'. Thinking something had gone wrong with his divination he thought he would try again. This time the verse he alighted on read 'go thou and do likewise'. It was perhaps the beginning of his learning how truly to do *lectio*.

◦❊◦❊◦❊◦

The Orthodox theologian Vladimir Lossky says that the scriptures contain a 'margin of silence' and that this cannot be understood by those who stand outside them. If we want to learn to read prayerfully, we must learn the art of prayer which is to listen to the silence.[15]

Learning how to read the gospels is one of the first fruits of meditation. In the fifth century John Cassian remarked that when he had begun this practice of imageless prayer he found it more demanding than he had expected. But he also discovered that scripture lay open to his understanding with a remarkable new freshness and clarity.

> For divine Scripture is clearer and its inmost organs, so to speak, are revealed to us when our experience not only perceives but even anticipates its thought, and the meanings of the words are disclosed to us not by exegesis but by proof. When we have the same disposition in our heart with which each psalm was sung or written down, then we shall become like its author, grasping its significance beforehand rather than afterward . . .

More is to come. Once this clarity has been reached it leads to 'pure prayer'.

> Thus we shall penetrate its meaning not through the written text but with experience leading the way. So it is that our mind will arrive at that incorruptible prayer (that) is not only not laid hold of by the sight of some image, but . . . cannot even be grasped by any word or phrase. Rather, once the mind's attentiveness has been set ablaze, it is called forth in an unspeakable ecstasy of heart and with an insatiable gladness of spirit . . .[16]

Cassian was a great reader of scripture before he found the method of meditation that led him to this. But even people who have no habit of *lectio* can find an unexpected thirst developing for scripture as a

[15] Vladimir Lossky, *In the Image and Likeness of God*, especially the essay 'Tradition and Traditions'.
[16] John Cassian, *Conferences*, 10: XI, 14, trans. Boniface Ramsey.

result of their work of silence. Others who have been reading scripture for many years sense a change in the way they are now read *by* it. Suddenly, hearing even such a familiar phrase as 'God is love' can startle the mind into a new constellation of all life's values.

Every spiritual practice—*lectio*, devotional or discursive prayer, meditation or the selfless service of others—is a way of faith. With the *eye of faith* opened and purified, another dimension of consciousness is awakened. We read the gospels and all the sacred scriptures of humanity with this eye of faith.

Faith enhances freedom because it is not the same as logical certainty. We read the gospels with reason enhanced by faith not in competition with it. With pure logic there is no personal freedom. The mind imposes logical truth. If, with your rational mind, you see that ten divided by five equals two you are not really free to believe it or not. To deny it is absurd. But faith invites a personal response that we are free to choose or reject. So with love. When you realise that you love or are loved a disturbing challenge enters your life. You are confronted with a vast space of freedom in which to affirm or deny that truth. This means reordering the values and priorities of life and personal commitment becomes a central issue. The challenge of faith, like love, is an experience that can cause moral vertigo at first. It is the price of freedom.

The gospels are a guidebook to this new space of human freedom. We read them according to the 'Law of White Spaces': a rabbi was approached by a group of his students who had been wrangling over the meaning of a difficult part of the Torah. He asked them to show him the page and then asked what they saw there. The words we are disputing about, they replied, the black marks on the page. Right, he said, well, the words contain half the meaning. The white spaces between the words are where the other half of the meaning is to be found.

ᔧ 5 ᔨ
The Life of Jesus

On an island seven miles long and three miles wide and with a population of less than two hundred there is space to live and time to remember your ancestors. You can drive from the east to the west end along a narrow road between the hedgerows in less time than it takes to move a few yards in a city traffic jam. But every tumbledown cottage you pass, every modernised villa, (someone who came back with money, or a Dubliner's holiday home), every field and crossroad is a place where ghosts congregate waiting to be remembered. Before understanding the psychic density of these places the stranger needs to have heard and accumulated the stories of the lives lived there, and to hear them many times and to sense how they are interwoven. My grandmother's scandalous atheistic brother who became a friend of Bernard Shaw and edited a radical newspaper of ungodly views in Canada. The unmarried girl who became pregnant and disappeared without trace and without comment—in England, perhaps, or in the bog on the wild side of the island facing the ocean? The old woman with the evil eye baited by the children but whose isolation must have given her a rare independence of mind because she feared no one, not even the priest. The man who stayed out too late drinking and playing cards and was chased back home by the devil as a black dog with flaming eyes.

There is also the deeper ache of more painful memories. The evictions. When the landlord's thugs came like storm troopers in the dead of night to turn the poverty-stricken hungry families out of their homes and burn their cottages to the ground. So many lives and vivid stories in a place where nothing much happened that ever made the world's headlines; but where life was often lived with an intensity and passion unmatched in the noisy and distracted cities. The events of individual lives surviving in the collective memory are skillfully selected with the genius of centuries of story-telling, by the heirs of the anonymous bards and shanacees. The stories illustrate judgements long made. They probe ever-wider circles of meaning around familiar events. And as in all biographies they are only the tip of the iceberg of identity, rare glimpses of the mostly hidden lives of people who were known before they were born. And whose deepest privacies death still preserves.

Jesus was raised in Galilee, a prosperous and fertile part of Israel. He was born into a country painfuly conscious of foreign domination. In 63 BC Pompey incorporated Palestine into the Roman province of Syria. Herod the Great ruled with autonomy in internal matters (37-4BC) but was controlled by Rome with regard to foreign and military policy. Herod Antipas ruled Galilee (4BC-AD39) with a similar political accommodation to the imperial presence. The Romans were as powerful and as unwelcome to the mass of the people as the English in Ireland or the Chinese in today's Tibet.

Before the Romans there stretched the long history of the Jewish people recorded in its great Book, a turbulent and violent history of war, mass exile, ethnic cleansing and repeated foreign domination. At the heart of the Jews' identity there was the sense of their special covenant with God as the 'chosen people'. They were proud to claim that they were the first to have worshipped the one true God. Even if they had frequently been unfaithful to God He never abandoned them. This 'jealous God' that they imagined so vividly in their stories and poetry allowed no idolatrous image to represent Him and even His name was too sacred to speak aloud. Religion and politics were inextricable. Scholars and theologians continue to debate to what degree Jesus should be interpreted in his historical context as a political or spiritual messiah.

The life that has changed so many other lives through history is largely unknown to us. His first thirty years were lived in obscurity. Once he appeared publicly, every event of his life that is recorded was selected to illustrate a perception already formed about him. We will never know most of what we might like to know about him. But the gospels insist that what we are given to know about his life, what happened and how, is enough to know him as he is now.

She was expecting a child and while they were there the time came for her baby to be born, and she gave birth to a son, her first-born. She wrapped him in his swaddling clothes and laid him in a manger, because there was no room for them to lodge in the house...

...After the angels had left them and gone into heaven the shepherds said to one another, 'Come we must go straight to Bethlehem and see this thing that has happened which the Lord has made known to us.' So they went with all speed and found their way to Mary and Joseph; and the baby was lying in the manger.[1]

The story of his birth as told in the gospels of Matthew and Luke must be the most illustrated story ever told. Luke makes it clear that he was telling the story for the same reason he wrote his gospel, to deepen the existing faith of his readers. After so many infant school nativity plays the story of the birth of Jesus may seem naïve to us. But the innocence of the story is not so transparent. It is as densely theologised as any passage in the gospel with rich echoes and associations of the entire Bible.[2] The virgin birth—a universal mythological theme—expresses an early Christian belief in the extraordinary nature of Jesus' physical conception and illustrates his special identity. Matthew is silent on the question of whether Mary later had other children, but Jesus is her first-born. Jesus is to be 'God with us', the *shekinah* or presence of God personified. How his conception and birth are described is therefore not merely historical but theologically crucial.

Finding no room at the inn, Jesus begins his life in poverty. From the beginning he is an outsider. His birth in a manger, an animal's eating trough, symbolises the inner poverty which Jesus and his followers will have to embrace. It also shows how he will be sustenance for the world. The three wise men from the East (Persia or Arabia), who later Christian tradition turned into kings, were *magi*, 'associated with the interpretation of dreams, Zoroastrianism, astrology and magic'.[3] They represent the ancient wisdom traditions of the Gentile world which will recognise in Jesus the fulfilment of their hopes and prophecies. Some early Christians were scandalised at the role of the guiding star which suggested astral religion. Their gifts of gold, frankincense and myrrh testify respectively to the kingship of Jesus, his cosmic priesthood and the sacrificial death he would suffer.

The shepherds represent the ritually unclean. They were stereotypes of low criminality, the marginalised and poor, those who would

---

[1] Lk 2:6-7, 15-16.
[2] Raymond E. Brown, *The Birth of the Messiah* (London and New York: Doubleday, 1993).
[3] Raymond E. Brown et al., *New Jerome Biblical Commentary*, p. 635.

be the first to respond to the message of Jesus. They are also the first to communicate the good news of his birth with the world. The closely related accounts of Matthew and Luke demand deep and continuous reading. If we cannot penetrate their meaning immediately we are not different in this from Mary the mother of Jesus who also does not at first grasp their full significance. She 'treasured up all these things and pondered over them.'[4] In Christian art Mary is often shown reading, the model of the Christian into whom the Word enters, becomes enfleshed and grows to maturity.

In their highlighting of detail the gospel stories of Jesus' birth may be compared with the accounts of his death which occupy a disproportionate amount of the whole text. We learn more in detail about his birth and death than about the major part of his life spent in obscurity, perhaps in Nazareth, an insignificant town with a population at the time about that of Bere Island today. The stories however, are not told to satisfy our biographical curiosity or our demands for historical proof. The historical reality is inseparable from the style of the story. Fact and interpretation can of course never be absolutely separated. Everything is told from a point of view. In the gospels the point of view is faith. But faith is not merely an opinion or interpretation. It is a way of seeing depth and meaning in the ordinary. The purpose of telling the life of Jesus is not just to give information but to disclose the experience of meaning: who Jesus really is for the gospel writers, their readers and for all humanity.

◦»◦»◦•

> During a general baptism of the people, when Jesus too had been baptised and was praying, the heaven opened and the Holy Spirit descended on him in bodily form like a dove; and there came a voice from heaven, 'Thou art my Son, the Beloved; on Thee my favour rests.'[5]

Jesus steps out of the obscurity of his hidden life as the carpenter's son to be baptised: not at first to declare his vision or mission but to bow his head to another human being. He is at prayer as he will be when the curtain of death falls.

[4] Lk 2:19.
[5] Lk 3:21-22.

The first event of his public life is his baptism by John the Baptist in the River Jordan. The synoptic gospel-writers[6] describe the event very differently but agree on it as the moment when Jesus became a noticeable presence on the religious and political stage of his time. The Baptism was a delicate subject for them to handle, however, because there was rivalry between the disciples of the two teachers. The Baptist's followers claimed precedence because it was Jesus who had bowed his head to him. From the beginning, then, Jesus, the teacher of equality and humble service, has been the object of rivalry. The disciples of the teacher who said that the first will be last continued to fight to be number one.

Despite this the Baptism is portrayed as an epiphany moment.[7] The heavens open, as they did at his birth. When Jesus emerges from the waters of the Jordan the Holy Spirit descends on him in the form of a dove. The dove was a dense symbol for the first readers of the gospel: its cooing poetically associated with the pains of childbirth; its gentleness, purity and high flight expressing the longing of humanity for love and for union with God. In Jesus this profound longing is, in faith, seen to be fulfilled. All who have faith, the implication is, will see this as clearly as they can see any physical reality. The Father's voice is heard with biblical echoes (for example, Psalm 2:7 and Isaiah 42:1) recognising Jesus as the beloved Son. This also empowers him for the journey from Galilee to Jerusalem in the course of which he will reveal by his words and actions how close God is to people.[8]

Jesus chose to be baptised by John and to be identified with the Baptist's mission. Later when his own authority was challenged he turned the tables on his opponents with an embarrassing question about John's authority: was John a prophet, he asked them If so, why had the religious leaders rejected him? If not, then the people must have been wrong. His own authority, however, did not derive from the Baptist, but directly from his own experience. This was his

[6] The *Synoptic* gospels are the first three, by Mark, Matthew and Luke which share a large amount of common subject matter and similar phrasing. As an example of the difference in approach between John and the synoptics notice how, in the account of the baptism of Jesus, John omits altogether the scene of Jesus asking to be baptized and places his entire emphasis on the epiphany.

[7] Brown, NJBC, p. 687.

[8] Lk 3:21.

'abba-experience' of communion with the Father. It is attested to in the synoptic gospels but most fully developed by John. Explicitly, however, his life was both personally and spiritually associated with the Baptist. Jesus and the Baptist are closely associated in the gospels even before their birth. They are even related by blood because Elizabeth, John's mother was a 'kinswoman' to Mary the mother of Jesus. In Luke a literary parallelism also unites them in the stories of their conception and birth: Jesus is miraculously conceived in a virgin, John miraculously conceived through the fertilisation of an old couple.[9]

The close historical and theological link between Jesus and the Baptist highlights their role as prophets. But it also distinguishes them. John is portrayed as the last of the Jewish line of prophets, anticipating the coming of the messiah. Jesus recapitulates the prophetic power of that whole lineage in himself and so expresses the fulfilment of the ancestral covenant between God and humanity. Later this 'recapitulation' of history in himself will be extended beyond that of a particular ethnic group onto a cosmic scale.

Jesus stood out in the crowd of people coming to be baptised. He instantly attracted John's notice. Later, after John had been imprisoned, he sent messengers to Jesus to ask him if he really was the expected messiah. John, who had leaped for joy in his mother's womb when she had met Mary during her pregnancy, needed to verify this new voice on the crowded stage of Jewish religious politics.

Why did Jesus choose to ride out of his Nazarean obscurity into public life on the Baptist's wave? There was a volatile spectrum of many other Jewish sects and parties. He could have chosen from among the Zealots (the terrorist wing), the Pharisees (mainly lawyers), the Essenes (the monks) or the Sadducees (some of whom were priests). His close initial association with the Baptist may have been influenced by considerations of social class or level of education or even by family connections. Jesus, many scholars think, was a lower working-class man. Thus, as Hans Kung remarks, Jesus lacked the material resources available to the other great religious founders such as the royally born Buddha or the politically and financially powerful Mohammed. But no doubt also the prophetic voice in John struck a deep chord in Jesus' self-awareness and served as a catalyst for the message he was burning to communicate.

[9] Lk 1:36.

Matthew's gospel gives a graphic description of what John stood for.[10] He lived frugally in the desert—with its overtones of the Jewish exodus from slavery in Egypt; its role as a place of personal meeting with God; and its reputation as a gathering place for discontents, rebels and mystics. The Baptist called the crowds to repentance and to a change of life before the retribution which was coming. When, in Luke's gospel, people asked the Baptist what they should do in those apocalyptic times he responded with a prophetic image of a new society built on radical standards of equality, charity and justice. Tax gatherers he told to be honest. Soldiers he told to desist from bullying the weak and running protection rackets.

> The man with two shirts must share with him who has none,
> and anyone who has food must do the same.[11]

This vision foreshadows Jesus' own message of a kingdom of peace built on justice. In the Baptist we hear something of Jesus' own teaching on the correspondence between morality and spirituality. There is the radical call to spiritual and religious authenticity, the denunciation of the double standards that allow religious hypocrites to justify themselves when they oppress the weak or powerless. And there is also the crucial call to personal repentance and change of heart. Inner and outer life must be reintegrated before the kingdom of God can come.

We also see in the Baptist two other characteristics which strongly mark the direction Jesus was to take. Firstly, his call to repentance was *universal*. It was not directed to one sect or chosen party. It did not aim to create a sect like the Essenes with whom the Baptist shows similarities. Secondly, the call to repentance was *individual*. The baptismal rite itself was communal but it marked out as unique each person coming to be immersed in the waters of the Jordan.

Jesus and the Baptist also shared a religious sense of the prevailing social crisis, even perhaps of an impending catastrophe. Shortly after the birth of Jesus, a Roman general had crucified two thousand Jewish insurgents outside the walls of Jerusalem. On one occasion Jesus invoked the still-fresh memory of a similar incident for which Pontius Pilate was responsible but about which we know no more.[12] The apocalyptic tone of much of the Baptist's teaching and some of Jesus' own

[10] Mt 3:8.
[11] Lk 3:11.
[12] Lk 13:1.

was justified less than a generation later by the destruction of Jerusalem which shattered the Jewish homeland and scattered the Jews
into the Diaspora for nearly two millennia. What Jesus saw, therefore,
when he left Nazareth was a society on a knife-edge. It was in this
social climate that his teaching found expression and he could hardly
have escaped its influence, both on its content and style.

For John the Baptist the crisis of the time presaged a cataclys-
mic collective punishment. The retribution would sweep in on the
tidal wave of God's anger. This is Old Testament rhetoric, easily misinterpreted today because of its association with the fundamentalist
who in his own anger claims to speak on God's behalf. Apart from
them most people today feel that they have had enough of vengeful
Jehovahs. But we should not dismiss the apocalyptic mood of the
Baptist too lightly. It is not the projection of human wrath onto an
externalised superego image of God. A quite different sense of the
prophet's warnings is felt when divine anger is understood in terms
of individual and collective karma. The 'retribution to come' is not
the cruel punishment when we see how it is triggered by our own
actions. A God who rewards and punishes, even though this is not
Jesus' preferred metaphor for God, is still an effective symbol for
describing the consequences of our actions and our responsibility
for them.

A deeper reading of the teaching of Jesus reveals a God that
does not, cannot punish. But every thought and action eventually
comes home to roost, every one of them. Today we are being
confronted, for example, with the complex karmic consequences of
our abuse of the environment. Similarly, the study of history, when
it is not written by the conquerors, describes the laws of *karma* and
the ravages of *sin*. History analyses the tragedies of Belfast, the
Middle East, Rwanda, Cambodia or Serbia, attempting to show how
each action led to the current maze of interrelated consequences.
For the Jewish mind a God shifting from anger to gentleness was perhaps a simpler and more powerful personification of *karma* than historical or psychological analysis. If today we find such an image
untrue and distasteful it is because it has been so often abused by
kings and priests in order to suppress and control the powerless
through a psychology of guilt and fear. This is not the intention
when it is found in the words of the Baptist or Jesus. The urgent image is not meant to instil fear but to awaken the listeners to their
own moral responsibility.

·◌··◌··◌·

Jesus taught his simple message by word and example. The authority that people experienced in his teaching flowed from a correspondence they felt between his words and deeds. Our *lectio* of the gospels needs to be sensitive to this especially in the description of the miracle stories. Jesus clearly did not want his message to be authenticated only by an extraordinary power of healing. At times he concluded a healing by instructing those who witnessed it to keep silent about it. He healed not to impress his authority but to reveal its source in the power of compassion he called his Father. Once when a large crowd was leading him to a recently bereaved household he felt this power go out from him:

> And while Jesus was on his way he could hardly breathe for the crowds. Among them was a woman who had suffered from hemorrhages for twelve years; and nobody had been able to cure her. She came up from behind and touched the edge of his cloak and at once her hemorrhage stopped. Jesus said, 'who was it that touched me?' All disclaimed it and his companions said, 'Master, the crowds are hemming you in and pressing upon you!' But Jesus said, 'Someone did touch me, for I felt that power had gone out from me.' Then the woman, seeing that she was detected, came trembling and fell at his feet. Before all the people she explained why she had touched him and how she had been instantly cured. He said to her, 'My daughter, your faith has cured you. Go in peace.'[13]

What *really* happened? What does the story mean? What does it show about Jesus? How does it help us to listen to his redemptive question? What does it tell us about who he is—for us?

What happened is a personal healing, something more than a mere physical cure. A suffering woman whose physical condition made her ritually unclean and a social outcast was restored to health and also to wholeness of life. Jesus felt power go out from him without knowing to whom. It suggests that the 'power' had an objective reality beyond his conscious control. But even more importantly he says that the healing was not the result of good magic but the woman's pure faith.

In Luke's gospel, which is always sensitive to the marginalised of society, the story also emphasises how Jesus transcends the ritual

[13] Lk 8:42-48.

purity rules that subordinated compassion to legalism. In the incident that follows this story Jesus makes himself technically impure by touching a corpse. His proximity to women even in his close circle shows how he fearlessly broke religious rules when they blocked the Spirit of God.

The deepest level of the story, however, might be found in how Jesus, stopping in the milling crowd, asks who touched him. The outcast woman should not have been in public at all and must have been cringing in fear of being exposed. It seems cruel to shame her into the open. And yet this is the greatest healing. Strengthened by his acceptance she declares herself cured. She has recovered her place of self-determination within the community and shed the shame of secrecy. Her faith and his grace restored her dignity.

⋅◦⋅◦⋅◦⋅

> When he came in sight of the city, he wept over it . . . Then he went into the temple and began driving out the traders with these words, 'Scripture says, "My house shall be a house of prayer"; but you have made it a robbers' cave. 'Day by day he taught in the temple . . . '[14]

As in every life there were special events in the life of Jesus that were recognised in retrospect as turning points. The gospels select for special attention events such as his Birth, Baptism, certain healings, miracles and teaching moments, his Passion and Death. The cleansing of the Temple, when he threw out the moneychangers, is also pivotal in both theological and biographical senses. The synoptic gospels describe this incident as occurring at the end of his life and suggest it was a direct provocation to the religious authorities which led them to their determination to finally get rid of him. In contrast, St John places the story early in Jesus' public life and characteristically 'reads' the incident in a way symbolic of the Resurrection itself:

> 'Destroy this temple,' Jesus replied, 'and in three days I will raise it again.' They said, 'It has taken forty-six years to build this temple. Are you going to raise it again in three days?' But the temple he was speaking of was his body.[15]

To understand the significance of the event we must grasp the religious and nationalistic symbolism of the Temple. Herod had begun its re-

[14] Lk 19:41, 45-47.
[15] Jn 2:19-21.

construction trying to recreate another great Wonder of the World. The Temple embodied the Jewish people's national consciousness, their religious passion for God and political passion for independence. When Jesus entered it however he was unimpressed by its extravagance and conspicuous wealth.

> Some people were talking about the temple and the fine stones and votive offerings with which it was adorned. He said, 'These things which you are gazing at—the time will come when not one stone of them will be left upon another . . . '[16]

What caught his eye were not the columns and porticos, the lavish use of gold and the processions of its rich visiting benefactors, but an old widow:

> He looked up and saw the rich people dropping their gifts into the chest of the temple treasury; and he noticed a poor widow putting in two tiny coins. 'I tell you this,' he said, 'this poor widow has given more than any of them.'[17]

His attention was drawn not to the rich and powerful in the Temple but to the sick and lame who dragged themselves there to find healing. But after his public display of anger against the Temple traders he was marked out as a dangerous rabble-rouser. Even more than his ideas, it seems, it was his brief popularity with the masses that sealed his fate.

There have been many renderings of the Temple scene in Western art, some immortalized in Christian art by paintings like El Greco's masterpiece. A modern retelling of the story in the film *Jesus of Montreal* extols the prophetic courage of exposing injustice. In the film the Jesus figure with cool composure smashes the television equipment being used to make a sexy beer commercial that debases both the actors and technicians—a crime for which he is later arrested and tried and which leads directly to his death. Jesus taught in the Temple day by day.[18] He prayed there and healed the blind and lame.[19] His protest against the desecration of the Temple was neither an attempted political uprising nor an attack on institutional religion. It was a way of affirming the real nature and pure purpose of religion.

[16] Lk 21:5-6.
[17] Lk 21:1-3.
[18] Lk 19:47.
[19] Mt 21:14.

Jesus observed the religious conventions of his time and culture. After his death his disciples continued going to the Temple. His anger at the corruption of religion protests at the misuse of religious power. Religious leaders, he declared, can abuse their authority turning it into an obstacle to people's spiritual growth and freedom. (He never blames the Romans for blocking the people's spiritual life.) The commercialization of the sacred area of the Temple symbolized how it had become an actual sacrilege against the sacred. It was a totem of human power fuelled by the fantasy of immortality. The Temple, like many religious institutions since, denied the religious humility which the acceptance of death demands. To bolster our denial of death we build our towers of Babel, Trump Towers or Millennium Domes, our great corporations and empires. So we defy and deny reality itself. Nothing more squarely sets itself against Jesus' teaching on the Kingdom of God than the denial of death expressed in the raising of power structures that oppress the poor. Spirit and truth, the purity of religious worship, demand that we live each day keenly aware of the impermanence and fragility of our selves and all our constructs. St Benedict said we must 'keep death constantly before our eyes'—not so that we should live morbidly but to show how to live fully in honesty and compassion.

If we go to church, temple, mosque or synagogue it is only to learn how to do this. But if going there merely reinforces our denial of death then the spirit of religion has been swamped by dependence on egotistical power-systems. Jesus once told a story to make this point. A rich man who has had a good harvest to make him even richer falls prey to the common illusion that material power bestows immortality:

> I will pull down my storehouses and build them bigger. I will collect in them all my corn and other goods, and then say to myself, 'Man, you have plenty of good things laid by, enough for many years: take life easy, eat, drink, and enjoy yourself.' But God said to him, 'you fool, this very night you must surrender your life . . .'[20]

The Temple was a spiritual storehouse, a barn of religious merit. Like other immortality projects, people clung to it as to a sea wall against the incoming tide of death. So it became a denial of life's true meaning. Characteristically, Jesus not only spoke of the need to refute the lie,

[20] Lk 11:18.

he also acted out his teaching. But he did not fly around the Temple in frenzy. In Mark we see how coolly calculated his behaviour in the Temple scene really was:

> He entered Jerusalem and went into the Temple where he looked at the whole scene; but as it was now late, he went out to Bethany with the Twelve.[21]

The next day he returned to the Temple and began driving out the traders and moneychangers and all those involved in the roaring trade in sacrificial animals, nor would he allow anyone to use the temple court as a thoroughfare for carrying goods. John goes further and describes Jesus making a whip to drive the traders out. Then, after the furore, he calmly began to teach. The crowd was 'spellbound by his teaching'. This combination of courageous action and charismatic appeal won him both fickle admirers and bitter enemies.

Jesus warned people to be ready, to stay awake for the day of reckoning, to live mindfully. It was a teaching based on his personal experience.

> Be alert, be wakeful. You do not know when the moment comes ... What I say to you I say to everyone: Keep awake.[22]

All the gospels agree Jesus knew of a conspiracy to eliminate him. At some stage in his public life he was forced to become a fugitive. He could not move about openly;[23] Herod was trying to eliminate him;[24] he could not walk freely even in the villages of Galilee;[25] he sent his disciples ahead secretly to arrange accommodation[26] and he was safest in a large crowd.[27] For a while Jesus succeeded in slipping through their stratagems to arrest him just as he had once slipped through an adoring crowd that had been intent on making him king.

⟨·✧·✧·✧·⟩

> They beat him about the head with a cane and spat upon him, and then knelt and paid mock homage to him. When they had

[21] Mk 11:11.
[22] Mk 13:35.
[23] Jn 11:54.
[24] Lk 13:31.
[25] Mk 9:30.
[26] Mk 14:12.
[27] Mk 14:2.

finished their mockery, they stripped him of the purple and
dressed him in his own clothes. Then they took him out to cru-
cify him.[28]

Like Shakespeare playing with time or Michelangelo changing the pro-
portions of space the gospels are selective. They bestow a dramatically
disproportionate amount of attention to the final days and hours of
Jesus' life: his passion, crucifixion and post-Resurrection appearances.
Commentaries on the life of Jesus reflect this—a recent book on these
sections of the gospel by a New Testament scholar runs to over a
thousand pages. The last hours of his life are described, like his first,
as an expression of faith. We are not given a transcript of courtroom
proceedings. In fact it is not even certain what exactly were the legal
charges that led to his arrest and execution.

The audience they were written for again determines the different
accounts. Mark, for example, who was writing for a Roman audience
portrays Pilate, the Roman governor, in a gentler light than might
have been expected: a sensitive if weak figure with an inkling of Jesus'
real identity but manipulated by the jealous Jewish leaders who
whipped up the mob against Jesus. Historical sources suggest a very
different Pilate, a ruthless administrator who was eventually recalled
to Rome for what, even by the standards of his time, was regarded as
excessive cruelty.

The spiritual truth of the Passion narratives is embodied in the
literary power of the gospels. Through this power they have been
etched into the collective consciousness of humanity. These sublime,
moving, simple words later inspired many of the greatest works of
western art. We read the Passion and Death of Jesus with the eye of
faith but the truth of the text has also passed into other forms and
media such as Bach's *St. Matthew Passion* or Handel's *Messiah*, Pasolini's
Gospel According to Matthew, Cimabue's *Crucifixion*, Michelangelo's *Pieta'*,
Rembrandt's *Christ on the Cross*.

History and art unite in the gospel narratives of the trial and
execution of Jesus. It is not clear what his crime was but the weight
of destiny bears down upon him in every verse: his betrayal by a close
disciple; his abandonment by his followers; his torture and humiliation;
the brutal power of the police state turned upon him as in the worst
of Kafka's nightmares; his agonising death. His life's work, embodied
in his disciples, had instantly fallen apart. His passion is not just

[28] Mk 15:19-21.

physical. His psychological crucifixion and sense of failure are also mortally wounding. His life and person are broken on the Cross. Nothing is left at the end except for a few of his women followers and, in John's account, his mother and his beloved disciple. The rest scattered and waited trembling for the knock on the door that would signal their own fate. As he hung defeated on the cross Jesus' influence on the world seemed to all intents and purposes to end with his life.

> Even the bandits who were crucified with him taunted him in the same way. From midday a darkness fell over the whole land, which lasted until three in the afternoon; and about three Jesus cried aloud, 'Eli, Eli, lama, sabachthani?' which means, 'My God, my God, why have you forsaken me?' ... Jesus again cried aloud and breathed his last.[29]

The story of his short tragedy seemed over.

<O··O··O>

> They went into the tomb where they saw a youth sitting on the right-hand side, wearing a white robe; and they were dumbfounded. But he said to them, 'Fear nothing; you are looking for Jesus of Nazareth who was crucified. He has been raised again; he is not here; look, there is the place where they laid him.'[30]

For many people the next step in the story, the Resurrection, seems unnecessary. It seems to break from real life into fantasy, from fact into myth. It demands not just empathy with suffering but a hope born of faith.

For many readers of the gospels over the centuries the additional demand of the Resurrection on our credulity is an optional extra. All that is really necessary has already been given in the story that ends with his deposition from the Cross and burial in a nearby cave tomb. Why not let it end as all human stories do, in death? The crucified Jesus gives all we need to live with a satisfying sense of human dignity in the face of rejection, suffering and death, the final tragedy of all human life. His history is of an extraordinary human being who was also sufficiently ordinary to have universal meaning and who bestows rare nobility on the shameful muddle of human existence. His teaching expresses one of the sublime visions of human existence. His Kingdom

[29] Mt 27:45-50.
[30] Mk 16:5-6.

is perhaps a beautiful Utopia. But his life ended with all the doomed beauty of a Greek tragedy. His story should be allowed to end on Golgotha, just as Socrates's ended when he drank the hemlock. Socrates lives on in his thought. Let Jesus live on in his gospels.

The disturbing mystery is that the meaning of the life and death of Jesus is only revealed in the Resurrection. In the Cathedral museum in Siena there is a beautiful sequence of paintings of gospel scenes by the fourteenth-century master Duccio di Buoninsegna. I find a childlike enjoyment in picking out and identifying the stories that have been painted, drawn, sculpted, acted and put to music over the centuries. In Duccio's small wood-paintings the Nativity, the feeding of the five thousand, the cleansing of the temple, the washing of the feet breathe with the freshness of the gospels themselves and glow confidently with their faith. These are scenes of stories that over the centuries have become essential to the way people discover meaning. They are simple and inexhaustible. Every retelling or new portrayal of one of these scenes recreates it. It reconnects us to the original event in a timeless or 'tempiternal' way. Such nonverbal readings of the gospels disclose the mysterious spaciousness of their meaning. We know we do not know everything about Jesus' life. He, however, extends beyond any factual accuracy we could imagine. We could never say it all anyway. Perhaps this is the point of one of the concluding remarks of St John's gospel:

> There is much else that Jesus did. If it were all to be recorded
> in detail, I suppose the whole world could not hold the books
> that would be written.[31]

At the summit and centre of Duccio's series of pictorial chapters there is a Crucifixion of deep pathos and beauty. The Resurrection is also represented but to one side of the sequence. Anyone reading the pictures without knowing the whole story could conclude that it ended with the death of the hero and that his meaning is in his death. But why, at least in most western Christian art and theology, is the Cross at the centre?

The accent of most Christian retelling of the gospel has been on the teaching and redemptive death of Jesus rather than the Resurrection. And this neglect or devaluation of the Resurrection in theology and teaching reveals much about contemporary Christianity. The Resurrection exacts a more demanding response from us than any other element in the gospels. (Partly, perhaps, because it is a story we do not see happen.) If it is mythical, why bother with it? If it is not what can it mean? Each gospel, though treating the experience of the Resurrection differently, presents it as the defining conclusion, the piece of the jigsaw that completes the whole picture. It must be taken as part of the story if we take the story as a whole. Crucially, the Resurrection is no less historical or real than any other story in the whole gospel narrative sequence.

Many interpretations of the Resurrection evade its challenge to faith. Because it is *de facto* unbelievable should we not assume the gospel is asking us to believe something else? Some of the early critics of Christianity asked provocatively if Jesus had risen from the dead why did he not appear to those responsible for his death (Even to the Roman Senate!) and display his triumph? Pagan thinkers like Porphry and Celsus who satirised Christian faith claimed that the Resurrection was like any other myth of a dying-rising god. Why should Christians be so naive, so unsophisticated, as to take it literally? Other theories argued that the body of Jesus was likely to have been stolen from the tomb and so the evidence of the empty tomb is invalid. In fact, the story of the Resurrection does not rely on the evidence of an empty tomb but on the testimony of eyewitnesses. Still others have offered rational alternatives: Jesus was not really dead when he was taken down from the cross. He survived, was seen by his disciples and then disappeared to live to an old age in India (a nineteenth-century theory) or alternatively in Japan, Rome, Glastonbury or Masada. It is natural to try to explain the Resurrection away even though the explanations effectively cancel each other out. St Augustine said that the incredible thing is that people should have believed something so incredible.

The gospels do not describe the Resurrection as an event in the same way as the Baptism or the Cleansing of the Temple. We do not see Jesus climbing out of grave. Yet the gospels are unambiguous. They ask us to believe that his disciples, most of whom could not believe it when they first experienced it, actually met him after his death. The Resurrection is an *event* but unlike any other event in time and space. Jesus himself was changed, body and mind. He is explicitly described as *not* a ghost or mental projection. Seeing him was at least as real as the evidence of the physical senses. The point is that in his new form of being he is even *more* real. A higher level of reality than we are used to has been achieved and is now impinging on our world.

Could he have been photographed? Was it a vision or apparition? Was it only a theological insight into his meaning or a psychological experience at some kind of collective level of hysteria? The gospels do not address these questions. Nor do they say that the Resurrection only affected those who saw him. The point of the story is, disturbingly, that the reader or listener too is intended for the same experience. Were it not for what was experienced in the Resurrection, we would never have known about his birth and baptism, his healings and teachings, the Passion and death. Historically he would never have made it out of the obscurity of his origins and the disaster of his end. The Resurrection insists on its actuality—however much we try to demythologise it. We may not be able to see the Resurrection as an event but the Resurrection is the light in which we see everything else.

This is more important, for *lectio* anyway, than scientific evidence that will never be available anyway. It is still tempting to explain everything about Jesus in the same historical-critical-scientific terms. Where the scientific method fails, however, other tools are needed. Too much analytical commentary will miss the subtlety of the gospels' pivotal event and so misread the whole gospel. Perhaps only the purest *Imagination* (in William Blake's, not Walt Disney's sense of the word) can perceive it: the imagination of faith to believe what cannot be imagined and must remain at one level forever unimaged and incredible. This is why Eastern Christian theology, with its preference for the *apophatic*, the inexpressible, places the Risen Christ, not the cross, at the centre of its prayer, worship and thought.

Certainly something happened to Jesus after his death that changed the minds of his followers—actually changed the way their minds perceived reality. And the Resurrection effect has not yet ceased to be felt.

·❂··❂··❂·

His life continues as self-communication through his spirit: his ever-present reality as personally alive.

The newly alive Jesus worked a revolution in consciousness in his first disciples. This got them communicating among themselves in ever-more diverse media. First by word of mouth, later on bits of papyrus. Papyrus had been used in Egypt and later dominated writing methods throughout the Graeco-Roman world until the fourth century. From that period papyrus began to be replaced by vellum, a parchment material of greater durability and cost made from animal skins. The earliest complete gospel manuscript is made of vellum and dates from the fourth century. The type of writing used was uncial which allowed no choice, for example, between capitals and lower case—son of god or Son of God, word and Word. And so, after the breath of human speech it was vegetable and animal fibre that carried the words of Jesus, those words that are spirit and life, into history. Today it's silicon chips and fibre optics that communicate the same message.

The telling of the story remains essentially oral, person-to-person. It is the same story which the woman from whom Jesus once cast out seven devils was the first to tell:

> Mary of Magdala went to the disciples with her news: 'I have seen the Lord!' she said, and gave them his message.[32]

The life of Jesus still expands beyond the confines of his historical individuality and so beyond his death. Listening deeply to his question—who we say he is—connects us with the incredible reality of his Resurrection even before we have the answer to his question or know what it is to believe. Yet as we see him more clearly the more he seems to disappear. The act of listening is faith. It dissolves objectified mental states and perceives the one who can never be clung to with the mind. The faith that is in the listening is also the faculty of seeing the invisible and believing the incredible. It centres us in the true Self through the free choice we make to listen to something deeper than the ego's doubts, opinions and arguments. Only in the *community* of the true Self, by the power of grace and faith are we content, even able, to savour the truth of a story often told.

---

[32] Jn 20:18.

∽ 6 ∽

The Kingdom of Forgiveness

*I*do not know much about Bere Island and I cannot claim it as a home with all that mix of rights and duties that a home entails. It is for me only a place where I have glimpsed what home means. Soon after I became a monk I was disturbed by one of the Desert Fathers' sayings that no one can be a monk in their own country. It means, I think, that the bonds and memories of one's home need to be broken if one is to enter into the acosmic, totally liberated state of the sannyasi or true monk: the state which is not defined by any label or external sign, the state we are closest to in life, perhaps, at the hour of death. Which is also every moment, because every passing moment is a separation from what went before and gives way to the next. And so each moment is a death. Even the most physically stable of monks (or meditators) is essentially a wanderer. We don't ever know for sure where we are going. The followers of the Son of Man, Jesus said, will have nowhere to lay their head. True enough, within a couple of years of becoming a novice I left my own country.

When years later my wanderings brought me to Bere Island for my first extended period of solitude there it was at a time of great personal disruption. My community was going through turbulence, with personality conflicts and problems. St Benedict, a wise monastic founder, foresaw and legislated for them all but they had left me confused, angry, hurt, ashamed and self-questioning. I was no advertisement for meditation. Bere Island was not consoling. But it was harshly, beautifully truthful. Part of its beauty was its lack of pretty consolation and its refusal to discuss the situation with me. It waited, with its rocklike patience, the ever-unhurried sea lapping and pounding its shores, for me to find the key out of the prison of anxiety. The abandoned cottages were my silent sermons on the passing of passion. I wandered on one of my afternoon walks in the roofless cottage of my mother's childhood. Fragments of my childhood scenes in London with tones of voices unregistered at the time of hearing regrouped themselves in my mind and a new unauthorised family history began to form. I noticed deep unexamined fissures of pain that must have accompanied the fun and boisterousness of the bevy of O'Sullivan girls. I sensed the influence of their fiery matriarch of a mother condemned to life on an obscure island while over *the years she imagined, and her talents mourned in her, the lost opportunities of America. I shared my grandmother's birthday but she had died a few weeks after my birth.*

My emotional distance from the events, my own problems and the wash of time released compassion. An unasked-for grace of healing forgiveness rose in me affecting my family's past and my own present. Then I found, to my jackdawish delight, a rusty key among the rubble on the kitchen floor where the feet of generations had crossed and criss-crossed, bumped into each other, embraced, fought and … somehow must have learned to love. Because love there was in my family. They must have learned to forgive one another. As I pocketed the key for my treasure box I saw for an instant of clarity that home has two dimensions. It is where we are vulnerable and hurt others and where we are hurt ourselves. Stuck only in that dimension we are creatures of misery and home is a hell, a family Christmas everyone wants to end. Another dimension hidden within it is the realm of forgiveness, where the past is redeemed, history is given new meaning and the dead are reborn. Deep sadness, which no one can celebrate like the Irish, must be traversed in order to enter that kingdom of joy. Forgiveness is the door. And the key.

⟨◦•◦•◦⟩

Who we say he is does not entirely depend on the recorded facts of his life. Nor is it reducible to knowing what he believed and taught. But to *believe* what he taught—what he meant by the 'kingdom of God'— begins our knowing who he is.

His teaching conveys wisdom and compassion to all humanity. He offers a piercingly pure insight into the structure of reality in terms not of philosophy, science or art but of simple (all-demanding) human holiness. In the Sermon on the Mount he called holiness happiness or 'beatitude'. In becoming holy, happy and whole, the human being is fulfilled by seeing God. With that the universe rejoices and achieves its purpose.

The compassion and insight of Jesus are fully human. Yet as a teacher he embodies an experience of the divine that transcends the human because it fulfils the human. It is the teacher himself not just the teaching that captivates us. Whenever a teacher truly embodies his message the authority of their love draws us into the person. An authentic person carries infinitely more conviction and persuasiveness than the cleverest of ideas.

⟨◦•◦•◦⟩

Who was he speaking to as he walked between town and village on his way to his destiny in Jerusalem? He spoke to the poor, the blind, the lame and crippled, the lepers, the miserable, the hungry, to sinners, prostitutes, tax collectors, and demoniacs. When he spoke to the arrogant rich and powerful, the learned and clever, he exposed hypocrisy and spiritual blindness.

He revealed the 'secrets of the kingdom of heaven' to the persecuted, the downtrodden and captive, the overburdened, the rabble and the crowd 'who knew nothing of the law'. His most attentive listeners were the most marginalised and they relished the attention he gave them. They were those who had come in last in the race of life or who had never been allowed to enter the race at all. They were the least important members of society, the uneducated and powerless who were always overshadowed by the learned and articulate: the lost souls who had drifted to the fringes of life far from the warmth of human companionship.

Most democratic politicians today exhibit concern for influential minority groups with valuable votes. They are politically correct when they speak to the media on behalf of the marginalised. Jesus was not a politician. His society was not democratic and did not pretend to respect minorities or the marginalised. If you were excluded that was your fault. His concern for them was not politically correct or expedient. He did not use the misfortune of others as a way to lever power in his own interest. The reverse is true: the crowd that briefly adored him eventually demanded his blood. Jesus seems to have been driven to identify with the poor, the suffering and the rejected simply from heartfelt compassion. He had come for them not for the well to do, for the sick not the healthy. This is the key to understanding Jesus and his meaning for humanity. It is only from our own need, often concealed in shame, and not from our pretended self-sufficiency, that we connect with what he communicates and who he is.

⋅◦⋅◦⋅◦⋅

He was above all scandalously associated with 'sinners'. He said he came to them as a doctor to the sick. The righteous and successful were as always happy enough, for the time being, with their denial of death. His concern for sinners may seem to us a normal 'Christian' attitude for Jesus to adopt but if we are to really hear his teaching and his question we have also to appreciate how shocking it actually was.

To recover the original shock of his teaching we need to understand what it meant to be a 'sinner'. The term did not carry only the sense of someone who breaks moral codes or at least is unlucky enough to get caught. Sinners belonged to castes as strictly demarcated as in India (or an English village). To be a sinner could mean, for example, to belong to one of the despised professions—prostitutes and robbers obviously, but also shepherds, tailors, barbers, tax-collectors and butchers. Workers in these trades found themselves in the religious equivalent of an economic poverty-trap with no upward mobility. Being outcast they could never fulfil the obligations of the Law's ritual purity and so they were in permanent exclusion from their community. They could never become respectable. Being a sinner was fate, your karma in life.

The hopelessness of sinners is illustrated in an incident in the Temple in John's gospel.[1] Jesus healed a man born blind. People who had witnessed it questioned Jesus about the machinery of fate that had caused the man's blindness. Surely, they said,—this is expressed as a point of view too self-evident to question—to be born blind is a sign that you or your parents had sinned. God who favours the righteous also punishes sinners. To be born blind is obviously a punishment for personal or generational wrongdoing. Life after all is not random. Everything must have an explanation. Causes have effects. Actions carry reward or punishment. What other meaning can misfortune have?

> It is common knowledge that God does not listen to sinners. He listens to anyone who is devout and obeys his will.[2]

This is the 'prosperity gospel' of some modern Pentecostal churches and TV evangelists who trade the secrets of spiritual and material success. So common was this belief in divine retribution in Jesus' time that even his own disciples were dumbfounded when Jesus proposed a radically different way of looking both at suffering and well-being. Good fortune, being well-off and comfortable might in fact, he said, be a curse in disguise. The respectable, the affluent and the righteous can carry a burden greater than any material misfortune when you consider it in the light of the kingdom of God. Wealth brings dangers that can impede your spiritual progress far more seriously than moral

[1] Jn 9:1ff.
[2] Jn 9:31.

misbehaviour. Sins can be forgiven. Who can 'forgive' the anxiety and aloofness that wealth can bring?

> 'It is easier for a camel to pass through the eye of a needle than for a rich man to enter the kingdom of God.' They were more astonished than ever and said to one another 'Then who can be saved?'[3]

It is difficult not to think, perhaps unconsciously, that health and prosperity is a reward for good behaviour. From childhood we are rewarded with pleasures for being good and deprived of pleasure for being naughty. The TV evangelist conception of God is of an external power that rewards us materially for keeping the commandments and brings suffering on us for breaking them. This image, often falsely justified by biblical misreadings, perverts the human relationship with God. It makes an idol of the living God. Yet we prefer the gods we have fashioned ourselves because we feel we can control them. Because we are complex and self-contradictory beings irreconcilable images of God can inhabit the same mind and surprising absurdities of belief and practice can result. A good, observant, religious person suddenly becomes bitterly angry with God when they lose their job, break up with their spouse, notice ageing or get cancer. 'Why me? Haven't I always gone to church, kept the rules and paid my tithes? I might just as well have always done what I wanted to do!' The other side of reward is punishment. As Jesus emphasised in some of his parables, it is often the respectable and self-righteous who most strongly insist that the wicked be punished both in this life and the next, with capital punishment or hell for all eternity (or, if the crime is sufficiently offensive, both).

⋅◇⋅◇⋅◇⋅

The Judaeo-Christian theology of sin and the Asian doctrine of karma are comparable ways of explaining the mystery of suffering and evil. 'Whatever measure you deal out to others will be dealt back to you'[4] is a saying of Jesus which any Hindu or Buddhist would understand within the framework of cause and effect. But his insight into the law of karma opens up new meaning through his teaching on forgiveness, the grace of unconditional and transformative love.

[3] Mk 10:25-26.
[4] Mt 7:2.

Both the Asian and the biblical doctrines express a cosmic law of moral compensation. Something somewhere eventually balances all of life's accounts, even the most secret ones. They explain the unfairnesses and tragedies of life that we desperately need to explain. More than anything, more even than rectifying mistakes, when something goes wrong we want to be able to explain it in order to ward off the terror of meaninglessness. Sin or karma explains the mystery of suffering. Despite the important differences between them, each theory helps countless people around the world to express the natural law that the fruit lies hidden in the seed. For every action there is an equal and opposite reaction. Both doctrines represent the moral equivalent of Newtonian physics.

The Biblical and Asian doctrines are perhaps more closely related than they appear at first sight. When Jesus met the blind man in the Temple his disciples asked him what for them or a Hindu was a perfectly normal question:

> 'Rabbi, who sinned, this man or his parents? Why was he born blind?'[5]

In his answer Jesus shifts their attention from a mechanical, karmic view of the moral universe. Jesus is like a quantum physicist who does not deny the Newtonian universe but sees deeper laws of reality. He proposes a challenging, more inclusive explanation which gives more than rational satisfaction because it also offers *meaning*.

> 'It was not that he or his parents sinned,' Jesus answered, 'he was born blind so that God's power might be displayed in curing him.'[6]

Life, he says, is more than an intricate system of cause and effect. The truth of suffering is not the *explanation* that it is punishment, the consequence of ours or others' actions. The full *meaning* is found in the encounter between human suffering and divine compassion. 'My meaning is love,' Jesus says to Mother Julian. The law of karma is not denied by the answer Jesus gives. Karmic forces can continue to explain *how* things happen, but not *why* they happen. His response shows that the strongest force of the universe is not the impersonal law of karma. The heart of reality is outgoingly personal. It is compassionate

[5] Jn 9:2.
[6] Jn 9:3.

not merely efficient. God is love. Love overrides karma. It dispels the ego's idea of justice projected onto a divine superego. It is all-embracingly just and nonjudgemental because it balances all moral books. Love covers a multitude of sins. This is the force that reconciles the duality of mercy and justice. If we think this is cheap consolation, we need only recall the cost of Jesus' own suffering and the extremity of his cry of abandonment.

Jesus teaches that, however its cause may be understood, the *meaning* of suffering is found in the way it is healed. Simone Weil believed that the meaning was found in the freedom to love God even when we are deprived of the feeling of divine joy and peace—even when we don't feel loved.

Jesus speaks of a power greater than karma. He then claims even more radically that the power of karma can be reversed and dissolved at its root by forgiveness. From his first public appearance in the gospel Jesus is identified with the strongest of human hopes, that the wall of karma encircling life can be dismantled. John the Baptist expressed this in his cry of recognition when he first saw Jesus coming to him for baptism:

> 'Look,' he said, 'there is the Lamb of God; it is he who takes away the sin of the world.'[7]

St Paul calls karma 'the law of sin and death'.[8] In relationship with Jesus, he says, we are set free from this law by another law. This new law overrides all others because it the life-giving 'law of the Spirit'. Sin and death may continue to beset individuals through their personal weaknesses. The human family may have to live with its sins of in-humanities and injustice as well as its daily catalogue of petty egotism. The law of sin and death is not instantly dissolved. Yet the hope, recognised by the law of karma itself, is confirmed that there is eventually an end to suffering. And the way that hope is realised takes human form. If one human being can reach the root of karma and apply the consciousness of the higher law to its sufferings, he does it for all.

In Jesus' vision we are not criminals in relationship to a judge. The *good news* is not that humanity has a more lenient judge but that the charge is dropped altogether. Sin is deleted by the very freedom

[7] Jn 1:29.
[8] Rom 8:3.

of love which sin ignores, rejects or forgets. Karma *is* actually dissolved and can be because its constituent elements are themselves impermanent. Humanity can awaken from its ancient nightmare of self-inflicted punishment.

The thirteen major healing miracles of Jesus described in the synoptic gospels express this liberating power as present in Jesus. They describe him healing by word or touch conditions of particular human misery from leprosy and blindness to haemorrhaging and paralysis. Like the exorcisms he performed they manifest the *dynamis* or power present in him. They were seen as signs that the power flowing through Jesus was able to heal the whole human being not just on the physical plane. Even the sicknesses then have a symbolic meaning. Whether it is physical or mental suffering that Jesus addresses, whether he *cures* or *heals*, the *meaning* is the same. The law of cause and effect, biological or religious, is shown to be subordinate to a higher law of love. To experience this law is freedom from the self-alienation which suffering can inflict.

The higher law of love is experienced as an *intervention*. Something unexpected, undeserved and even unaskable suddenly happens out of the blue and becomes really present. It is manifested most powerfully, however, not in the supernatural but in human acts of compassion and forgiveness. These too are miracles. To be touched like this is to experience personally the meaning of salvation. It makes sense that the word 'salvation' derives from a root word for 'healing'. To be healed is to be saved.

⋘⋅O⋅O⋅O⋅⋙

Jesus shares his knowledge of the pure love of God's mercy intervening in the universe of human experience. Intervention does not signify impetuous interference, random action or preferential treatment. God does not change his mind; and so in a sense God does not even 'act' in our temporal and relative sense of action. God *is*. In God's isness all action is simultaneous.

It disturbs the institutional religious mind to think it, but this is Jesus' teaching: God forgives. To express this as a choice on God's part, a change of mind, a relenting is only a necessary anthropomorphism. We are unable to conceive the utter simplicity of a divine act or to imagine how one act of God is inseparable from every dimension of the divine movement that is love. Forgiveness cannot be fully understood merely as God's 'reaction' to sin. If God is the reconciliation of all paradox, as Nicholas de Cusa said, then the duality of action and reaction is transcended in God.

> And I have learnt that the place wherein Thou art found unveiled is girt round with the coincidence of contradictories; and this is the wall of paradise wherein Thou dost abide.[9]

God neither acts nor reacts in a human sense at all. God is 'I AM'. Yet how else but through the forgiveness described in the parable of the Prodigal Son or in Rembrandt's painting of the same story, can we express this felt truth: that, when we penetrate into the heart of reality, sin and karma are destroyed? We *feel* forgiven. We *are* rendered free. It is a central part of Jesus' teaching that we should be 'perfect as the Father is perfect'. Therefore we can learn to be co-redeemers with Jesus. Even we in our Godlike turn can dissolve karma by forgiving. Forgive those who offend you, Jesus said, 'seventy times seven times' (beyond measure) and curtail your judgement of others.

The gospels see Jesus and his self-embodied teaching as the historical intervention of God's ahistorical love: an 'act of God' that appeared in the 'fullness of time'. For his disciples he is the human unfolding of the compassionate heart of creation, the creative-redemptive love that is God within human existence, the human 'I AM'. This is the source of his *dynamos*. It is why he, through the word of his teaching, can so radically dissolve the law of sin and punishment—why the slate can be wiped clean.

·◇·◇·◇·

Christian theology has developed complex views about sin, some mortal some venial, and diverse ways of being purified in this life and in purgatory. Indian thought also distinguishes at least three kinds of *karma*.[10]

According to St Augustine and St Thomas Aquinas the punishment for sin is contained within sin itself. Sin is 'separation from God'. This does not diminish the consequential suffering inherent in the karmic baggage for oneself or others. Nor does it absolve the individual from personal responsibility for transcending the tendency to repeat negative patterns. Sin is an all-too-painful reality by whatever name it goes

[9] Nicholas of Cusa, *The Vision of God* (New York: G. P. Putnam's Sons, 1951), Ch. 9.
[10] *Sanchita* is the total load of karma to be worked out. *Prarabda* is that part of karma (good or bad) with which the body has taken shape to be enjoyed or suffered now. *Agami* is that part of karma which will bear fruit at a later time.

and however it is analysed. The *Cloud of Unknowing* says we should not think of it too abstractly. Sin is something we should feel, almost physically, in its totality.

> Mean by 'sin' the whole lump of it, not particularizing about any part, for it is nothing other than yourself.[11]

Where do we feel this 'lump'? Not only in our individual actions. Sin is also found in social institutions and political or religious structures that perpetuate or cover up injustice. It is found in our unconscious relationship to ourselves in the dynamics of self-rejection and self-deception, addiction and compulsion. It is expressed in all our relationships, with our friends as well as with our enemies, towards all forms of life including animals and the environment. The damage sin does derives from its blindly selfish nature. Sin is punishment for that alienation from the true Self and that objectification of others that sin itself causes. The cycle of evil. Sin and its punishment are a single transaction extended through time. But God cannot punish.

Mystics of all traditions have seen how the supreme law of love intervenes through union with God to eradicate sin and break the cycle. Julian of Norwich frequently remarks how seeing this leads to an eternal laughter even in the dark face of evil. She looked for sin, she said, but could never find it. It does exist as an independent force but only in its effects.

> I believe it has no real substance or real existence. It can only be known by the pain it causes. This pain is something as I see it which lasts but a while. It purges us and makes us know ourselves, so that we ask for mercy.[12]

Reflecting on her revelations, Dame Julian came to understand that sin can even be worthwhile.[13] It has a role to play in awakening us to the reality that love is the meaning of the universe. This led her to sense a cosmic moral balance beyond the mind's power fully to understand. Sin is suffering but it is eventually balanced with joy in heaven to, and beyond, the degree of pain it caused on earth. She knew that people do not freely choose to sin. Sin is a consequence of unmindfulness, of not knowing what we are doing. This does not mean that we are relieved of all responsibility for sin. We are responsible for

[11] *The Cloud of Unknowing and Other Works*, Ch. 36.
[12] Julian of Norwich, *Revelations of Divine Love*, Ch. 27.
[13] Ibid., Ch. 38.

becoming more mindful so that we create less pain for others and ourselves. But because sin is the result of ignorance and illusion it does not merit any more punishment than it contains in itself. Sin, she says, is the sharpest scourge that any of us can be flogged with. It makes us loathsome in our own sight and makes us condemn ourselves to hell. But then the touch of the Holy Spirit brings us to contrition and turns our self-directed bitterness into hope of God's mercy.

Inevitably we fall because of our weakness and stupidity. Just as surely we get up with even greater joy because of the mercy and grace of the Holy Spirit. When she understood that the devil loses more in our getting up again than he gained in having us fall, it made her laugh. Seeing it all so clearly she is convinced that sin is no cause for despair even though 'we still need to recognise our sin and weakness'.[14] God courteously forgives our sin when we repent but, she insists, he also wants us to forgive our own sin as well—and along with our sin our 'foolish despondency and doubting fears'[15]. We should therefore learn to accept the discomfort of sin as casually as possible. There is no role for guilt here at all. The less importance we give to it the less pain we will experience.[16]

> Our courteous Lord does not want his servants to despair even if they fall frequently and grievously. Our falling does not stop his loving us.[17]

In one passage she plays with the idea of sin as an accidental falling. Like Clement of Alexandria she compares sin to a man falling into a ditch. Clement had said that you fall into a hole either because you do not see it or because you do not have the strength to jump over it. In her allegory of the Lord and his servant, Dame Julian describes the servant rushing off to fulfil the Lord's command. But in his enthusiasm he falls headlong into a deep ditch and injures himself badly.[18] He struggles to get out but is wedged in so tightly that he cannot even turn his head to look at the Lord who loves him. He gives vent to his feelings as he suffers torment and the worst is to feel so utterly alone in his sin. The Lord, however, regards the suffering of

[14] Ibid., Ch. 78.
[15] Ibid., Ch. 73.
[16] Ibid., Ch. 64.
[17] Ibid., Ch. 39.
[18] Ibid., Ch. 51.

his unfortunate servant with compassion and gentleness. He wants to console him for his ordeal with something greater than anything he had enjoyed before he stumbled into the ditch of sin.

Dame Julian saw with brilliant theological clarity that the servant represented not only Adam or Everyman but also Christ. When Adam fell, God's Son fell, she says, because of the primordial unity between humanity and God through the second person of the Trinity. God never *began* to love humanity. He always loves all that is. When Adam fell, therefore, God's Son fell with him. Becoming Word made flesh Jesus fall into the depth of the womb of the Virgin who was herself the 'fairest daughter of Adam'. Because of this identity between the Son and humanity God cannot blame us for our sin any more than he blames the Son. In Jesus God has made himself responsible for the Adam and Eve in all of us.

Clearly this view cannot completely satisfy the modern mind. It rests too comfortably in the mythic imagination for us. But Dame Julian's teaching is both a soothing and intellectually coherent insight into the traditional Christian metaphors of salvation,

> Jesus is everyone that will be saved, and everyone that will be saved is Jesus—all through the charity of God; and through virtue, obedience, humility and patience on our part.[19]

Few of us can laugh like Julian in the face of sin and its devastation. But in the work of self-knowledge we slowly learn to see how sin and punishment are one and the same. A spiritual practice like meditation, *gradually* and even imperceptibly dissolves the roots of sin embedded in mental patterns and physical habits. The 'sin of the world is taken away' by encountering the healing love of God at the centre of all being. In the gospel vision this love is translated into human consciousness through the indwelling of the risen Jesus.

This is clearly not how a Zen meditator or Jew or Hindu would describe it. But sin and the taking away of sin is a felt reality in every person's life whatever their belief-system. Sin, like forgiveness, transcends religious barriers. It unfolds at different levels of the person simultaneously and reaches completion only through time. Liberation, *moksha*, salvation, like enlightenment, take time. Through time the faith that saves us grows. Origen said that Jesus would remain hanging on the cross until every creature, even the devil, was saved: so inclusive

[19] Ibid.

is the love of God which as Jesus taught creates and saves in one nondual act of love. This is good reason for spiritual laughter.

◦◦◦◦◦◦

> From that day Jesus began to proclaim the message: Repent for the Kingdom of Heaven is upon you.[20]

Jesus forgave sinners and his own enemies even from the Cross. One of the ways we listen to his question is by following his example of forgiving those who hurt us. To do this is to enter the reality which Jesus places at the centre of his teaching: the experience of the Kingdom of God.[21] The Kingdom is the place outside space, the moment outside time, where sin and all its consequences have been totally absorbed beyond the effects of fear and pain. The Kingdom, one could say, is the way God intends us to live. It is our natural home. Jesus speaks of this Kingdom-experience as his ancestors spoke of the Promised Land or the messiah, as a Zen master speaks of enlightenment or as the Buddha speaks of nirvana. He also embodies the Kingdom as a personal reality experienced through relationship. To know him as he really is, is to find oneself in the Kingdom.

To see Jesus in this clear depth we must see how central the Kingdom is to his vision of reality.[22] It is not a system of morality. The Kingdom is not a place we are going to. Nor is it a reward we are to receive for good behaviour. The Kingdom upsets normal ways of thinking more deeply than the strictest of moral commandments. It is a fundamental experience of reality *as it truly is.* To be in the Kingdom is to live in harmony with heaven and earth, with friend and foe, with body and mind. It changes the way you even *want* to live. It is to live in the continuous consciousness that we are born and die under the *basileia* of God. *Basileia* does not mean Kingdom in the sense of place but reign or power. The Kingdom is power in the sense of bonding relationship. *Where* you are, especially if you are *in love* matters less than *who* you are with. To be in the Kingdom is to know ourselves in relationship.

---

[20] Mt 4:17.

[21] Kingdom translates the Greek *basileia.* It is not gender specific and could also be translated as the Reign of God. In fact in Aramaic the word *malkuthakh* is feminine and so could be translated 'queendom'!

[22] The kingdom is mentioned 122 times in the gospels, 90 of them by Jesus.

The Kingdom is experienced when we acknowledge the loving power of God over the power of egotism and all the ego's personal and social manifestations or structures. This is precisely what Pontius Pilate could not understand when he tried, in his own way, to find out who Jesus was:

> Jesus replied, 'My Kingdom does not belong to this world. If it did my followers would be fighting to save me . . . My Kingdom belongs elsewhere.' 'You are a king then?' said Pilate. Jesus answered, 'King is your word. My task is to bear witness to the truth . . .' Pilate said, 'What is truth?'[23]

‹❍··❍··❍›

The Kingdom, Jesus says, is within us, among us and between us. As an anonymous prophet once wrote on the wall of Paddington station in London, 'Faraway is near at hand in images of elsewhere.' Everywhere and nowhere. This is pure *utopia*, which means literally *no where*, which is how the *Cloud* describes the place where the work of contemplation is performed. Jesus told Pilate: 'My Kingdom is not of this world.' And an apocryphal gospel has Jesus say,

> Whoever is near me is near the fire, and whoever is far from me is far from the Kingdom.[24]

Utopian maybe, but not imaginary. The Kingdom is no less *real* than those dark forces of the psyche that can pull the human mind into the terror of destruction and death: ignorance, greed, pride, illusion, insecurity, anxiety, despair, impatience, intolerance, isolation. Humanity is pulled into its all-too-common inhumanities by these dark forces. In contrast to these forces the teaching on the Kingdom offers an inexhaustible hope and liberty. In the experience of the Kingdom Jesus offers humanity a realistic vision of happiness and a convincing hope that we are meant to be happy.

The Kingdom has been discovered and described in many ways in all cultures. The Vedic seers found it in the atman, a reality the size of a thumb in the depth of the heart. Many symbols have tried to express its intimate immensity, and its interior cosmicity, and the means of realising it: the philosopher's stone of the alchemists, the

[23] Jn 18:36ff.
[24] The Gospel of Thomas, 82.

diamond centre of Chinese wisdom, the kundalini serpent of tantra, the soul-centre of Plotinus, the source of inner strength for Marcus Aurelius, the Grail of the Middle Ages, the Force of Star Wars.

Although the two terms are not interchangeable, the *Kingdom of God* is the Christian insight into reality which corresponds most closely to the Buddhist *nirvana*. The teaching of Jesus on the Kingdom, like the Buddha's on *nirvana*, is one of humanity's greatest affirmations of fundamental hopefulness. They breed an optimism that unites heaven and earth, inner and outer. This teaching affirms life as meaningful and purposeful despite its tragedies and banalities. It affirms and celebrates the human aspiration to perfection and wholeness. It expresses our irrepressible intuition that fullness of being is our destiny. It consoles us with the only consolation that is not deceptive (which is the truth) that fullness of life *is* the intentional meaning of life.

Belief in the Kingdom is not wish-fulfilment. It arises from a sure conviction about the essential *goodness* of human nature and about the meaning of that goodness. Whenever this conviction is expressed in acts of compassion and forgiveness or in words of wisdom and truth it becomes self-authenticating. People act well because they are essentially good. Acting generously teaches us that we are capable of forgiveness and compassion. The example of goodness is infectious and enhances the self-worth of those who witness it. When people act badly they expose how much they have forgotten that they are good. Any sign of human goodness therefore contests our general assumption that human nature is essentially selfish. Simple goodness and honesty as much as heroic deeds of selflessness invalidate the cynical conviction that we are unredeemable.

Words and deeds which express the *good heart* of human nature reveal the true Self of the person and simultaneously manifest the Kingdom. They destroy karma and liberate human beings for life 'in all its fullness'.[25] In what he said and did Jesus, too, not only preached the Kingdom: he embodied it even within the imperfect, fallen and complex world in which he lived and died—our world. The gospels show that ordinary people of good will who met him, heard him, touched and spoke with him were moved to their depths (a dangerous thing for the one who so moves them) by his affirmation of the original innocence of human nature.

[25] Jn 10:10.

By revealing the Kingdom, the answer to all questions of meaning, Jesus raises many questions. Is the Kingdom *inside* us; so all we need is to find a remote and peaceful cloister to meditate in? Or is the Kingdom an *external* reality to be struggled for in the life of the societies and institutions of our time. Do my human intimacies end in the Kingdom; or are they consummated there in a personal identity beyond anything I can imagine? Or does the Kingdom exist at all? Is it like the colours which are irrelevant to humans because they are outside their range of perception?

The Kingdom-teaching resolves these questions for those who practice it. It deals with one of the strongest dualities of all religious thought: the tension between mystic and politician, contemplative and activist, monk and social worker, celibate and spouse. The question of Jesus refocuses the blurred vision these apparent contradictions create. 'Who do you say I am?' invites a resolution in the integrated reality of a single, ego-transcended person. In other words, when we see the inner and outer dimensions of the Kingdom unified in Jesus we look at these problems and all dualities in a different way. Seeing him in the Resurrection experience, we can believe that everyone is capable of fullness of life and that the way there is to be redeemed by love. Turned towards him, by his question, we see how all-inclusive, hospitable and forgiving the Kingdom is.

The Kingdom is hardly believable outside the experience of self-knowledge. When we have come to know ourselves (by renouncing everything we are not), we see clearly what the Kingdom is *not*. The Church is not the Kingdom, for example. Human excellence or moral perfection or fulfilment of religious laws are not the Kingdom. The Kingdom is not a reward for good behaviour. Mystical experience is not the Kingdom. In relationship to Jesus we see that the Kingdom, like God, simply *is* love, is everywhere, within and among us simultaneously, transcending the mental constructs we label time and space and cause and effect. In the Kingdom there are no passports or identity cards because there are no longer any frontiers to cross, no divisions to separate. Neither male nor female, Jew nor Greek, Catholic nor Protestant, Christian nor non-Christian, gay nor straight, Arab nor Israeli, Serb nor Croat, Hindu nor Muslim, black nor white, rich nor poor, conservative nor liberal, Tutsi nor Hutu. In the Kingdom each individual being is inseparable from every other in the divine web of Being. The fullest self-knowledge dawns in awakening to the oneness of the human family and its oneness with God.

⟨∘⋆∘⋆∘⟩

Shortly after Jesus' death and the failure of his mission, two of his disciples were despondently walking the road from Jerusalem to Emmaus.

They were deeply disillusioned and were discussing the meaning of all that had happened in Jesus' brief career. No doubt they felt betrayed by Jesus in whom they had invested such high hopes. Then Jesus quietly joins them walking along the road but they fail to recognise him. He asks what they are talking about. (He is still, even now in his risen form, asking questions.) As he walks along the road with them, his question makes them more conscious of what they are trying to understand. He enters into their journey, their search and their conversation. Then he opens their minds to the meanings of the scriptures which had foretold that the Messiah would have to suffer before he entered into his glory. Until then these two unhappy disciples still thought of the Kingdom as worldly dominion, a political cause or a social reality:

We had been hoping he was the man to liberate Israel.[26]

When Jesus spoke to the crowds, just as when he taught his disciples privately, he was frequently misunderstood. The people, Luke tells us, 'thought the reign of God might dawn at any moment'.[27] Even after the Resurrection they asked him, 'Lord, is this the time when you are to establish once again the sovereignty of Israel?' His reply echoes the advice of the leaders of the first-century Christian community to its impatient members: 'It is not for you to know about dates and times which the Father has set within his own control.' Instead of a timetable for the end of the world they would receive 'power when the Holy Spirit comes upon you.'[28] The Kingdom is more than the end of the world or even the perfecting of *this* world.

When the Pharisees asked him when it would come he replied that the Kingdom could not be observed or objectified. It could not be identified in space or time because the 'Kingdom is within/among you'.[29] The crucial word here is the Greek preposition *entos*. It means

[26] Lk 24:21.
[27] Lk 19:11.
[28] Acts 1:6.
[29] Lk 17:21.

both *within* and *among*. The Kingdom transcends even the duality of inner and outer.

⋯◦⋯◦⋯◦⋯

The Kingdom is freedom from all inner and outer domination: the 'glorious liberty of the children of God'. It is the power of God flowing freely in every human dimension both social and personal. It is the fulfilment of the individual both as a unique individual *and* as a part of the whole that is indivisible from all other individuals. It is the end of the tragedies of alienation and isolation, the two most powerful causes of suffering and of human inhumanity. It is the reconciliation of all opposites. As the pure primal energy of the Creator it integrates the wave and particle. In the solitude of the human heart it is discovered as the 'stream of living water' that is the Spirit. In the social dimension of human relationships it bursts into consciousness through the selfless practice of forgiveness and compassion, generosity and loving kindness.

Where the Kingdom is *among* us, there is neither hatred nor selfish competitiveness nor any other sources of division. Where the Kingdom is *within* us, our true nature has dispelled all ignorance about ourselves and established harmony and integration between the conscious and the unconscious. We are then free to act in accord with our essential goodness: as the image and likeness of God that we are. As individuals we have been reunited with the common truth of human nature. The Kingdom is realised when the internal relationships of the human psyche have found harmony with the true Self. Then the individual can relate to others as to himself. The full potential of spiritual growth has been reached.

A Gentile, weary of endless Jewish wrangling over the Law, once asked Hillel, a liberal rabbi contemporary with Jesus, for a summary of the Torah. Could he recount the essence of the Law while standing on one foot? Hillel replied: 'whatever is hateful to you do not do to your fellow man. This is the whole Torah. The rest is commentary. Now go and study'. As an observant Jew, Jesus also saw the Kingdom of God in relation to the Law. But he summarised the Law in a brief and simple formula, loving God with one's whole strength, loving one's neighbour as oneself.

⋯◦⋯◦⋯◦⋯

Communicating this vision of the Kingdom was itself the work of an artist. Jesus was a master of the story and of the unforgettable image. In the parables of the Kingdom he describes its multi-dimensional nature. A seed growing. Bread rising. Birds settling into branches. Crops coming to ripeness. Pearls being discovered. Seas being fished. People cancelling debts. Wayward sons coming to their senses and returning home. Stubborn petitioners getting what they ask for. People being forgiven. Children being children.

In the great art of his parables the Kingdom is expressed through radiantly simple images of growth and transformation, of discovery and the final judgement or settling of life's accounts. The Kingdom is the experience of *natural* growth because the Kingdom is neither a static nor an other-worldly reality. It is the experience of *discovery* because the Kingdom is always new. It is the experience of *mercy* and having your debts forgiven because the Kingdom of God is God's boundless compassion. It is the experience of being *childlike* because the Kingdom is genuinely simple, a unitive, nondualistic state of consciousness. To put it both most simply—and also most provocatively because it sounds so simplistic—the Kingdom is both the source of life and its goal.

By reaching out especially to the marginalised and despised Jesus showed that the Kingdom is the banquet of life to which all are welcome. One of the parables employs just this image of a general invitation extended to the untouchables of his time, to come to the great banquet of the Kingdom.[30] Life is a feast, a concert enjoyed in the midst of mortality. As we see on the walls of Etruscan tombs, even death transposes but cannot end the party.

Because the invitation to the banquet can be communicated *to* all it can also be extended *by* anyone. Jesus once prevented his disciples from stopping a man who was not 'one of us' from using the name of Jesus to drive out devils. If someone was not against him, Jesus, like a true liberal, said they were on the same side. Thus no kind of sectarianism can ever justify itself in his name. When Christians arrogantly draw a sharp line between Jesus and other people it soon becomes obvious that it is actually Jesus and the sectarians who are standing on opposite sides. Whenever a Christian judges or excludes others he condemns himself as a disciple. The paradox of 'being a Christian', as we will see in the following chapter, is precisely that

30 Mt 22:1-14.

it is a distinct but never a sectarian identity. It does not prevent you from being anything else compatible with the teaching of Jesus. Simone Weil said the tragedy of Christianity is that it came to see itself as replacing other religions rather than adding something to them all. An essential part of this contribution is Jesus' teaching on the Kingdom.

In the 'parable of the anonymous Christians', as it has been called, Jesus associates the Kingdom with behaviour rather than beliefs. He identifies himself preferentially with the afflicted, the unvoiced and the underprivileged.

> For when I was hungry you gave me food; when thirsty you gave me drink . . . And he will answer, 'I tell you this: anything you did for one of my brothers here, however humble, you did for me.'[31]

The irony highlighted here is that those who minister to Jesus in the sick, the hungry, the thirsty and imprisoned, may not know to whom they are doing it. You can be in the Kingdom without calling it that. To be with Jesus you do not have to think about him. Christian identity, we will see, is not an exclusive club. All sit at the table of the Kingdom. Christian identity is a certain and enlightening way of naming.

◦❍◦❍◦❍◦

It is difficult to imagine any Jew speaking about religion as if it did not matter. But it is even more difficult to imagine a Jew who could not also joke about their relationship with God. Apart from the simple humour in many of Jesus' stories there is a kind of pun at the heart of his manifestation of the Kingdom. It is a timeless Word of God that expresses itself through human words, a man who is like and unlike all others, a king who is powerless. Like a good comedy the story revolves around a mistaken identity:

> He was in the world; but the world, though it owed its being to him, did not recognise him. He entered his own realm, and his own would not receive him.[32]

And like all good comedies it ends in a marriage, in a permanent and happy union.

[31] Mt 25:35ff.
[32] Jn 1:10.

I will be with you always, till the end of time.[33]

For the Word of God to be misheard by those to whom it is addressed is a joke on a cosmic scale. Like comedy it walks the razor edge of tragedy. Like the stories of Zen masters and Desert Fathers the gospels use irony to convey the deepest insights. The purpose of a koan, like the redemptive question of Jesus, is to bring the mind to the absurd and laughable limit of its attempt to be master of the reality it reflects. It shows that words can never equal the reality that they are striving to express. There is both pain and laughter in that shortfall. Enlightenment is achieved in a moment of keen laughter: when we discover that the car keys we have been looking everywhere for were in our pocket all the time. Or when, after years of self-wasting hostility, we learn that the person we hated because we feared them had feared us even more.

The humour of the gospels is not comic. But like much humour it revolves around an absurd human misunderstanding. Sin and illusion are basically absurd in the light of the Kingdom. This absurdity is most clear in the way those who sat at his feet drinking in his words misunderstood what Jesus was saying. Time and again they were impressed and fascinated but missed his main point. We can hardly consider this without wondering whether we have really got the point ourselves. The meaning becomes most intelligible when we see how all his words are turned towards his hearers with a penetrating intimacy by his redemptive question concerning himself. None of our apparent certainties about who Jesus is can go unexamined if we keep this in mind. We will never take him for granted or replace his original presence with an image.

This is why another warning remark of Jesus hovers over all our thinking about him:

You know how to read the face of the sky, but you cannot read the signs of the times.[34]

We can never rest complacent that we have fully understood him in himself or in his relation to our own times. Nor can we ever be certain that our interpretation of the meaning of the kingdom corresponds infallibly with his. Yet this humble self-doubt, that defeats the pre-

[33] Mt 28:20.
[34] Mt 16:3.

tensions of fundamentalism, is the door to wisdom. We can never trust appearances or first impressions. Stories can have unexpected endings. The laughter hidden in the master's teaching is the compassionate irony of life we so often misinterpret as impersonal cruelty. It teaches us to seek the consummate joy of being that lies at the heart of even life's worst tragedies.

◦❍◦❍◦❍◦

In the Kingdom it is all or nothing.

There is no room for compromise in face of the overwhelming generosity of the gift of consciousness. The real wonder is not that we are like this or like that but that we *are* at all. What is more, somehow we possess all the means necessary to bring consciousness to its fullest development.

Or, better put perhaps, the Kingdom is all *and* nothing.

All, because we must give everything—a condition of compete simplicity demanding not less than everything, as Julian of Norwich said. And *nothing*, because it is the no-thing of the Self (the nonexistence of the isolated, autonomous self). We must continuously return to this poverty of spirit and detachment the instant we begin to reacquire possessions. The Kingdom is nothing whenever we are possessed by what we possess—whether the possessions are material things, psychological states or spiritual experiences. We cannot be a follower of Jesus, he told us, without renouncing *all* our possessions. The experience of *all* and the experience of *nothing* are not as self-contradictory as first appears.

One can feel this paradox at work in all dispossession, all letting-go. After clearing out the basement and giving away all the unnecessary stuff we have accumulated we get a glimpse. There is often a sharp pang of attachment, a silly final clinging before the cleansing relief of letting-go. Many have experienced the liberty of the Kingdom in the horror of financial or social failure. Like Viktor Frankl, Alexander Solzhenitsyn has described the terrible beauty of finding peace in the gulag or meaning in a concentration camp. Ramana Maharshi described the mystery of fullness and emptiness, the riches of poverty, that he experienced in the days following the death of his ego. He was sitting naked on the side of the road receiving alms from passers-by and was filled with the overwhelming conviction that he had everything. They thought I was a beggar, he said. But he knew he was a king. He was full *because* he was empty.

Fullness and emptiness share the same disturbing and exhilarating characteristic of being *boundless*. In fullness there is no limit to fullness. In emptiness there is no limit to emptiness. The Kingdom experience is not in the emptiness or the fullness but in the boundlessness. There are no deals to be made with fullness and emptiness. This becomes most powerfully obvious in the experiences of death and of love. In the deepest states they are known as one. Only they, at that depth of mystical oneness, empower us for the absolute, selfless commitment to the Kingdom that Jesus says is necessary.

Jesus communicates the Kingdom in the absolute inclusiveness of his love—his tolerance, compassion and generosity. But his selfless death also incarnates his teaching on the Kingdom. It was a fully human love, a fully human death. Esoteric 'spiritualisers' of the gospel later denied that the Son of God could know fear, suffer physically, shed tears or feel affection or grief. They portrayed him as wandering through life wrapped in the knowledge of his divinity as if it were a fireproof covering against suffering. They said he wore humanity like a cloak and claimed that just before he died he shed it and flew up to heaven. One can understand the dilemma of these Docetists who struggled so hard with the paradox of a human, suffering God. But only the paradox of the humanly divine can express the truth of human nature. It is not just a theological quibble therefore. It changes the way you think about yourself. And once its truth has been felt it determines your path to self-knowledge, your whole way of life. For long the subject of theological controversy, today the divinity of the man Jesus also stimulates interreligious dialogue. But the full emptiness of Jesus, his human divinity, is more than an idea to debate. It is a grounding truth of our relationship with him. If it is true then it is also a truth about ourselves that shapes how we respond to one other.

Human beings prefer their gods to be set safely above them out of reach and beyond human weakness. Perhaps this was Judas's dilemma. Like him we can feel let down by seeing how vulnerable Jesus is. Those who feel let down are the most likely to betray. When Jesus, the hero from whom we hoped so much, so readily accepts the humiliating failure of the Cross we tend to disassociate from him. Like the Grand Inquisitor in Dostoevsky's *The Brothers Karamazov*, we want to tell Jesus how he should have handled it better. Why didn't he summon the angels to rescue him when Pilate challenged his kingship? Why not take the way out Pilate seemed to be offering? Ordinary mortals, the Inquisitor believed, need infallible and invulnerable authority figures. If they don't exist they must be invented.

Deep down we are fascinated by the idea of the Creator as a suffering servant consoled by a creature. But it is also deeply unsettling because of what it reveals of the insecurity of our ego. Through his love and death Jesus forms in our minds an image of a God who is incompatible with our egos: both less aloof and more vulnerable than egotism. Our relationship to Jesus means precisely this—how we see God. And seeing God is what conversion in the Kingdom is all about.

·◇··◇··◇·

Most Christians inevitably experience conversion long after their baptism as infants.

Until conversion, the meaning of which we will explore in Chapter Eight, we will be disturbed by the understanding of God that emerges through listening to Jesus' question. It is so different from the god of our early training, the patriarchal, judgemental and punitive personification of karma. Conversion shatters this image. God is seen to be more than karma, more than the enforcement officer of the moral law. Contemplative prayer supported by better religious training helps us cross the desert that separates the living God from the God we were taught to fear, serve and obey. But could never truly love.

Bringing these early pre-conceptual images of God up to date is the ongoing work of conversion in the spiritual journey. Behind a lifelong accretion of images of God, there always remains the direct experience of God we knew as children. In contemplation this childlikeness is restored. We do not regress to childhood but we become 'like little children'. Unless we do, Jesus warned, we cannot enter the Kingdom of God. Simplicity is the essence of contemplation. Childlike prayer and the mature reading of the gospel advance the conversion process. When the mind becomes still we effortlessly cease clinging to images. Silence then empowers us to hear Jesus' question with original clarity and childlike attention. His gospel teaching also then begins resonating with our personal experience. Gradually this experience purifies all ideas of God in the mystery of God itself. We enter Jesus' experience of God.

The main idea we have to shed is that of a punitive God:

> Love your enemies and pray for your persecutors; only so can you
> be children of your heavenly father who makes his sun rise on

good and bad alike, and sends the rain on the honest and dis-
honest ... There must be no limit to your goodness, as your heavenly Father's goodness knows no bounds.[35]

You must love your enemies and do good; and lend without expecting any return; and you will have a rich reward: you will be
children of the Most High, because he himself is kind to the
ungrateful and wicked. Be compassionate as your Father is compassionate.[36]

The symbol of God is the most powerful of all the symbols the mind
clings to. It constellates our entire symbolic universe. It influences and
interprets all personal and social life. However we may think, or even
refuse to think of God, whether we are theists, atheists or agnostics,
the idea of God is the most comprehensive of all symbols. I once sat
next to a physicist at a dinner. After we were introduced, he opened
the conversation by saying 'Of course I believe in God—but not in the
way you believe in Him.' He assumed he knew what I meant by God.
I discovered that however different our meanings might be we could
share 'God' as a symbol of ultimate reality and truth. It was an interesting conversation.

Even the image of the God that non-believers say they do *not*
believe in is a very potent symbol. As a compound symbol 'God' has
been under construction from our earliest moments of consciousness.
At the deeper levels, in our unconscious, it is inextricably involved
with all the encounters with authority absorbed from parents, older
siblings, teachers, priests, police, customs officers and ticket inspectors.
The fear of rejection or punishment associated with these authority
figures cut deep, leaving lingering wounds in our psyche. This fear is
transferred in the child's mind to the metaphysical symbol of God—
the supreme authority—which the child has learned from its daily
culture, at home, in school, in church, from the media. In this way
the God-symbol descends into an idol serving human power systems.
It is robbed of the grace needed to evoke wonder, to explain and
enlighten. It blocks rather than ushers us into the mystery of our
existence.

We go on to tailor this symbol to our needs and prejudices. For
example, the masculinity of the God of Semitic religion has shaped
the domestic and political structures of the societies that believe in

[35] Mt 5:44ff.
[36] Lk 6:35.

Him. Think instead for a moment of God as a 'She Who Is'.[37] Then not only the church and priesthood but also the power structures of business and politics have to be reimagined. Perhaps men are not naturally born to dominate if God is not male. Once we are ready to see a God in which masculine and feminine are integrated, the human power systems based on male domination are fatally undermined. They can no longer be metaphysically justified by the commanding symbol of reality. We then see the *dishonesty* of all gender domination and eventually of all forms of oppression. Human sexuality itself is freed from cultural repression by the discovery of a God who creates 'Man' equally as male and female. Men and women are freed from their cultural stereotypes. They are freed to develop all sides of their personality. Prejudice about sexual orientation diminishes. Deep in the psyche, the symbol of God releases a healing, integrating, enlivening power. This is the effect of experiencing the Kingdom of God.

·○··○··○·

In the childhood of many Christians, God was once a living mystery. Their actual experiences of God were later clouded by the fear and guilt built into the ideas and images of God they absorbed. These images must be exorcised before clear experience can be regained.

As children, our capacity for the direct experience of the Kingdom is natural and spontaneous. Jesus said that *only* the childlike can enter it. For a young child it is an experience almost entirely without conceptual framework. Religion and family and other social institutions provide the conceptual structure. But the child's mind matures enriched and complicated by its capacity for self-reflection. Early in life the gap begins to widen between experience and concept as we think about what we are learning. Under the pressure of social conformity, feeling and thought lose their spontaneous and natural correspondence. We *pretend* to feel what we do not feel but what we think we should. We say what we don't *mean*. Even beliefs we may vigorously defend or promote may never have been *felt* to be true. Religious emotions such as gratitude and joy can be faked or formalised. For many people today, as the gap between the idea and the experience of God yawns wider, their sense of alienation from institutional religion increases also. Religious orthodoxy ceases to be a help to spiritual growth whenever conformity is imposed. And people today increasingly reject

[37] Elizabeth A. Johnson, *She Who Is* (New York: Crossroad, 1992).

this. Institutional rigidity appears to *deliver* a ready-made truth and while there are many today who find this seductive, the truly spiritual option is to *discover* it in our own experience.

The modern preoccupation with experience is not new. History tells many stories of religious renewal driven by personal experience in defiance of external authority. Experience, of course, can mean different things to different people. It can mean feeling ecstatically charged with charismatic energy. Or it can mean the deeper, slower pattern of personal transformation such as is undertaken in the discipline of contemplative practice. Experience bestows its unique and personal kind of authority. Religious institutions frequently perceive this as a threat but they can also help to train and develop such experience. They can exert a moderating influence on extreme manifestations of subjective experience that tend towards fanaticism or delusion. Generally, however, institutional religious leaders have discouraged contemplative experience for the many. It creates too many prophets and raises too many people with the authority of real holiness. Yet the tension is necessary. The inspirational witness of personal experience needs to be felt within the institutions, even when they condemn it. The majority of us come to holiness in the slow lane. But it is only deep personal experience which frees us from those engrained images of God which block spiritual growth and drain the spirit out of religion.

To find God, then, we must lose God—at least our primitive ideas and images of God. Detaching from these familiar images will be painful, individually and for the community of which we are part. It is a deep level of our psyche that is being changed. Even for the nonreligious person there will be the pain of feeling they are losing some kind of familiar and reassuring God. Pain as well as joy accompanies the discovery of the living mystery because the idols we must smash are so enmeshed with our images of ourselves.

The sense of separation from God, however, is necessary for spiritual individuation. It is particularly painful and confusing for religious people. Their first sniff of the Kingdom may feel less like a discovery of God than a loss or even a sacrilegious rejection of the God once so securely delivered to them. But through the awful emptiness of absence, God is encountered in the awe of pure presence. Slowly it dawns that losing the image is the prerequisite of finding the original. Losing your way is the very way of seeking God. This truth about the vision of God reveals another law we may not even be aware we are obeying:

that to find our true Self we must lose our ego selves. To deepen a relationship we must let go of the other. Absence then imperceptibly transforms into the mystery of presence. At last we realise that the absence of God is only the failure of our powers of understanding to grasp God's real presence.

All we can say accurately about God, according to Thomas Aquinas, is *that* God is, not *what* God is. Our relationship with God is therefore akin to the mystery that we are to ourselves. If it is true that God remains always a mystery to us, it is also true that we are a mystery to ourselves. The mystery is after all, that we even exist, that *anything* should exist. This wonder is a fundamental human quality and, according to Aristotle, the keystone of philosophy. The wonder of being human is contingent on the wonder of God's *mysterium*. This mysteriousness of God is the primary Biblical affirmation about God. Despite all the thought and ritual that it has accumulated, the knowable unknowability of God is the linchpin of Christian theology.

> 'If you can understand it,' says St Augustine, 'then it is not God. If you were able to understand then you understood something else instead of God. If you were able to understand even partially then you deceived yourself with your own thoughts.'[38]

This *radical* humility (and humour) before the ineffable mystery of God is the foundation of the Christian tradition. From the heart of that tradition there issues an authority that liberates. Its teachers point the way, with a wise unknowing, a learned and humble ignorance, into the Kingdom.

·⟨∘⟩·⟨∘⟩·⟨∘⟩·

The terms *Kingdom of heaven* and *God* are virtually interchangeable in the first three gospels. St John prefers the word *Life*.

The Kingdom refers to the life of God perceived through relationship with oneself and others. At the heart of Jesus' teaching, therefore, is his insight into relationship, expressed most intimately in his *abba-consciousness*. For Jesus the meaning of the Kingdom is inextricably involved in relationship and interdependence. His gospel cannot therefore be reduced to a system of ideas or commands. It is a life. The communication of his teaching *is* a living relationship with whoever receives it in the 'Word of Life' which Jesus himself embodies.

---

[38] St Augustine, *Sermon 52*.

This Word is a full self-communication of complete truth. Because it transcends even the greatest concepts it cannot be understood by the intellect alone. It demands imagination and feeling. Above all it needs that form of spiritual intelligence we call love whose symbolic organ is the heart. By calling forth a concerted human response from the whole person, therefore, the human expression of the Word of God in Jesus unveils the mystery *we* are within the mystery that God is.

Jesus calls the response to this mystery 'worship in spirit and in truth'. God, 'who is spirit', he said to the Samaritan woman at the well, wants *this* kind of worship not merely external observance.[39] The time has already come, he says, when you will worship the Father neither in this temple nor on that mountaintop, but in spirit and in truth. Prayer of this depth redefines and reprioritises all ritual though it does not dispense with it. Once we have begun to enter the mystery at this deeper level we recover the childlike capacity for pure worship. The 'simple enjoyment of the truth' is how Aquinas defined contemplation. The fruit of prayer is purer prayer in happiness and liberty of spirit. *We* are set free when *God* is liberated from our egotistical needs and idols.

Contemplation, meditation, worship in spirit and truth, the 'pure prayer' of the early Christian monastic tradition all describe how we begin to *see* the reality of the God of Jesus.

Happy are the pure of heart for they shall see God.[40]

Jesus' teaching on the Kingdom was delivered within a religious framework of belief and Jesus was an observant if radical practitioner of his religion. Yet the Kingdom challenges many ideas about religion. Firstly, it resituates the religious mind in a personal relationship to the truth. Relationship begins with *listening* to what the truth is saying. The very act of listening to his teaching about the Kingdom initiates a response to his redemptive question which in turn reveals the affinity between teacher and teaching. Just by listening, therefore, by paying attention, by being mindful, we embark on the purifying of the heart. The shedding of images of God and the ego begins with the silence necessary for listening. This relentless simplification will progress until we awaken to the Kingdom, the place of self-knowledge from which Jesus could say that 'The Father and I are One.'

[39] Jn 4:24.
[40] Mt 6:8.

Jesus shows that the Kingdom is not an abstraction outside of the web of relationship. God is not the isolated monad of human imagining with whom each individual has a separate relationship. Our personal relationship with God is enshrined in the family of all beings. God is the ground of all being. Every relationship of life is an aspect of our total identity rooted in that ground of being. The Kingdom is the grounding relationship of all conscious beings, the simple unity of an infinitely complex, interdependent universe.

⋖⋗⋖⋗⋖⋗

We begin in relationship. We make progress by staying open. This is why listening to the right questions is so important.

We are able to know whatever we need to know. The teaching of Jesus does not satisfy our curiosity about every kind of question we would like answers to. Nor did the Buddha or Ramana Maharshi. What it does is present us with the important questions which point to the fundamental inquiry of human consciousness: *Who am I?* The redemptive question of Jesus is neither speculative nor merely curious. It is not abstract but highly practical because it changes the way we live and think and feel. It invites an answer through a costly personal response expressed not in words but in a relationship where the meaning of words is embodied. Self-knowledge contains all answers.

The response to the question of Jesus bestows itself in the very relationship which it opens. Jesus himself is the Kingdom in person. As with all human interaction, relationship with Jesus begins tentatively and deepens and matures with time. The historical words of his teaching, as in the art of the parables, are powerful symbols that continually deepen and illuminate that relationship. But his words lead to spirit not to endless mental analysis. According to the Teacher, the words themselves *are* spirit and they *are* life.

Relationship with Jesus begins as soon as we hear his 'you' as a life-giving word addressed to *me*. His question is his knock on the door of our life. We soon find that it is not a closed relationship. It is not sectarian or individual or in conflict with other relationships based in truth and love. To be in relationship with him is to find oneself in clearer and more conscious relationship with other people, friends and strangers, with the environment, with history and tradition and even with the as yet unborn.

To be in relationship is to be in love. To refuse to love is to break out of relationship with those who hurt or displease us. It is an ultimately futile attempt. There are degrees of relationship but there is no one with whom we are not connected. When relationships fracture and cause pain, in marriage, friendship or between ethnic groups, it is because they have not learned how to elevate love above the demands of the ego. This insight into the Kingdom as universal relatedness is the fruit of all Christian prayer, indeed of all spiritual practice. Jan Van Ruysbroeck, a fourteenth century Flemish mystic, expressed it like this:

> We know well that the bosom of the Father is our proper ground and the source from which springs our life and being. And from our proper ground, that is, from the Father and all that lives in him, there shines forth an eternal brightness, which is the birth of the Son ... All those who are raised above their creaturely condition into a God-seeing life are one with this divine brightness. So they are that brightness itself and they also see, feel and find ... they are that same onefold Ground.[41]

⋯⋰⋱⋯

Reading the scriptures of the Christian faith dispels complacency. The first Christians grew their faith in Jesus by reading the scriptures. Mystical theology originated in the interpretation of the sacred texts. Eventually what is being interpreted, interprets the interpreter to himself. The words and stories, the symbols and poetry of the Bible penetrate and suffuse the mind of the reader. It is as if, to pursue the image of the Desert monks, the juices released by the mind's chewing of the cud of the word open the heart.

Contemplative practices in all traditions share a reverence for the power of the sacred words of scripture. They understand how reading scripture can deepen every form of prayer and purify every spiritual practice. The need today to regain this reverence for the Word is urgent. The opportunity to do so is at hand. Christians have never had such easy access to their own scriptures. To these we could add the non-canonical books, the apocrypha and Gnostic writings, many of variable value, many of them fallen by the wayside in the catholic tradition. In general, people who discover this more esoteric Christianity return to the New Testament canon with a renewed appreciation and a better understanding of why it came to be defined in this form. We may also

---

[41] Jan Van Ruysbroeck, *Spiritual Espousings, Selected Works. The Adornment of the Spiritual Marriage* (J. M. Dent: London, 1916), III.3.

find nourishment in the scriptures of the Eastern traditions, the Upanishads, Buddhist Sutras, Sikh writings, in which the same Word of God—there can only be one—also resonates. Tasting the Word in other traditions returns us to the gospels with a finer palate for truth. The familiar recovers a wonderful newness just as travelling abroad makes us love our home more.

Many Christians fear the idea of finding the living Word in other traditions. This fear, however, only blocks deeper relationship with the Word made Flesh. Jesus liberates from fear and opens his disciples to ever-wider circles of friends. His question leads us to great discoveries and painful renunciations. It discloses the very nature of God as relationship. Our personal sense of identity is altered by seeing how we are in relationship, in loving relationship, with all that is. No one can listen to his question without being led to ask, *who am I?* And at some point another irritating question will have to be faced, *what is a Christian?*

∾ 7 ∾
Jesus and Christianity

*O*nce in Thailand, I was sitting in a quiet corner of a Buddhist temple watching the devotees come and go, mainly women with children in tow and old men. They entered as into a familiar room, prostrated reverently but casually, made offerings and in their different ways beseeched the higher powers for help. It reminded me of a Catholic church. The educated Buddhist monks with whom I had just been in dialogue would, like many Christian clergy running parish churches around the world or temple priests throughout history, have lived a performer's distance between themselves and their audience of fellow believers.

On one of my first Sundays on Bere Island I was asked to stand in at mass for the priest who usually visited from the mainland. I felt happy and privileged to be celebrating mass in the church where my ancestors had worshipped, a pretty and devoutly tended sacred space in the quiet middle of the island. My grand-parents and uncles were buried in the graveyard. I felt some pride on my cousin's behalf. Recognising that I was probably seen as an odd kind of fellow who never wore a Roman collar, this liturgy might establish that I really was a priest and might bring my cousins a little reflected glory. A small return for the friendship and hearty meals they had shared with me. The preparations for mass were efficient. The local postmaster was the sacristan. When I asked him to do the readings, however, he recoiled in horror and I asked why. 'I'd never live it down,' he said. They'd think he was getting above himself. I began to sense that this mass was not going to be my gift of celebrating community and family that I had self-centredly imagined. The small church was about half full. But as I stood at the altar, vested in old-fashioned vestments I hardly knew how to put on, the first six rows in front of me were bare. The rows behind were sprinkled with women and children poised for mass as if on starting blocks for a hundred-metre race. The men of the island stood at the back of the church like rebellious schoolboys glaring impatiently. Even those who had been chatting outside with me a few minutes before seemed to be eyeing me now with inexplicable aggression. I felt the English half of my bloodline beginning to observe and comment. So this was the sacrament which had kept the faith alive through centuries of English persecution.

The mass that followed taught me a lot about institutional Christianity. The responses were delivered like rounds from a machine gun. The next response was half out before I had started my previous line. I declaimed the readings myself and felt I might as well have been reading the Cork Examiner classifieds. When I offered the sign of peace and came down off the altar to share it they stared at me as if I was walking towards them in my underwear. None of the standing men came to communion. Only in my homily when I braved a few words about what it meant for me to be there among them did I feel there was the glimmer of connection, a real listening, but no reciprocated eye contact. Yet after mass, outside, with the general relief of returning to the rituals of ordinary life, everyone returned to normal. Later I saw that the fault was mine. I was the guest, but as the officiant I had imposed my idea of how to have the meal. Nevertheless, it was all very odd. The dislocations between personal faith, friendship and the institution were difficult to understand.

The church, I thought later at a happy Sunday lunch with my cousin, is a family and most families, as we all know, are to some degree dysfunctional. But there's no escaping them.

◦•◦•◦•

So far, in listening to the question of Jesus, we have been focussed on the historical Jesus of Nazareth and his teaching.

We have seen that there is no authentic story to be told about Jesus without the light shed by experiencing Jesus risen—as in the personal encounters that transformed the first disciples. This Resurrection-experience had an overwhelming reality for the first Christians. It taught them that the history of Jesus rose with him and that his new transcendent reality meant that he could touch and be present to people of all places and times. St Paul refers to it as a collective as well as a personal event. Jesus 'appeared' to Cephas and to the Twelve, and to 'more than five hundred of the brethren at the same time' most of whom were still alive when St Paul was writing. Paul also says that Jesus later *appeared* to James and to all the apostles. Last of all, he concludes, 'he appeared to me'.[1]

The Resurrection was a transcendent reality, surpassing the normal limits of human experience; yet normal, sane living people experienced it. It meant that the historical life of Jesus and his teaching were extended indefinitely into time and space. When Christian thinkers

[1] Cor 15:5-8.

began to say that Jesus was the centre of history it was because the historical condition of humanity seemed to have been revolutionised by what had happened in Jesus. What from time immemorial spiritual seers from China to the Himalayas, from Ireland to Australia had intuited as the eternal in Man, our deepest current of Being, broke the surface of time's ocean in the Resurrection of Jesus. It had unique and universal dimensions. It broke as the single wave of an individual human consciousness that remained visible among the countless disappearing waves. But it also represented them all.

For those who recognise Jesus alive in the Spirit life is different. It is as if the sting of death is drawn out of it. We still live under the limitations from which his Resurrection has freed him but they no longer appear so all-controlling. Even now an intoxicating freedom and a revitalising hope is accessible. What happened in Jesus illustrates our own destiny—every human being will be 'raised from the dead'. The gospels put it simply: he has 'conquered death', the greatest and most terrifying of all human constraints. To live free from the fear of death is to live with the greatest of freedoms.

To recognise Jesus in the Resurrection-experience is to taste a new liberty of spirit. We are brought deeper into the present moment, rooted more firmly in the wonder of ordinary life. The ordinary is not abolished but recharged with depth and significance. The Resurrection is not an altered state of consciousness; it is a transition into a reality which, however gradually we may awaken to it, changes *us* unalterably. A luminosity enters our way of seeing things, sacred and profane. When, as William Blake said, we see anything as it really is, we see it in infinity.

The discipline of spiritual practices attunes us to this experience. Contemplative prayer (deeper than words, image and thought) and gospel *lectio* (the turning of spiritual attention to word, image and thought) are the midwives of the spiritual awakening in which the Risen Jesus is recognised. Worship and liturgy are seen to be expressions of the community of the True Self. Prayer awakens us to this by bringing us to self-knowledge. To see Jesus is to see the true Self which can only be seen in a state of union not as a separated reality; it means to see *as* the true Self, to see him as he sees himself, to see ourselves as we are seen by God. Only through another can we see 'the eye that sees but cannot see itself'. If it is true, as he tells us, that we cannot observe the Kingdom coming, nor can we see the Self as if it were another entity. Similarly, meeting with the Risen Jesus is not an isolated event.

It occurs in all dimensions of consciousness and perception. The gospel stories of the Resurrection appearances stress the ordinary ways he is recognised. What transforms these ordinary situations is *insight*. Reading the gospels, like meditation and all the rich forms of Christian prayer, is not meant merely to provide more ideas to think about or even more feelings to enjoy. It schools us in insight, the vision of faith.

꘎꘎꘎

But what really does it mean to call oneself a Christian? How does recognising the Risen Jesus with the purified eye of the heart relate to the institution of Christianity? Many, if not most, westerners by now are of the 'Jesus yes, church no' persuasion. To those who have *not* seen how rich and vibrant the life of a parish can be, or witnessed the altruism of personal lives serving the poor or sick, or shared in the contemplative renewal of Christian spirituality, it can even seem that Christianity and Jesus are cut off from each other. But the vitality of Christianity today is not limited to the headline-catching pentecostal churches or the political Christian Right.

Even these can be the place where beginners start a spiritual journey into deeper and more mystical explorations of the reality of Christ. Eastern religions have opened many to this spiritual dimension but often in time they rediscover a richer Christian tradition they imagined when they rejected the church for its shallowness or intolerance. Even so, in Western society today it is true that for vast numbers the Christian tradition has become incomprehensible, even redundant. Some may return: what is irrelevant at twenty looks more meaningful after the birth of your first child or the death of a parent. But most, once separated from the church, stay that way.

Most of the media take a hostile or mocking view of the Church: a relic of the age of superstition, subjection to clerical power, repressed sexuality, general eccentricity. Its rituals and local customs are presented as anachronistic in an age of virtual reality and globalisation. Its morality and use of authority seem locked into a Eurocentric imperialist, patriarchal past. Or, Christianity is regarded as actually dangerous and despicable, as it was for many first-century Roman intellectuals. (The historian Tacitus referred to Christianity as that 'pernicious superstition which has broken out not merely in Judea the home of the disease, but in the capital itself.') This dominant media image of Christianity is very different from the experience many have of it in their lives as providing community, inspiration and meaning. But the message continues to be hammered home by the media: Christianity, along with other world faiths, belongs to the past. Numbers have indeed plummeted. But there are also fascinating and unmistakeable signs of growth and new forms of 'being Christian'. Who is right, what way is Christianity headed?

What is significant is that even the most vitriolic critics of the church rarely include Jesus in their attack. Indeed their argument is often that Jesus has been betrayed by the institution of Christianity. Seeing that he was originally betrayed by one of his close disciples and abandoned by the rest of his followers, is it so surprising to see a huge gap of human fallibility and sinfulness between him and his church. Isn't it precisely for sinners that he came? If the institutions of the church have claimed (and pretended) at times to form a perfect society, immune from human failings, is not this very hypocrisy itself a sign of its being a community of sinners capable, however, as history repeatedly shows, of repentance and self-renewal?

How did Jesus and Christianity ever drift so far apart? The question is very pertinent in an age of anxiety and hyper-individualism that craves peace and community. It is especially relevant as the churches go through their process of purification and renewal.

⋅◦⋅◦⋅◦⋅

The Western church seemed to Carl Jung to have culpably failed in its role as a teacher of wisdom because it failed its mission of representing the true message of Jesus. Its institutions became objects of self-idolatry and were confused with the Kingdom that Jesus proclaimed was 'not of this world'. Despite a continual counterwitness to this self-idolatry from its saints, the churches' institutional leadership set itself apart in a self-defined realm of the chaste and sacred and declared all else, including the body, to be profane. When this tendency prevailed, true spiritual life declined until the next movement of renewal began. Today Christianity confronts its karma in the controversial issues that tomorrow will no doubt appear as self-evident as the evil of slavery or the right to vote. Until then, the equality of women, respect for sexual orientation, the right to participate in church government, friendship with other religions will continue to be the crucibles in which Christianity is renewed, the yardsticks of its integrity.

The charges levelled against Christianity by the media and many historians and are rarely counterbalanced by recognition of its achievements. Because this imbalance affects the way people think of themselves as Christians it is important to listen to the charges unflinchingly, humbly. They claim that where Jesus gave equal status to slave and master, Christianity legitimised the ancient divisions between the powerful and the powerless, rich and poor. Jesus shocked his contemporaries by sharing his table with the outcast and turned no one away. The churches pander to social respectability at the cost of spiritual truth, excommunicate one another and deny fellowship to outsiders. Jesus taught within a community of friends, his spiritual authority resting upon humility. The churches erect vertical power structures like any other institution, even claiming that its bureaucracy is divinely ordained. Jesus served. Clergy preside. Jesus taught. Churches preach. Jesus forgave and healed. Churches condemn. Jesus respected women. Many churches endorse their subordination. Jesus transmitted peace and joy. Christians fight angrily for succession and political power. The religious legalism that Jesus rejected quickly reestablished itself in the church. The history of Christianity compounds a catalogue of faults: Crusades against the infidel, persecution of heretics, warlike medieval papacies, Machiavellian politics, appeasement of dictators, silence over the Holocaust and other injustices. There is a response to all this. But the Christian of the twenty-first century cannot understand what it means to be a Christian without recognising the truth of much of it and feeling a profound and humbling sorrow for it.

This is indeed why the strongest criticism often comes today from those who love the church most. A contemporary Christian writer has written a litany for Christians to recite to ask forgiveness for the sins of the church. It is a painful, embarrassing cry of repentance but could only have been written by a Christian who anticipates a fuller realisation of the church's potential:

> For the Inquisitions
> For cruelty in the Crusades
> For the senseless killing of men of different faiths
> For the violence in Northern Ireland
> For the oppression of women
> For collusion with the powerful
> For the abuse of priestly power
> For cruelty to orphans
> For sexual abuse of children
> For ignoring the homeless

For ignoring the Holocaust
For corruption of the young
For pride and pomposity, (etc.)
Forgive us O Lord[2]

These are the Christians who are aware of the church's unique and barely realised potential. They can see the communion of Christian churches representing a rich historical and cultural diversity, a truly global and spiritual institution: generating a spiritual vision of humanity as a single family and facing its social problems. They strive for a church that is prophetic, independent, courageous and ready to sacrifice itself, quick to defend the defenceless, speak for the inarticulate, free the oppressed, feed the hungry, embrace the neglected, balance rights and duties, remind leaders of the true nature of peace and justice, respectful of the environment, the value of the homeless, the dignity of orphans, the handicapped and the unwanted elderly. Christian identity must be shaped by paradoxes: repentance and hope, recognising failure and believing in essential goodness. Being Christian does not mean a denial of the churches' sinfulness.

There are further noteworthy achievements made by Christianity which its critics often ignore. Ironically, the spirituality and theology of the church developed many of the values now often used by others to rebuke it: the fundamental concepts of personal liberty, human rights, universal education and social equality whose roots lie in the teaching of Jesus and the primitive church. The first dioceses were among the first organised welfare institutions for the homeless and sick. Christianity spearheaded many intellectual breakthroughs and encouraged the arts. Its mystical traditions have enriched the spiritual life of the whole human family. Despite the corrupt medieval popes there have been saintly and enlightened ones. Despite the proud princes of the church there have been the Helder Camaras and Oscar Romeros, the Maryknoll missionaries murdered because they stood up for the poor and refused to abandon them even when their own lives were threatened; despite corrupt monks there have been the St Francises and Mother Teresas. Despite the wars of religion there have been peacemakers reconciling conflicts, hostages who loved their captors, countless unsung missionaries defending peace and justice and raising the standards of life and self-respect among the people to whom they committed their whole lives while, shamefully, the church blessed napalm bombs headed for Vietnam. It also gave rise to the Northern Ireland man who in the name of Christ forgave his daughter's terrorist killers as she lay dying in his arms. As well as the silences over injustice there is the silent, patient, healing work of reconciliation performed by lay and clerical Christians in all the world's places of conflict. Without such people whose inspiration was the love of Jesus and solidarity with the church, human history would be a far more shameful affair than it is.

Furthermore, to get the balance right, one must question the way the charges are often addressed against Christianity. For example, what is 'the Church' or 'Christianity'? Do the accusations apply to ordinary Christians living out their faith today or in the past? Do these charges apply against *all* Christians or even all its clerical leaders? A blanket historical condemnation of the Church is an illogical generalisation. The fact that the medieval church used torture against heretics is as repulsive to us as is the torture used by a modern repressive regime. One could argue that the church should have thought and acted in a more enlightened way. But that assumes the church is a supernatural institution. It is the fact that Christianity has survived its own failings as well as it has that suggests the guiding presence of a faithful Friend and Teacher.

There is no doubt that being a Christian brings one into a difficult relationship with the institution of the Church. But being a Christian is more than belonging to an institution.

⟨O⟩O⟨O⟩

Christianity is both a flawed institution and a mystical Body. It embodies a way of life modelled on the life and teaching of Jesus. If one chooses to distance oneself from the institution this does not mean a total rejection of Jesus. It may simply be distaste for a very mixed bag of unglamorous people with whom the risen Jesus forms his spiritual body. Being a 'non-Christian' can have a spectrum of meaning as broad as Christian identity itself. You may respect, admire, love or worship Jesus while also rejecting the 'institutional church'. You may believe in the teaching of Jesus or hold beliefs about him which the church would condemn you for holding. Perhaps you even hold to those beliefs while still wanting to worship with fellow believers in a mainstream church. People have always responded to the question of Jesus in a way that defines them as much as it defines him.

Until modern times the church had the political power to suppress nonconformity. Today, pluralism flourishes (or is rampant, depending on your point of view). In Western culture the church has largely lost anything more than ceremonial political power. But, as in many other areas of modernity, hard searching is underway among Christians to reconcile pluralism with objective truth, tradition with personal conviction. Is pluralism always right, always the best? When does 'universal tolerance' become a mask for indifference or fear of commitment? There is an ancient wisdom in Christianity that has served it well in all its periods of change. This is the wisdom of a living tradition that returns people in times of crisis to their roots: to the early church and to the font of personal experience in the prayer of the heart. Contemplation awakens the power to read the signs of the times and develop the clarity needed for right action. But an historical and spiritual understanding of the primitive church is crucial, not because it was a golden age, but because in many ways it provides the Christian model of resourcefulness, adaptability and diversity in unity.

Christian identity is nourished by this sense of living tradition. It harmonises the individual and the community. This is why in such an individualistic culture tradition is so problematical. It is not nostalgia or history hijacked in support of the status quo. The practical test of how we relate to tradition is in personal growth in goodness and holiness and in how we are conscious of this growth being related to our relationship to Jesus. People can relate personally to Jesus either as an historical hero or as a living master and friend. Understanding their relationship with him may also change over the course of a lifetime. As this changes so will the person's understanding of the church. Relationship with him is subject to growth as well as decline, to years of stagnation or sudden rediscoveries. With Jesus, as with others you have long thought you knew, relationship can suddenly ascend above the horizon of your understanding. That new perspective changes everything.

⋅❍⋅❍⋅❍⋅

Throughout their history Christians have learned to define each other as representatives of 'orthodoxy' or 'heresy', often through violent conflict.

It is often claimed that orthodoxy is defined by those who hold power just as history is written by winners. While tradition does have an historical objective content it can also be deliberately misinterpreted for personal ends. Like any other adjective, the term 'Christian' can be abused by those who claim to be the only, the true or the better Christians. Yet those who run the institution cannot totally define what is or is not said to be 'true tradition'. Pendulums swing. And often it is great individuals who start them swinging. The biblical religions accord great authority to the prophets and saints of every era—though often not until they have persecuted them to death.

So in a time like ours where so many reject the institution while revering its founder what does the term 'Christian' mean? If, for example, you are a Christian must you be a member of one of the officially recognised churches? St Paul, who was not naive about the tendency of new Christians to go off the rails, nevertheless saw initiation of baptism as a definitive part of Christian identity.[3] It was at once both a mystical rite and a sign of belonging to a group of weak fellow practitioners. It is difficult to imagine, as a norm, being a Christian without a personal decision expressed by a sign of initiation. With this comes the grace to enjoy the friendship, support and solace of community with fellow believers. This then leads to an insight into where you and others fit uniquely in the Body of Christ and what your role, or ministry is meant to be. In this experience one sees that the church is not Jesus. But in a sense *he* is the church. It cannot be separated from him. When this profoundly personal and even mystical sense of belonging to the Body degenerates into a comfortable clubby feeling institutionalism and legalism soon supplant both community and spirituality.

Many less institutional ways of being Christian and enjoying Christian fellowship are being tried today. People are experimenting, selecting different degrees of distance from the institutions. The definition of Christian identity is being recast. But these experiments do not reject the idea of *being church*. They mean something different by 'church'. They are vitalised by encountering the Risen Jesus mystically and socially. To recognise him, to whatever degree and at whatever level of one's experience, forms a relationship with him which calls some kind of Christian identity into being. It is not only the gospels that must be read in the light of the Resurrection: the same light clarifies every personal relationship with Jesus. Being a Christian may sometimes be defined only in terms of going to church. But essentially

[3] Gal 3:26-28.

it means a personal relationship with Jesus. This relationship then leads inevitably into relationship with others who also know and seek him because to find him is also to continue seeking him. Being a Christian does therefore entail accepting oneself as a member of his Body the church. Unfortunately there will always be an imperfect organisational form to this. Certain defining characteristics are found in most of these forms (denominations) of the church: common prayer, baptismal initiation, breaking bread, reading the gospels, doing theology, living community, serving the poor. By listening to his question we may be led in a number of different directions of Christian identity and degrees of churchiness. Jesus opens many ways of responding to his question with our lives.

Christian theology reflects this diversity. The vast spectrum of ideas held about Jesus show how many ways there are of expressing intellectually what being a Christian means. We can see this in the different ways he has been believed in through history.[4]

Differing theologies once generated violent conflict and still arouse strong passion among their adherents. Even today the media is interested in the conflicts of Christian thought, if not in their actual ideas at least in the stories of theologians silenced or excommunicated. Ideas do, of course, matter and not all ideas are of equal value. But theological differences have to be discussed without forgetting the bond of shared reverence and discipleship. People who hold very different views about who he is may still share the experience of his life and Spirit and the mystery of God embodied in his teaching. Each type of Christian may claim the best way of answering his question. But, if the Resurrection is how we know him then his presence is the final word. The more clearly we hear him as the Word the more silent we become. The more silent we become the more our thoughts and words

---

[4] For example, Docetists believed that the Son of God assumed the human condition in appearance only: he walked around as God in disguise and someone else died on the Cross in his place. Patripassianists saw Jesus as the incarnation of the Father, not of the Son, and so it was the Father who really died on the Cross. Subordinationists believed that Jesus was divine but still subordinate to the Father. Arians believed that Jesus was the Logos but that the Logos was itself a creation of God. Adoptionists said that Jesus was indeed the Son of God but only by adoption because of his fidelity and moral perfection. Monophysites rejected the two-nature language of Chalcedon but believed that Jesus is 'truly divine and fully human'.

will reflect him as the Word. He is the Word behind all the words of the endless Christian chatter.

This does not mean theology should close up shop. But that contemplation prevents it from becoming a closed shop. It does, though, suggest the value of closing up the shop-shutters every so often (like twice a day for times of meditation) and turning wholeheartedly from the work of thought and dialogue to the work of silence. The passion with which different Christian views are presented, attacked and defended shows how easily the ego clings to them and uses them as ways of hurting others. Theological ideas can prepare the mind for prayer. They can be radiant as the dogma of the mystery of Christ, articulating the inexpressible with poetic and intellectual beauty. But they can also degenerate into party slogans.

Some movements identifying themselves as pure Christianity, including some very odd ones, have reflected particular lifestyles as much as theologies. In the second century, for example, the followers of Marcion saw Christianity as an entirely new revelation free of its Jewish antecedents and so rejected the God of the Old Testament; they also recognised some women as the incarnation of the Holy Spirit and may have ordained them as priests. The Ebionites, an ascetical sect of Jewish Christians believing that Jesus was the natural son of Mary and Joseph, settled beside the River Jordan and lived a life of radical poverty. The Carpocratians, probably with a waiting list for new members, believed not only in reincarnation and the natural birth of Jesus but also that the only way to overcome a sinful temptation was to indulge it fully. Today in Africa, Asia and South America, new churches are breaking with the white-European mentality and individuating within their own culture. Emphasising community, healing and equality in discipleship, they often proliferate with the fertility and turbulence of early Christianity.

Many theologies and many competing churches claim to be Christian or even more *truly* Christian than each other. Yet the gospel and the experience of deep prayer reveal a unity in Christian identity that transcends the divisions. It is felt when one sees that purity of heart communicates faith better than rational arguments. This essential identity is felt when one understands that the gospel is better lived in personal encounters in community than in the polemic of ideas. Hence the value of the Eucharist and of meditating with others in silence. These demand personal, physical presence. You cannot cele-

brate the Eucharist or meditate together in faith without being aware
of a presence that unites you with others and itself and that also
embraces you and all others present. As if he anticipated the confusion
and conflict that would follow, Jesus reminded his followers that
where two or three gathered he would be present. That he would
remain with them until time ended. That the test of being his disciple
is simply to love one another. To love and to pray *in his name* is an
adequate definition of what it means to be a Christian.

⋅᠅⋅᠅⋅᠅⋅

If Christians can be accused of a history of exclusivism and imperialism this applies not only to their attitude to other religions but even
to other Christians.

To simplify matters one could say that from its earliest days Christianity spawned two complementary but often conflicting schools
whose roots lie in the differences between the gospels. They laid different theological weight on the humanity and divinity of Jesus. The
Alexandrian School started from the divinity: a Christology 'from
above' as in the gospel of John. The Antiochean School started from
the humanity: a Christology 'from below' that reflects the tone of the
synoptic gospels. Neither could entirely reject the other. As a minimum, Christianity posits a dialogue between the divine and the human
in Jesus. But the disagreements of emphasis between Alexandria and
Antioch created deep fissures. These are still active today in institutional barriers between denominations and in the mutual suspicion
with which Christians can regard each other. The Church of the Holy
Sepulchre in Jerusalem illustrates this, pitifully and absurdly. A number of denominations worship *their* Jesus there on bitterly guarded
square metres of God. The atmosphere is of mutual rejection. No better
example need be sought for the human tendency to neglect the essential and to absolutise the external. The tension between Alexandria
and Antioch, however, can be creative. It also expresses an authentic,
catholic diversity in responding to Jesus' question.

The tension does not need to lead to bitterness or anarchy. It can
be held in the deeper unity of Christian faith experienced in contemplation, worship, service and scripture. In that experience of unity the
harmony of the divine and the human in Jesus is felt also in ourselves.
Yet, rather than centering in their unity as disciples of the same master, Christian churches have preferred to see themselves as Greeks or

Jews or Romans, as High or Low Church Anglicans, liberal or traditional Roman Catholics, Methodists, Baptists, Plymouth Brethren, Quakers or Pentecostalists. Differences there will always be. But where there is the courage to pray and dialogue together people discover that differences are easier to live with than they think. For many, however, it is still hard even to *want* unity.

The prayer of Jesus was *may they all be one*. To make this truly one's own, one has to believe in the *already existing* unity it expresses. The unity his presence creates. Like most human beings Christians do deeply want unity and peace—but on their own terms. Ulster Orangemen and Nationalist Catholics in Northern Ireland look at each other as demonic perversions of Christian belief. Or, at least they use Christian labels to justify their inhumane ways of relating to each other. Some monks on Mount Athos do not even accept the validity of baptism by outsiders and insist on rebaptising their converts. The refusal of intercommunion among many churches is a scandalous sign of disunity. The divisions among Christians are as terrible a denial of Jesus as the appalling history of Christian anti-Semitism. Divisions and intolerance will always arise from competing answers to his question. They are healed and transcended when we return from defending our answers to listening to his question.

By posing his question to all, Jesus bestows dignity and equality on each individual. By denying that dignity and freedom, any grouping of Christians separates itself from Jesus. To restrict, by force or condemnation, others' right to choose their kind of response also damages one's own freedom to respond to the redemptive question. Intolerance and prejudice is spiritual suicide because it prevents one from deepening one's own faith and leads to isolation in the mental prison of the ego and its prejudices. Throughout history the repression of the freedom of others to choose their own kind of Christian identity has accumulated a heavy karma for modern Christians to work off.

When Christians draw lines between themselves and others, Jesus remains a relentless and scandalous crosser of these lines. He quietly slips to the other side. Whenever an attempt to imprison him is made he disappears from sight and appears elsewhere. Thus is lived out the paradoxical nature of Christian identity. A Christian is simultaneously a member of a community and an outsider. It is as if Jesus still prefers to be with the outcast, however wrong their beliefs or behaviour, rather than with those who are self-righteously sure that only they are right.

The intolerant Christian isolates himself or herself from the Christ of universal tolerance. Jesus' truth is greater than all the opinions about him put together.

Perhaps Christians will learn this better in the coming millennium as they learn how to relate in a Christlike way to other faiths. One of the ironies of Christian identity involves finding Christ in what is non-Christian. Learning to revere the truth in other religions will help Christians to love one another. And in that tough work they will recognise and enter the embrace of the risen Jesus.

⋅◦⋆◦⋆◦⋅

Many people feel that they are Christian but are reluctant to label themselves. Yet their personal experience of the Risen Jesus has already begun. It is inseparable from their own growth in self-knowledge. So they do not worry much about the exact terms in which they express the beliefs that emerge from their experience of faith. They see that faith and belief though strongly interwoven are distinct. The contemplative experience shows that there are ideas and there is also that which lies beyond concepts altogether. Shallow faith creates rigidity of belief. Deep faith is itself a maturity that cannot be defined even by the experiences that it produces. It ever remains, as mere rationalists are infuriated to hear, a mystery.

Faith and belief, institutional orthodoxy and personal experience, all together help to define one's Christian self-identity. One of the Desert Fathers, Evagrius Ponticus, writing in the fourth century in the tradition of Clement of Alexandria and Origen, said that

> Christianity is the Teaching (*dogma*) of Christ our Saviour. It is composed of spiritual training (*praktike*), of the contemplation of the physical world and of the contemplation of God.[5]

Christianity is more than a belief system. More than an institution. More than a morality. More than a culture. It is also spiritual growth and development ('training') and necessitates a kind of contemplation that touches all aspects of reality (the physical *and* the spiritual world) as Evagrius pithily puts it. According to Gregory of Nyssa,

> If one can give a definition of Christianity, we shall define it as follows: Christianity is an imitation of the divine nature.

[5] Evagrius Ponticus, *The Praktikos*.

He continues this idea: Christianity 'brings human beings back to their original good fortune' of being created in the image and likeness of God. If to be a Christian is to imitate the divine nature we are dealing with much more than conformity of beliefs. It is about faith expressed in lifestyle. It demands serious personal spiritual practice. Jesus said he would recognise those who were his own and who lived his teaching even if they had not recognised him. Behaviour counts for more than belief. Actions are truer than words. Beliefs matter when they lead the mind to recognise what the heart has already seen.

Christianity is a *way*: a lifestyle trying for consistency between belief and action. It is modelled on the inspirational figure and teaching of Jesus who called himself the Christian's Way. It is a way of life based not just on imitation and admiration. It is a *participation* in his life, a mingling of the streams of his life and yours day by day.

⊷⊶⊷

Among the world's religions it is Christianity that is responsible for communicating the gospel of Jesus. Christians are particularly charged with affirming how he is with us until the end of time. No small responsibility for sinful human beings, however divinely guided, who bicker and squabble endlessly.

A rabbi once taught that it is impossible to pray when you are in a state of anger. So, how can religious institutions disturbed by anger transmit peace unless they are continually praying at levels deeper than even the best thoughts and noblest words? They cannot claim to *speak for Jesus*. They can speak in his name, but only to the degree that their own egoism is transcended. Otherwise it will be their own name masquerading as his. This is the responsibility of speaking from the experience of union with him. When this is authentic it will be self-evident that it is he who is speaking through his Spirit.

Society has the right to expect of Christianity this kind of authority—characterised by tolerance, compassion, humility and courage. It derives not from politics but prayer. It is the fruit of the self-forgetfulness and humility of prayer rather than self-assertion and competition. Defending theological integrity and interpreting tradition are necessary labours. There is no end to the writing of books and no sooner has a breakthrough been made than it is questioned and needs to be redefined. But this labour of the mind needs to be continuously anchored in the prayer of the heart.

Christianity is one of the mysterious religious institutions of the human family that, for all its failings, has the role of a teacher of wisdom. Across centuries and cultures it bears a message that seeks fresh means of expression in every generation. Those who love their church do so because they see in this humanly impossible task an extraordinary potential for serving and uniting humanity. One loves the church then even for its failures, when these are humbly confessed. In the end, we cannot be united to Jesus and at the same time belong to a church that lovelessly excludes or condemns anyone. This is what makes the church essentially catholic and ultimately more than a sociological phenomenon. In all its forms it is one and universal. Yet, however important the church's forms may be, Jesus cannot finally be equated with Christianity. That is the Christian's puzzling yet liberating realisation. It is the disturbing freedom of the Christian spirit. Its self-transcendence. Its sharing in the transcendence of Jesus as the Logos that is found everywhere. The church is, in the end, *not* the Kingdom. That is the church's humility.

Yet to listen to the question which Jesus poses to humanity, and which he *is* to humanity, inevitably brings us into relationship with the religion which, bearing his name, represents him across history and culture. The tension between Jesus and the churches is a paradox that reveals the true nature of both. Ideas or sectarianism do not bring us to this truth. The opening of the eye of the heart does. It is in the conversion experience that the union of Jesus with the individual and with his Body the church becomes clear and fully conscious.

∽ 8 ∽

Conversion

*B*etween *my cottage and my cousin's house, down the hill and across the fields,
I would pass another whitewashed home set back a good way from the path.
The worn track up to the front door was lined by strips of white cloth tied to
stones and fluttering like prayer-flags in the constant wind. Old Joseph lived
there alone. Since his wife died years before, he had followed the set routines of
old age, childless and alone but defending his independence and dignity against
his increasing blindness and other infirmities. The white cloths guided him to
and from his front door. He smoked and drank in moderate enjoyment and his
diet consisted mainly of fish and white bread. (Only overseas visitors and town
dwellers prefer soda bread to shop bread in Ireland.) Chris, my cousin's wife,
cared for Joseph as if he were a member of her family. His needs were calculated
into her shopping and cleaning routines. She fought a losing battle against the
grime and untidiness of his solitude. Once when he had to go to hospital for a
few days for eye treatment she and another woman moved in to his cottage and
swept through it cleaning, polishing, putting up new curtains, tidying the litter
away. When he returned and peered into his ravaged home he pointedly said not
a word of thanks, said nothing. Day by day thereafter when Chris took him up
his daily cooked meal she found one improvement after another reversed. Within
a week everything was back to normal and he, of course, could feel his way
around as well as before.*

*Age and infirmity and character made Joseph an outsider on the island. But
the island community, like the shop and pub that Chris drove him to for a weekly
treat, could not be imagined complete without him. His outsidership helped to
define the community. It also added to the island his own dignity that the island
appreciated and felt privileged to share in. He asked nothing, was humble enough
to receive favours; and his views, which he aired loudly in the pub after a pint
could be eccentrically amusing but were listened to with respect. He was not
antisocial but self-confidently unique. He indisputably belonged but his life was
his own. He had a solitude often seen in those close to death, but he was courteous
and friendly. He taught us all a lot about what it meant to belong and yet to
remain one's self. He had time for people and his community. He had time to
be himself.*

Getting this balance right is a long ordinary process with occasional dramatic interventions. It could be called *conversion*.

At some stage in listening to the question of Jesus—and as a direct result of the listening—a change is wrought in the listener. A turning of attention, a shift in consciousness, occurs which triggers a chain of events which taken together can be called conversion. In his lecture on conversion in *The Varieties of Religious Experience* William James subjected this form of personal transformation to rational analysis. He accepted conversion as an undeniable phenomenon in many lives, even in the lives of scientists.

> To be converted, to be regenerated, to receive grace, to experience religion, to gain an assurance, are so many phrases which denote the process, gradual or sudden, by which a self hitherto divided, and consciously wrong, inferior and unhappy, becomes unified and consciously right, superior and happy in consequence of its firmer hold upon religious realities. This at least is what conversion signifies in general terms, whether or not we believe that a direct divine operation is needed to bring such a moral change about.[1]

James begins his study of conversion with the case of young Stephen Bradley. At the age of fourteen he had a vision of Jesus 'in human shape, for about one second in the room, with arms extended, appearing to say to me, "Come." This set free a great wave of happiness within him, he reported, and a strong sense that he *was* converted. Nine years later he attended a Methodist revival. He felt nothing while there but when he got into bed that night he underwent an 'experience of the power of the Holy Spirit'. His heart rapidly increased its beating 'which soon convinced me it was the Holy Spirit from the effect it had on me'—an effect of unbearable happiness. His heart became 'unutterably full of the love and grace of God.' He must have been groaning because his brother came in from the next room to ask if he had a toothache. Eventually Stephen fell asleep and on waking the next morning he found he was able to resummon the bliss of the night before. He felt as if he were walking on air, far above even the

[1] William James, *The Varieties of Religious Experience* (New York: Triumph Books, 1991), p. 188.

fear of death. He spoke as one charged with the spirit of Pentecost and, after he had had breakfast, he felt it was his duty to speak with his neighbours about religion.

There are many interesting elements in this conversion story: the two-stage conversion over a nine year period, the sincerity and innocence of Stephen Bradley's tone, his lack of fundamentalist arrogance and the fullness of the experience as a body-mind event. But the reader wants to question, criticise and assess the story. A modern reader with knowledge of Eastern religion might ask, for example, was it an experience of *kundalini*? Could Bradley's experience be explained as the rising of this primal energy of the human person from the lower energy centres of the body, through the heart centre and finally to the crown of the head, the highest of the *chakras* or energy centres? Did he identify this experience with the Holy Spirit simply because he had read the story of Pentecost, because he was already, at least culturally, a Christian? Was his initial vision of Jesus in his room hysteria, 'merely psychological'? What happened to him later in life? Did it all wear off? How would a Muslim or a Buddhist understand and describe what Stephen Bradley went through?

The question of Jesus calls everyone who listens to it towards some kind of conversion, if not as suddenly or intensely as for Stephen Bradley. Conversion may unfold gradually and in a unique way for each person on many levels, intellectual, emotional and religious. One's relationship with oneself, with others and the wider world is altered. Solitude, the capacity to be at ease with oneself, replaces loneliness, the anxiety of not connecting with others. The sense and understanding of God is also changed. Personality and social conditioning are factors in conversion but they do not *explain* it away. We cannot just dismiss Stephen Bradley as an hysteric, any more than we can ridicule C. S. Lewis, the agnostic Oxford professor of literature whose mind slipped into faith in God on the top floor of a bus.

We make sense of experience through narrative. That is why we try to fit everything that happens into the story of our life. In fact we very much see ourselves today as unfolding stories and we love to tell the story to whoever will listen. Modern identity depends heavily upon this narrative sense of self and the urge to communicate it. But it is an instinct with deep roots in history. The experience of conversion has, in the narrating and embellishing of the story, helped shape the Christian tradition as well as our modern sense of selfhood.

We will look now at two stories of conversion, separated by two millennia, a man and a woman, both Jewish like Jesus and both transformed by the question of who Jesus was for them.

⋅❀⋅❀⋅❀⋅

Saul of Tarsus began his relationship with Jesus by persecuting those disciples of the failed messiah who first called themselves not Christians but *followers of the way*. But on the road to Damascus a light flashed from the sky and, falling to the ground, Saul heard a voice asking him 'Saul, Saul, why are you persecuting me?' Jesus, a luminous voice in Saul's consciousness, is again posing a question. It creates the first strands of the web of relationship: a 'you' and a 'me'. As in his encounter with Mary Magdalene in the garden, Jesus calls the person he is questioning by name. Saul is enticed to ask his redemptive question: 'Tell me, Lord, who you are,' Saul replied. 'I am Jesus,' the voice answered, 'whom you are persecuting.'

It is a profoundly meaningful story at many levels. By naming himself and by identifying himself with his followers the risen Jesus triggers the mutual recognition which is at the heart of the conversion experience. Those who undergo conversion through experiencing at first relationship, then union with him come to a new level of self-awareness. They feel themselves still themselves but, in addition, an extension of his being. They are now consciously part of the mystical Body of Christ. The convert can now begin to recognise the risen Jesus in the awakening to deeper self-knowledge that results from the experience of being *informed* that he, the new disciple, is recognised. Blinded by the light he had seen (his companions only heard the voice), Saul was led to Damascus and began to pray. He was visited by Ananias, a 'follower of the Way', who laid hands upon him and filled him with the Holy Spirit. Saul's sight returned and he was baptised. His new being was expressed in a change of name. Before long he was proclaiming Jesus publicly in the synagogues. The persecutor had changed sides and become one of the persecuted.[2]

The 'apostle to the Gentiles' had a bizarre preparation for his vocation, as if a zealous SS officer active in rounding up Jews should suddenly have announced he wanted circumcision so that he could become a rabbi. Perhaps Paul's unsuitability however was his recommendation. Christian discipleship attracts outsiders and forms a com-

[2] Acts 9.

munity out of them. Paul, the fanatical conformist in his own religion, could not have been further removed from the family group of Jesus or the close disciples and friends of the Master who formed the nucleus of the early church. We are told, not surprisingly, that it was a long time before they trusted him.

Whatever being a Christian may mean in terms of discipleship and church affiliation, it is always essentially linked to being an outsider, someone who does not quite fit in. The Christian senses that the Kingdom, though within everyone here and now, is still 'not of this world'. It is not that they are social misfits. They conform in many ways. They 'do not live apart in separate cities of their own, speak any special dialect nor practice any eccentric way of life,' according to a first-century writer.

> Nevertheless, the organisation of their community does exhibit some features that are remarkable, and even surprising. For instance, though they are residents at home in their own countries, their behaviour there is more like that of transients; they take their full part as citizens but they also submit to anything and everything as if they were aliens. For them any foreign country is a motherland and any motherland is a foreign country.[3]

The early Christian converts were often enthusiastically prepared for persecution by civil and religious authorities and even for martyrdom. But persecution is only one expression of the distance which the Christian feels to exist between himself and the world. In societies that tolerate religion or are merely indifferent the Christian outsider's sense of detachment will look and feel different. Christian identity in Western society, for example, is lightly tolerated as a private leisure activity provided it does not interfere with one's life or that of society. Restricted to Sunday sermons or christenings and funerals it is not newsworthy. Trivialisation, dumbing-down and misrepresentation are a liberal society's form of persecution. Being thrown to the lions has dramatic appeal, being dismissed as laughable may hurt one's feelings more. Either way outsiders suffer. In any society the conversion experience, the awakening of self-knowledge, reveals a tragic dimension in the way the 'Kingdom' and the 'world' fail to fit each other. Spiritual and materialistic values part ways at certain crucial points in life and thought. The cause of this can perhaps be found in inner space: in the

[3] Letter to Diognetus, N 5-6.

distance between the ego and the true Self. Yet it is through the courage to embrace the path that conversion opens up that joy becomes an integral and undefeatable part of one's life. There is paradox and irony in this as in all aspects of Christian identity. It is reflected in the irony of *belonging* to a group of outsiders.

◌◦◌◦◌

Paul's conversion continued until he paid the supreme price of his faith, martyrdom in Rome. He left behind one of the greatest marks on history made by any individual through his intense, visionary *imagining* of the church. He saw how the networks of small house-churches that he tirelessly nurtured were forming the mystical Body of Christ. For him they were not a mere local cult but had a cosmic meaning far beyond petty rivalries, marginal status and small numbers. Paul saw this community growing in the Spirit. He knew that it would survive its own internal contradictions and shortcomings by the same grace.

Despite his commanding vision of community, however, Paul never lost the abrasive individuality of the outsider. His conflicts with the more conservative disciples are recorded in the Acts of the Apostles. He was not an easy team player. His personality was never perfected by conversion. He even admitted he was difficult. He acted on his own authority distinct from an embryonic Christian curia that had begun in Jerusalem: the 'pillars of our society, James, Cephas and John' as Paul calls them.[4] 'I am a free man and own no master', he proclaimed but he used his freedom to serve all.[5] He claimed that he received his revelation and mission directly from Jesus and not through any third party. This kind of claim to direct personal experience has always worried institutional church leadership. But in Paul's eyes it gave him an authority equal to that of one of the original Twelve who had accompanied Jesus on his teaching journeys thirty years earlier.[6] God freely chose to reveal his Son 'to me and through me'. That is Paul's unshakeable first-hand confidence in the authority of his conversion experience.

In one of his letters to the Christian community in Corinth, Paul reveals a glimpse of the mystical element of his faith, although Jesus

[4] Gal 2:9.
[5] I Cor 9:19.
[6] Gal I:II.

is not specifically mentioned in this context.[7] Speaking of himself in the third person he describes how he

> was caught up into paradise and heard words so secret that human lips may not repeat them.[8]

In the volatile world of Paul's psyche there seems to have been a movement across inner space between an intimate love affair with Jesus on one hand and on the other, though not separate, an experience of the intoxicating freedom of pure spirit. The risen Jesus for St Paul is the centre of his personal life. His own personality has been transformed by union with that of Jesus. Yet belief in the extraordinary truth of Jesus does not turn him into an idol. The radical other-centredness of the Jesus of the gospels, the teacher who points beyond himself, finds expression in the Pauline mystical Christ dwelling *within* the human person. For Paul Jesus is not just another new god for the shrine corner. He does not even require a new temple because it is his followers who, as St Peter said, are themselves the Temple of the new era, a temple of 'living stones'.[9]

The Pauline Jesus refreshes the spirituality of Jewish faith which is grounded in the sense of the pure, interpersonal mystery of God. Out of this mystical perception flows the extraordinary, dizzying liberty which Paul communicates. The law and the legalism of all institutional religion are transcended in one bound through the person of Jesus the Christ. The freedom released in this transcendence transforms every aspect of personal, social and religious life. Religion need never again be the 'collective neurosis' that Freud later denounced. There is no need to be trapped in the guilt complexes of religion or to suffer crippling anxiety about the problems of life. We are not freed from pain. But suffering takes on different meanings once we are unhooked from guilt and anxiety and we know a union with one ready to accompany us in our suffering. To suffer with freedom is to find peace. Christianity, as Simone Weil claimed, uniquely finds a use for suffering. The dissolving of karma in the Resurrection gains freedom from sin and death. Human consciousness is boosted out of a self-centred orbit and the addictive need for its self-created prisons. In Paul's vision the freedom won in this breakthrough in the human condition has more

[7] 2 Cor 12.
[8] 2 Cor 12:4.
[9] 1 Pet 2:5.

than an individual meaning. It enjoys a cosmic boundlessness. But it takes the process of conversion—a formula that includes time and faith—for the individual to realise what this entirely means.

It has happened, this great breakthrough, but it is still unfolding. It is an upward evolution to greater consciousness, a 'new creation' as Paul calls it. The new freedom is not a licence to indulge every whim and fancy. That has often been tried and found to fail. It is a mature freedom, a responsible liberty, empowering us to respond to deeper levels of reality. St Augustine's insight into the same liberty of Christ which intoxicated St Paul led him to formulate one of the pithiest statements of theology, as strong in its existential freedom as in its moral demand: 'love and do what you like.'

> We know that no one is ever justified by doing what the law demands, but only through faith in Christ Jesus; so we too have put our faith in Jesus Christ, in order that we might be justified through this faith, and not through deeds dictated by the law . . . the life I now live is not my life, but the life which Christ lives in me; and my bodily life is lived by faith in the son of God, who loved me and gave himself up for me. I will not nullify the grace of God; if righteousness comes by law, then Christ died for nothing.[10]

❧❧❧

Paul's letters convey an intensely focused, some would say fanatical, personality. It is not an easy or attractive one: passionate, volatile, angry, even crude. At times the religious extremism of the former persecutor shows through in the way he lambastes and denounces his opponents. Yet for all his faults he conveys a fundamental goodness of purpose and a genuinely transcendent vision of love and compassion. Meaning and purpose in him derived from the continuous surrender of himself, body and soul, to Jesus and the work that he saw Jesus still performing in the world through the Spirit. There is more love than ideology in Paul, more about personal conversion than dogmatic or moral theology. His theology was a passionate attempt to communicate and articulate his deepest experience. This experience of the love of Jesus was a consuming passion and, just as all creativity is driven by passion, so was his religious originality:

[10] Gal 2:15ff.

> For as I passionately hope, I shall have no cause to be ashamed,
> but shall speak out boldly that now as always the greatness
> of Christ will shine out clearly in my person, whether through
> my life or through my death. For to me life is Christ, and death
> gain ... This indeed I know for certain: I shall stay and stand by
> you all to help you forward and to add joy to your faith, so that
> when I am with you again, your pride in me may be unbounded
> in Christ Jesus.[11]

Paul's 'thorn in the flesh' remains part of his personal mystery. Was it
a physical or even a moral impediment? It is the human imperfections
of such heroes of faith, like Martin Luther King's sexual weakness or
Mahatma Ghandi's long struggle with himself, that can make them all
the more persuasive and trustworthy. From them we learn that conversion is not about perfection. It is about the discovery of one's essential human goodness and the confidence that, despite weaknesses
and faults, we are acceptable, even lovable to God. And so why not to
ourselves? It is the beginning of the healing of self-hatred. Through
self-acceptance, conversion must eventually complete the whole person, intellectually, morally, religiously, emotionally. It is a process of
change, sometimes dramatic and instantaneous, sometimes gradual
and mundane.

> And so, to keep me from being unduly elated by the magnificence
> of such revelations, I was given a thorn for the flesh ... Three
> times I begged the Lord to rid me of it, but his answer was: 'My
> grace is all you need; power comes to its full strength in weak-
> ness.'[12]

A new influx, or a raising, of consciousness triggers the transformation
of self-awareness in the conversion process. The inrush of experiential,
nonconceptual knowledge, called *gnosis* by the New Testament and recognised subjectively as love, brings an authority rooted in the humility
that is self-knowledge. Different levels of knowledge then need to be
realigned. Values and priorities get reexamined. Life has to regroup
around a new centre and for most people this is a life-long process.

Conversion raises a necessary distinction between levels and types
of knowledge which interfaith dialogue can help clarify. The Christian

[11] Phil 1:20ff.
[12] 2 Cor 12:7ff.

idea of conversion and holiness and the Eastern idea of *moksha*, of enlightenment or liberation are distinct and perhaps happen in different dimensions of consciousness, perhaps simultaneously. This does not mean that Christians do not become enlightened or that Buddhists or Hindus may not be holy. For the Christian, however, conversion and the enlightenment intertwine as unfolding operations of consciousness by listening to the question of Jesus. Then, by recognising him, as we realise that we are recognised by him. Paul does not strike one as having reached a steady or permanent state of enlightenment but the force of holiness is with him and there are strong flashes of the wisdom and compassion of enlightenment. Anyway, he was certainly converted. The ongoing conversion depicted in his letters illustrates in a surprisingly intimate way this twin process of spiritual growth: the transforming grace of spiritual insight and the dogged discipline needed to live it day by day.

The Pauline letters show how the goal and the path, alpha and omega, interweave in ordinary life. They illustrate how mystical insights into reality grow in the ground of the domestic round. They show too how the ego can at any time make one forget the insight gained and regress into behaviour that is driven by the blinding passion of desire rather than the enlightening passion of love. Paul's letters are indisputably essential to the canon of Christian scriptures. Yet they make curious reading alongside the Upanishads or the *Dhammapada*. They are so unabashedly, fallibly human, almost a kind of mystical soap opera, the reality of life with other people and in the cloister of the heart. The Hebrew passion for God never took great metaphysical flight rather than the official version of how things should be. St Paul remained very Jewish. Yet his contribution to Christian scripture, as part of the 'new' testament, creates a new kind of scripture that democratises the higher reaches of the spiritual journey. Perhaps the signification of the domestic that is a characteristic of modernity begins here in early Christianity. His letters illustrate a religion of incarnation and the material and psychological world that is incarnated is not conceptually neat. They see God in the constant, daily interactions between the higher and the lower self, between new knowledge and old instinct, spirit and flesh.

<O*O*O>

Union with Christ, according to St Paul, initiates a new creation, a new *way* of seeing, knowing, living and feeling. We do not see anything different or anything that was not always there in front of us. But we see *more* of what is *really* there and progressively less of what is illusory. We see God more clearly. In the Christian conversion experience Jesus pervades the physical and psychological texture of all life. Life is thereby opened to what Jesus himself is now experiencing 'in the realms of light'.

> Adapt yourselves no longer to the pattern of this present world but let your minds be remade and your whole nature thus transformed. Then you will be able to discern the will of God and to know what is good, acceptable and perfect.[13]

> I pray that the God of our Lord Jesus Christ, the all-glorious Father, may give you the spiritual-powers of wisdom and vision, by which there comes the knowledge of him. I pray that your inward eyes may be illumined, so that you may know what is the hope to which he calls you, what the wealth and glory of the share he offers you among his people in their heritage, and how vast the resources of his power open to us who trust in him.[14]

St Paul shows how Christian identity is born in vision. 'Am I not an apostle? Did I not see Jesus our Lord?' he asks.[15] But this vision is not an *apparition*. It is more even than insight. An 'appearance' was what convinced Paul that nothing in any realm, human or heavenly, could separate him from this experience. It had led him to know the love of God flooding—not merely filling—his inmost being through the mind of Christ. He knew, more strongly than any language could express, that the consciousness of Christ was a living presence in his own existence and inseparable from his own self-identity. The mind of Christ refers not to a disembodied presence, a concept or archetypal symbol at work in the unconscious. It is the resurrected humanity of Jesus expanded beyond the limits that he lived within during his thirty-three years of historical existence.

So, Paul discovered, we now know Christ no longer 'after the manner of the flesh'. Perhaps this is why he shows little interest in the historical Jesus. Not that we do not still know Jesus in a *bodily* way; it is a different kind of bodiliness. His body now is coextensive with the material, mental and spiritual realms of reality. Wherever the body

[13] Rom 12:2.
[14] Eph 1:17-18.
[15] 1 Cor 9:1.

or mind of man can reach, therefore, it will encounter the risen body
of Jesus. The 'mind of Christ' to which Paul refers is not a merely
cerebral reality but the whole, incandescent humanity of Jesus. It is
'in us' and therefore opens us to all worlds. Eventually our own physical body will undergo the same transformation which Jesus underwent and receive a 'form like that of his own resplendent body'.[16] This
is the 'hidden wisdom' of the gospel Paul proclaimed so openly.

> God has made known to us his secret purpose, in accordance
> with the plan which he determined beforehand in Christ, to be
> put into effect when the time was ripe: namely that the universe,
> everything in heaven and on earth might be brought into a unity
> in Christ.[17]

To appreciate Paul's passionate love for the Jesus who had both mastered and liberated his life it helps to remember how much Paul himself was an outsider, an exile in his own culture. Jewish followers of
Jesus had been expelled from the synagogues and were regarded as
dangerous, absurd fanatics by the Romans. Few had any social status.
Today we must read his exalted language with an historical imagination remembering that 'church' for Paul did not evoke an image of St
Patrick's in New York or St Paul's in London. Church meant community,
belonging to a spiritual and social 'village' network. *The church* was not
a centralised multinational corporation. It was still a persecuted,
mainly low-caste minority, a fragile web of house-communities full of
bickering and backsliding yet somehow enjoying the peace of Christ.
To become a Christian, however, did not yet mean giving up the identity of a Jew, a Greek or Roman. There could be conflict between these
distinct forms of identity. But it could be lived with. Then as now the
'Christian' was first and foremost a disciple of Jesus, a member of his
body the church, a citizen of the universe, a child of God.

To be 'in Christ' who is 'in us' means to be an outsider to everything that is less than the universality of his wholeness. Conversion
thus redefines all relationships but rejects none that are life-giving and
truly compatible with the whole. Clement of Alexandria and the other
early 'Christian humanists' insisted that nothing that is not contrary
to nature could be contrary to Christ. Despite its *outsiderliness* Christianity can never be reduced to an esoteric cult because, while keenly

[16] Phil 3:21-4:1.
[17] Eph 1:9-10.

aware of the distance between the Kingdom and this world, the Christian does not separate himself from the world. Being outsiders does not mean they feel love turn cold. Their role is not to judge or condemn the world. They understand that in a world of intrinsic impermanence, constantly passing away before our eyes, all are in fact outsiders. However much we may deny it, no one under the passing moon lives in an 'abiding city'. Conversion helps us to see ourselves as we are. It therefore enhances rather than removes freedom. We can then choose freely who we *will* be: desperate wanderers across the face of the earth or pilgrims of hope in the spiritual realms.

·◌··◌··◌·

No one has understood her Christian identity as outsider in a more extreme way than Simone Weil. And no one more sharply saw the dangers of institutionalism within the religion of Christianity. Her conversion is peculiarly modern because institutionally it never happened. She *saw* Jesus but refused baptism. She has been called, as a consequence, the most post-modern of saints, the patron saint of outsiders. Like her great contemporary Dietrich Bonhoeffer she struggled with Christianity as a social structure which (they both felt) had tragically fallen short of its mission and potential. Both died as victims of the war, one hanged by the Nazis, the other almost by her own hand because, in solidarity with her countrymen, she refused to eat more than the rations allowed them in occupied France. Like their master, both died before the age of forty.

We know of Simone Weil's spiritual life, as we know of St Paul's, largely through letters, the letters she wrote to her priest friend and director, Fr. Perrin. She was born in Paris in 1909 into a middle-class Jewish family. Her exceptional intelligence was recognised early. Her writings, mostly published after her death, in England in 1943, have since established her as one of the major philosophical minds of the century. She was driven by a fierce and highly idiosyncratic passion for truth and a thirst for integrity which can make her seem at times both sublime and almost absurd.

She claimed that she had never 'sought for God' but that from the beginning she had 'always adopted the Christian attitude', growing up and remaining within a Christian inspiration for her practical decisions both about life and thought. In a not untypical Jewish way she could be anti-Jewish. She thought less about an after-life than about the life of truth. But from childhood she 'believed that the instant of death is the centre and object of life'. At fourteen she fell into a dark night of the soul, 'a bottomless despair' because she felt that her gifts were no more than mediocre compared with those of her brilliant and more acclaimed brother. She suffered agony at the thought that her mediocrity might exclude her from the 'kingdom of truth'. She eventually crawled out of this wretchedness by the insight that anyone, however ordinary, can enter that kingdom simply by longing for truth and by steadily concentrating all his or her attention upon it. Any truly attentive and dedicated person 'thus becomes a genius too, even though for lack of talent his genius cannot be visible from outside'.

⋅◌⋅◌⋅◌⋅

Soon after this dark period of her life she fell in love with St Francis of Assisi. She felt that like him she was fated to be a vagabond. In her holiness there burned a pure and sometimes harshly self-rejecting egotism that led her to declare herself someone with whom it was unwise for anyone to link their destiny.

She identified herself with outsiders: the poor, the marginalised and rejected were at the compassionate core of her faith and her thought. Her sense of belonging to those who belonged nowhere was intensified by the times she spent working alongside workers in a car factory, with fishermen in a Portuguese coastal village and with itinerant grape-pickers in French vineyards. In 1937 she spent two days at Assisi where, she said, she first fell to her knees in prayer. This was followed by ten days over Eastertide at the French Benedictine monastery of Solesmes. Here, while suffering from agonising headaches, she was led by the beauty of the chant and liturgy to understand how God can be loved in the midst of affliction. Here too she met a young English Catholic who introduced her to the poem *Love* by George Herbert which she learned by heart and recited often as a mantra.

> I used to think I was merely reciting it as a beautiful poem, but without my knowing it the recitation had the virtue of a prayer. It was during one of these recitations that, as I told you, Christ himself came down and took possession of me.[18]

A similar experience in prayer occurred while she was working in the vineyard. She had developed the habit of reciting the Our Father in Greek as she picked the grapes.

[18] Simone Weil, *Waiting on God*, p. 35.

The effect of this practice is extraordinary and surprises me every time for, although I experience it each day, it exceeds my expectation at every recitation. At times the very first words tear my thoughts from my body and transport it to a place outside space where there is neither perspective nor point of view. The infinity of the ordinary expanses of perception is replaced by an infinity to the second or sometimes the third degree. At the same time, filling every part of this infinity, there is silence, a silence which is not an absence of sound but which is the object of a positive sensation, more positive than that of sound. Noises, if there are any, only reach me after crossing this silence.... Sometimes, also, during this recitation or at other moments, Christ is present with me in person, but his presence is infinitely more real, more moving, more clear than on that first occasion when he took possession of me.[19]

Despite her experience of the Risen Jesus, Simone Weil resolutely refused baptism. She said she was more willing to die for the church than to enter it as long as it rejected outsiders and repressed its own members. She was also convinced that baptism was not God's will for her because to be baptised would entail separation from the whole multitude of nonbelievers. Her decision to remain a Christian outside the church expresses the peculiar intensity of her faith in Christ and her willingness to embrace suffering. She exemplifies how deeply, at times agonisingly, solitary is each one's responsibility for dealing with the separation between self and other. For Simone Weil, this separation was a terrifying distance. But a false union would have been a worse affliction for her. She knew how easily an inauthentic decision could activate her own capacity for evil: how easily, for example, she could be caught up in the imperialism of Christianity or even the demonic emotions of Nazism. Her vocation, she concluded, was to be forever alone and anonymous. Only so could she be 'mixed into the paste of common humanity'. The only way to be *in Christ* and *with others*, for her, was to remain faithfully a perpetual outsider.

I feel that it is necessary and ordained that I should be alone, a stranger and an exile in relation to every human circle without exception.[20]

[19] Ibid., p. 38.
[20] Ibid., p. 23.

Her agonising refusal to enter the Church is simultaneously one of the greatest criticisms and the strongest affirmations of Christianity in modern times.

⊸⊙⊸⊙⊸⊙⊸

She loved God, she said, and the Catholic faith, the saints, six or seven Catholics of genuine spirituality whom she knew, Catholic liturgy, hymns, architecture, and all its rites and ceremonies.

Perhaps only an intelligence so French in its idealism, and a cultural Jewishness so ambivalent about its origins could live with such contradiction. Her reasoning, however, was clear, filled with self-knowledge and innocent of self-deception. She declared she had not the slightest love for the church in the strict sense of the word 'apart from its relations to all these things'.

What frightened her most was the church as a social structure. This meant the institution that could deny the sacraments to sinners and the spiritually needy, persecute heretics and refuse to confess its own sins of past and present. The church's attempt to force 'love and intelligence to model their language upon her own' was for her an abuse of power that defied the divine. It derived from the 'very fact that it *is* something social'. She feared church nationalism (us and them and we are better) because she feared to catch it herself like a virus. The devil, she said, always manufactures a false imitation of the divine, an ersatz divinity. The church must be a social structure; she did not deny that obvious truth. But 'insofar as it is, it belongs to the Prince of this world'.

Through her difficult and idiosyncratic personality, Simone Weil focuses many of the themes we have been exploring about Christian identity. What makes her relation to Jesus so modern? Perhaps both that it originates in the solitude of mystical experience and that it felt so estranged from the institutional church. We need not conclude from this that spiritual experience automatically alienates people from the church. There are innumerable examples of Christian women and men of equal integrity as Simone Weil for whom this is palpably not the case and who love the church, institutional warts and all. But for Simone Weil in relation to the church of the war period experience and institution were incompatible.

Her experience of Jesus 'possessing' her combined with her intellectual clarity and emotional certainty helped to shape her own unique kind of discipleship. Yet her outsidership is not merely rebellious or disobedient. Simone Weil is not alienated from the Christian community, but from a particular form of the church. She does not base her faith on her mystical experiences alone, any more than the New Testament says that we must have physically *seen* the risen Jesus in order to be Christian. 'Happy are those who never saw me,' Jesus said, 'and yet have found faith.'[21] She does not describe her experience in detail. Yet in whatever the way the Resurrection *happened* to her, for Simone Weil it possessed an integrity as self-authenticating as for Mary of Magdala or St Paul. Whatever the nature of her encounter with the Risen Jesus her faith partook of the essential nature of all Christian experience which tastes *now* but also awaits fulfilment. Her penetration of this paradox purified her faith of all sentimentality and wish-fulfilment.

> You have not seen him, yet you love him; and trusting in him now without seeing him, you are transported with a joy too great for words, while you reap the harvest of your faith, that is, salvation for your souls.[22]

To refuse to belong to the church, Simone Weil argued, does not mean to disown Christ. For some people at least, she argued, to be Christian means precisely *not* to join the institution. It can mean that, as an outsider, you carry out his precepts, shed abroad his spirit, honour his name when occasion arises and even be ready to die out of loyalty to him. The solitary authority of her Christianity carries the fragrance of her own intensely unique response to Jesus' question.

Deep prayer or, as she calls it, 'attention' underlies her kind of Christian discipleship just as Bonhoeffer's 'secret inner discipline', that he said needed to be restored to the Christian life, underlies his prophetic vision of Christianity in a post-religious culture. Attention is focussed through the lens both of solitude and relationship: an unqualified uniqueness redeemed from estrangement from God by an awareness of belonging and participation. Attention purifies and is redemptive. Both kinds of awareness derive from the contemplative practice of 'attention'. Her faith led her to stand apart from the Christian structures of her day but she does not insist that everyone should imitate her. True outsiders are not so eager to tell others what to do. Accepting of how different *they* are, they do not try to get others to

[21] Jn 20:29.
[22] 1 Pet 1:8.

be like them. More conventional Christians however cannot sidestep her prophetic witness merely by pointing to her eccentricity. The very oddity of her outsidership sheds light on the essential outsidership of all Christian identity. Like any saint her uniqueness shows that Christian identity incorporates the solitude of each individual created and loved by God.

Simone Weil was entranced by the image of the Mystical Body of Christ. But she also believed that the way this image was understood by the church of her day illustrated the degeneration of Christianity as a social structure. By loving its own structures and hierarchies more than Christ, the Church misses the organic mystery of itself as a spiritual body. Misunderstood in this way *Body* becomes *machine*. True human dignity does not consist in being part of a machine, she said, but in being an integral organ of the Body. For Simone Weil human value consists above all in the universal vocation to holiness and the church is meant to be the sign, the sacrament of equality and fraternity helping all to respond to this call. Such a vocation means that we live no longer just in or for ourselves but that Christ lives in us. Through our becoming holy in the wholeness of Christ, in his oneness, he truly becomes each one of us.[23]

Few modern writers have described with more passion and clarity than Simone Weil the recognition of the Risen Jesus. Her conversion helps the Christians of the third millennium to understand better the essential Christian meaning of holiness. Holiness, as she sees it, is reached only by a total, sacrificial truthfulness to oneself in cooperation with grace. As the completion of relationship with ourselves, with others and with God, holiness is the secret contained in the redemptive question Jesus poses to humanity. Helping people to reach holiness is therefore the meaning and purpose of the church: a meaning that can only be realised by finding the optimum distance between one's self and the church as a social structure.

Simone Weil's life and thought also highlight the centrality of contemplative consciousness for modern Christian identity. Having long been relegated to the periphery of the Christian vocation and limited to specialists in monastic or eremitical life, today the contemplative dimension of Christian discipleship is being undertaken and practised daily by people in every walk of life. Karl Rahner's belief that the Christian of the future would be a mystic or nonexistent

---

[23] Simone Weil, *Waiting on God*, p. 46.

echoes the example of all the great Christian prophets of the twenti-
eth century.[24]

From St Paul's searing insight that everyone without regard to
religious or racial origin is called to recognise and share in the life of
the risen Jesus, to Bonhoeffer's sense of the era of a more silent and
'religionless' Christianity rooted in prayer and action; from Merton's
discovery that monastic contemplation and the world of action are not
mutually exclusive but interdependent; to Bede Griffith's practice of a
Christianity faithful to its traditions but freed from intolerance towards other religions and able to engage in their wisdom; to John
Main's recovery of a Christian contemplative tradition that can be practised by people in daily life: all these modern teachers and witnesses
to Christian identity sound a major theme. It is that the roots of
conversion lie in contemplation and the ordinary Christian of the future will be contemplative. New purified forms of the church are born
out of this contemplative conversion of heart.

◦◦◦◦◦◦

An early Christian monk whose conversion led him to abandon everything to seek God in the solitude of the desert was once asked what
a monk was. He replied that a monk was someone who asked every
day what it meant to be a monk. The Christian disciple in his or her
community of solitude is also continually asking what it means to be
a Christian.

A Zen master was once examining his student. Pointing to the
book of Buddhist scriptures beside them he asked the student how
much of their content was the Buddha's and how much came from
the demons. The student immediately replied 'they are all the demons.'
'Excellent,' said the teacher, 'now no one will be able to pull the wool
over your eyes.' This is helpful hyperbole of the kind that Jesus employed. Relationship with Jesus is opened and developed by his asking
a question that like the Zen master's shocks us towards self-knowledge
and self-transcendence of a disciple's daily living. Jesus asks the question. But he also *is* the question which each of his followers
encounters. And, in the cosmic extension of his identity, he embodies
the redemptive question to all humanity. He asks not for a dogmati-
cally orthodox response but for the *conversion* of wholehearted atten-

[24] Karl Rahner, *Christian of the Future*, trans. W. J. O'Hara (London: Burnes & Oates,
New York: Herder & Herder, 1967).

tion. A question has power to open the mind only when it is listened to. Simone Weil reminds us how urgently we must learn again to pay attention.

We are disciples of what we pay attention to. As William James said, what we pay attention to *is* what we believe. Ramana Maharshi's description of the guru-disciple bond helps us to understand more clearly the nature of attention. When Ramana's disciples were taking their leave of him they would often complain that they needed his presence to maintain their spiritual motivation. They would say that once they left his presence, their fervour and insight began to decline. Within a few days they were once again embroiled in the mire of worldliness and egotism. His influence seemed to wear off. Ramana would always challenge this defeatism. He reminded them that the guru was within them. Yes, they would reply, we know that, but we need the visible presence of the outer guru. It is the outer guru, he would respond, who is telling you to find the guru within.

In Christian terms, he was speaking of the Holy Spirit whom Jesus promised to send to his disciples and who would 'call to mind everything he had taught them'. The Spirit would be the medium in which he would be present to them 'until the end of time'. Conversion is the result of an encounter with the Spirit.

~ 9 ~
Spirit

Nothing is more palpable than the spirit of place, the atmosphere that strikes you as you walk into a room, discover a new city, step on to a magic island. Bere Island has a strong silent spirit. The hill that runs like a spine down the island protecting the populated land side from the wild Atlantic seems to say something you cannot understand. But its speech is not difficult. It is isness: 'I am here.' It is only saying itself. I have always envied people who live in places whose natural language they understand. They seem to me the wisest of people and often the most silent. They know a language whose entire vocabulary is all around them and whose meaning they will never exhaust. Walking the lanes and fields of Bere Island, I felt I was being taught its language and the only way you can learn a language is to love it. Then the most familiar places never fail to refresh and delight even if, like old friends, they may excite you in calmer ways than before.

One day I found a new path, actually a road built by the British engineers who belonged to the military post on the island. Their road wove around the hillside and over to the wild side. It led to one of the many protruding tips of the island where the dramatic beauty of the coast, the pounding surf and sudden, frightening cliff edges wait to be discovered and understood. Here, too, stood a stocky little white lighthouse. Its usefulness now exhausted by other technology, its light had gone out long ago but its silence and stillness was an eloquent enduring statement. It was a symbol of itself, preaching nothing, demanding nothing. Its value could not be measured economically. If it fell into ruin and one day was blown piece by piece across the ocean so that no trace was visible it would still be there, part of the spirit of the place.

On another visit I made to the island some years later a family gathering took place for a wedding. One of my aunts from Canada had returned for the first time in fifty years to the island where she had been born and reared. Now she was dying, physically stunted by bone cancer, stooped and in pain but still enjoying her vodkas. She was the indisputable matriarchal life of the party—and its soul. I suggested that a group of us walk up to the lighthouse thinking the idea would attract just the younger fitter ones. In fact everyone came and Aunt Peggy would certainly not think of staying back. From my place at the end of *the group I saw the line of O'Sullivans hiking resolutely up the steep incline and Peggy battling her way stubbornly and quietly, without ostentation or self-pity, simply determined to get to the top and see the view. She did. The lighthouse said nothing when we turned the corner and found it waiting, as always, on duty. A faithful friend and advocate. But we heard it. A simple sign of spirit, reminding us of our tragic weakness as well as our incredible grandeur, it would outlast us all.*

·◦❀◦❀◦·

Jesus, knowing his death was fast approaching, told his friends that a new way of knowing him beyond the boundaries of space and time was at hand. This would be revealed by the 'sending of the Spirit'.

> I tell you the truth: it is for your good that I am leaving you. If I do not go, your Advocate will not come, whereas if I go, I will send him to you.[1]

If it is not insane to say that we can personally know someone who died two thousand years ago, it is because the Spirit makes it a reality. Through the Spirit, therefore, Jesus confronts us with the meaning and purpose of death and the paradox of resurrection. He educates us about how presence and absence are twin aspects of all relationship. A Filipino migrant worker who has to spend months or years away from her family experiences the pain of absence but remains present to her distant husband and children for whom she is working. Friends can meet after long absence and forgetfulness and suddenly be reminded that they have always been present to each other. And, conversely, in the closest unions there is the infinite distance of otherness. I am never you and can never make you mine. Presence does not disprove absence; absence does not dispel presence.

Jesus promised to return after death and to remain with his disciples until the end of time. Time ends whenever, by paying full attention, we pass over the wall of the objectifying ego into insight. We step beyond space-time into the present moment. He said he would not leave us orphaned and bereft. 'I will come back to you ... you will see me again.'[2] For many this is the fantasy part of Christian faith, its offer of false consolation. It is easy to accept Jesus as sage, teacher, avatar, or archetype. And these *are* valid ways of relating to him. But

[1] Jn 16:7.
[2] Jn 13:18.

they do not exhaust all that the gospel says about him. His continuing presence within the absence created by his death is the gospel's essential message. His disappearance in death and the absence of his visible form are the conditions of his presence in the Spirit. His absence is a *necessary* aspect of his presence. That is why we cannot focus only on the Resurrection and deny his death; why we should not settle only for the heroism of his death.

It is also why his question is such a bombshell. Listening to it confronts us with the painful reality of mortality and the value of life. The denial of death, our most powerful repression, burdens us with anxiety and drains life of meaning. Any repression or anxiety within the psyche inhibits all our relationships and may prevent any from reaching their fulfilment and this includes relationship with Jesus. This is why Jesus is presented so strongly in the gospels as a liberator, a bringer of peace, a healer—and why time and again he tells people not to fear.

The clarity and freedom of our self-knowledge determines how clearly we can *see* Jesus in the Spirit. If we remain unconscious we stay in a dreamlike state and will not see what can only be known in the wakefulness of the Spirit. The Gospel accounts of the Resurrection appearances—Mary of Magdala, the disciples on the Road to Emmaus, doubting Thomas, the unbelieving or terrified apostles in the upper room—all show how difficult it is, with our chronic inattentiveness and weak self-knowledge, to recognise Jesus in the new form of his presence.

> He said to them, What you look for has come, but you do not know it.[3]

◦◦◦◦◦

As the 'guru within', Jesus is seen in the light of self-knowledge. He is not seen with mortal eyes but with spiritual vision.

Spirit, however, is neither abstract nor merely interior. Teillhard de Chardin calls it 'matter incandescent'. It is nonspatial, nontemporal, polymorphous. It is as much within as outside, as much male as female. To be here and everywhere at the same time is like being nowhere always. This nowhere (the 'elsewhere' of the Kingdom) is a favourite paradox for mystical writers trying to communicate their

[3] *The Gospel of Thomas, The Hidden Sayings of Jesus*, trans. Marvin Meyer (San Francisco: Harper Collins, 1992), no. 51 p.43.

experience of this realm. The fourteenth-century author of *The Cloud of Unknowing* speaks of the nowhereness of God in order to deter his readers from imagining that the spiritual can ever be limited to tangible experience or mental image. It is an experience but unlike sensory or mental experience. Space and time—even our most valued spiritual 'experiences'—are metaphors for spirit, forms of the formless. They are invested with spirit and become significant only when we perceive this. To make matters even more subtle, the contemplative tradition teaches that experience in the spirit can neither be described nor remembered.

In the realm of spirit whatever we perceive sensorily or mentally takes on a symbolic character. It *is* real but it also points to something else. It contains something that cannot be fully known with the senses or understood by the mind. This is why art which operates in the symbolic realm is so close to the spiritual but often has difficulties with religion. Art and prayer both point to a deeper or higher intensity of reality beyond themselves. Whatever the mind can predict, define or understand points beyond these ways of perception into the cloud of unknowing. Reality is, paradoxically, clearer in this cloud where the God whom the rational mind cannot grasp can be known by love. The greatest power of human consciousness is its capacity to transcend (not disown or undermine) its mental operations, to go beyond its greatest thoughts, and so to be spirit.

Now that he has 'become a life-giving spirit', as St Paul declared, Jesus is known 'no longer after the manner of the flesh'. After his Resurrection he still has bodily form but it is no longer bound to the material world though he is present there too as in all dimensions. St Paul speaks straightforwardly about the spiritual body when he refers to the different types of body, earthly and spiritual, in a way which Asian thought readily understands.

> But you may ask, how are the dead raised? In what kind of body? How foolish! The seed you sow does not come to life unless it has first died; and what you sow is not the body that shall be, but a naked grain, perhaps of wheat or some other kind; and God clothes it with the body of his choice, each seed with its own particular body ... There are heavenly bodies and earthly bodies ... So it is with the resurrection of the dead. What is sown in the earth as a perishable thing is raised imperishable. Sown in humiliation, it is raised in glory; sown in weakness, it is raised

in power; sown as an animal body, it is raised as a spiritual body. If there is such a thing as an animal body, there is also a spiritual body.[4]

The early Christians related their experience of Jesus to Jewish prophecy. Jesus was seen to have fulfilled those ancient hopes and insights. Christians today can also be moved to a sense of fulfilment by other traditions.

> As fire, though one, takes new forms in all things that burn, the Spirit, though one takes new forms in all things that live. He is within all, and is also outside.

> And beyond is Purusha, all-pervading, beyond definitions. When a mortal knows him, he attains liberation and reaches immortality.

> His form is not in the field of vision: no one sees him with mortal eyes. He is seen by a pure heart and by a mind and thoughts that are pure. Those who know him attain life immortal.[5]

⋅◦⋅◦⋅◦⋅

Jesus fulfilled his promise to return to us in two essential dimensions of human experience: by the 'interior' sending of the Holy Spirit and by his spiritual Body taking 'exterior' form in the community of his disciples. Wherever two or three meet 'in his name', when the Eucharist is celebrated, in reading the Gospels, in human friendship and works of mercy, he is present. At first his presence may be only glimpsed as potency, something we have simply to hope for, like an unborn child. Gradually this seed of potency called faith grows into knowledge and experience. Jesus is formed and comes to birth in us. Openness to the news of the Resurrection and attentive listening to the whole of his story starts the seed-clock ticking. Faith germinates deep in the ground of our being. The ensuing process has less to do with intellectual understanding or submitting the will to dogma and far more with a transformation of consciousness:

> And what is faith? Faith gives substance to our hopes and makes us certain of realities we do not see.[6]

[4] I Cor 15:35ff.
[5] The Upanishads, Katha Upanishad.
[6] Heb 11:1.

> Again I tell you this: if two of you agree on earth about any
> request you have to make, that request will be granted by my
> heavenly Father. For where two or three have met together in my
> name, I am there among them.[7]

As this transformation process unfolds, relationship with Jesus deepens. Faith deepens commitment to that relationship and faith pushes
consciousness further into spirit. Spatial metaphors—in, up, deep and
so on—are difficult to avoid. *Through* him, *with* him, *in* him, we are lifted
up above ourselves. We feel simultaneously pushed deep down and
lifted on high. Life feels very different with the opening of these apparently contradictory perspectives. The Spirit feels like a game with
space and time. Values and priorities long accepted are reevaluated.
Qualities we thought ourselves incapable of—patience, empathy, compassion, tolerance—develop in our character and behaviour. One day,
almost casually, we see that our image of God has been overhauled.
Antipathies and aversions, such as former Christians can feel towards
the church or fundamentalist Christians towards other religions, yield
to a new spirit of reconciliation and friendship.

The 'downward' movement of the Spirit involves all human relationships with the presence of Jesus. The 'upward' movement illuminates the Cosmic Christ. Living out the response to his question
recharges our relationship to the whole universe:

> We shall see with a wave of joy that the divine omnipresence
> translates itself within our universe by a network of organising
> forces of the total Christ . . . a centre of radiation for the energies
> which lead the universe back to God through the humanity (of
> Jesus).[8]

So his question leads to another door to push open: what on earth do
we mean by *Spirit*?

⟨⟩⋯⟨⟩⋯⟨⟩

Ruah, the Hebrew word for spirit, is one of the key words in the Bible.
On the first page of Genesis the Spirit of God hovers over the waters
of chaos before cosmos, order, appears with time and space. Through-

---

[7] Mt 18:19-20.
[8] Teilhard de Chardin, *Le Milieu Divin: Essaie de vie interieure* (Paris: Editions du Seuil,
    1957). *The Divine Milieu: An Essay on the Interior Life* (New York: Harper, 1960).

out the Bible the Spirit of the Lord 'comes upon' people revealing truth and transforming personalities. It can also 'depart' from people, as it did from King Saul when he sinned. It brings people back to their senses. The Spirit 'fills the whole world', strengthening, testing, correcting, healing, wounding with love, inspiring with wisdom, leading ordinary, sinful, fickle human beings through the labyrinths of their personal, tribal and global histories towards their common destiny.

In the New Testament the role of the Holy Spirit is even more central. The 'sending of the Spirit' after his Resurrection concludes his mission. It has many dimensions. It opens consciousness to the Risen Jesus. It is a friend to all humanity. It is the energy of Jesus at work everywhere until the end of time. Pentecost, the feast of the transmission of the Spirit upon the disciples fifty days after the Resurrection, is celebrated as the birthday of the church as the visible form of the mystical Body of Christ.[9] Until the End when the Big Bang folds back on itself the Spirit will remain the medium in which the compassion of Jesus reaches into the smallest detail of human need and suffering. After that, who knows? Through the Holy Spirit Jesus works to unify the dual and the nondual, the one and the many.

◦◦◦

Ruah also means wind or breath. Immaterial but life-giving and always present. Breath is the sign that we are alive. Someone else's breath can restore us to life. Watching or following the breath, in some Eastern forms of meditation, stills the mind. In the Hesychast tradition of Eastern Christianity repeating the name of Jesus interiorly in rhythm with the breath brings the mind into the heart. To become more mindful we have only to remember that we are breathing. The very way we breathe determines both how we live and what we feel. We breathe short and hard when we are angry or frightened. We breathe long and deep when we are peaceful and when we meditate. Yet we do not have ultimate control over the breath. It is gift, the basic gift of life. And we take breath for granted, like a good friend we trust to be there when needed.

When we see the world afresh after a bout of despair we are breathing in the Spirit. When clarity replaces confusion and doubt, when joy replaces boredom, when harmony overthrows conflict, when

[9] Jn 16:7.

a conviction of basic human goodness dissolves cynicism and pessimism about human nature, the Spirit is becoming manifest. The Spirit is also the air in which the resonance of Jesus' question sounds.

◦•◦•◦•

Like the metaphors used to convey the meaning of spirit—air, wind and breath (and the dove whose natural habitat is the air)—the biblical writers also used the elements of water and fire.

John baptised with water for the repentance of sin. The descent of the dove of the Holy Spirit on Jesus after his own baptism signified another kind of baptism would come through Jesus. This would be the definitive initiation: the baptism of the Spirit. 'He will baptise you with the Holy Spirit and with fire' the Baptist prophesies.[10] One baptism liberates from the karmic consequences of sin. The other bestows holiness by participation in the Spirit of God—because as Jesus had earlier said 'only God is holy'. While sin, the action deriving from egotism, binds to the laws of karma the Spirit introduces us to a subatomic world where duality is transcended: where God and humanity are one.

In the Spirit unity and diversity are reconciled in simplicity. St Paul saw the unity of mind and heart among the early house-churches as the gift and sign of the Spirit. Unity is not uniformity however because 'where the Spirit is there is liberty'. In the Spirit *we* experience that *you and I* are one, but that we are still free to be ourselves. The Spirit permits different aspects of the truth to coexist harmoniously. Spirit is the foe of all kinds of repression. In the Spirit cause and effect, which the mind separates and polarises, are a *single* event. Events that seem sequential to the mind are known simultaneously in the Spirit. In the Spirit the infinitely small is also the infinitely great: 'the heavens have opened', mind and heart are one, the tiny mustard seed grows into the mighty tree of faith.

In conversation with Nicodemus Jesus spoke about the nature of spirit. If, he says, human beings are to 'see the kingdom of God' they must be born over again from water and spirit. Without this dual baptism, an external moral and interior ontological initiation, we remain bound to the 'flesh'. Flesh (like 'world' and 'devil') here means not just the physical body but the ego-centred mind and its complex interaction with the body, its desires and instinct for self-survival. If

[10] Lk 3:16.

we do not experience the Spirit we remain stuck in sense-gratification and pain-avoidance.

Spiritual knowledge boosts us out of the egocentric orbit. Flesh can only give birth to flesh, Jesus tells Nicodemus. It is the perpetual cycle of *samsara*, endless as the pursuit of desire. This self-circling mind cannot achieve transcendence. We cannot *think* our way into spirit. It is 'spirit that gives birth to spirit'. The sending of the Spirit sparks an awakening to the depth of our true nature.

Spirit is unthinkable. It cannot be measured or given an end or a beginning. Jesus says it is like wind or breath, free to blow where it chooses. You can hear the sound and feel it on your skin but you cannot define it, analyse its parts or plot its course. The Spirit is not locked inside us like a ghost in a machine. It is the air we breathe in and breathe out. It conveys our capacity for self-transcendence. Mind and body thus exist in the Spirit as fish exist in the sea—and as the sea flows through the fish. We breathe the Spirit as the Spirit breathes us.

After his conversation with Nicodemus Jesus meets a lonely Samaritan woman at Jacob's well where she has come at noon, the least sociable hour of the day, to draw water. She is one of the very few people in the gospel to whom Jesus unambiguously says who he is. 'I am he,' he replies when she suggests he may be the promised messiah. He is the 'living water' which quenches human thirst. In the same breath he tells her that 'God is spirit' and that to truly worship God we must do so 'in spirit and in truth'.[11] These conversations with the learned Nicodemus and the outcast village woman convey St John's sense of the nature of Jesus' self-disclosure. They also prepare us for the dramatic contrast Jesus will later draw between spirit and flesh and his definitive assertion that life derives not from flesh but directly from spirit.[12] Whatever is open to the Spirit and 'in the Spirit' is truthful. And the food needed to nourish the life of the Spirit is the truth. Truth is more necessary to the *human-ness* of our nature than physical food. It is the bread of life.[13]

Speaking in the synagogue in Capernaum, where he lived for a while, Jesus described the relationship between spirit, life and truth. His own words, he said, were spirit to those who listen to them.

[11] Jn 4:24.
[12] Jn 6:63.
[13] Jn 6:27.

> The words which I have spoken to you are both spirit and life.
> And yet there are some of you who have no faith.[14]

From this time, according to John, many of Jesus' followers abandoned him while his core group of disciples drew closer around him.

◌◦◌◦◌

By saying that his *words* were spirit and life Jesus opens a new way of understanding both his identity and the nature of spirit.

In the theology of the Trinity the Holy Spirit means primal communication. She is the love exchanged between Father and Son in that communion which is Being itself ('I AM') and which we call God. Spirit is not only the bond of the Trinitarian communion but its very oneness. Flowing as the mutual love of Father and Son she could, in another culture, call to mind the terms Mother and Daughter. All relationship, sentient and insentient is an expression of this primal relationship. The structure of all existence is thus essentially Trinitarian, dynamic and fluent. The Spirit is the relationship subsisting between all that exists and so holds all *in* being. She makes everything whole (and holy). Nothing real can be outside relationship. The Spirit is essential relationship and makes all relationships holy. Spirit is communication: the self-revelation and self-giving of one to another which unites and transcends both 'I' and 'Thou'. Spirit is not only the *I-Thou* of relationship but the *we* as well. We cannot *see* communication. We feel its consequences. One of the characteristics of Spirit is that her form and content are one. She discloses herself within the very person who is trying to observe her. She is always present, but cannot be pinned down.

Communication is not merely linguistic or conceptual. But when it does work through these means it suffers from the inevitable gap that always occurs between saying and hearing, between receiving the message and interpreting it. Those who do not wish to speak the truth exploit this gap for their own purposes. In the time-lapse involved in all communication, *mis*communication happens easily. Some degree of misunderstanding or confusion distorts most relationships much of the time. In conscious silence, however, there is no time-lapse between transmission and reception. In the present moment, the 'I AM' of God, communication *is* spontaneous communion. The perfection of all communication therefore is silence and in true silence spirit is most purely

---

[14] Jn 6:63.

perceived. When all forms of language have been transcended in the fullness of silence, the tap is turned completely on. Words can communicate miraculously. But they also reduce the flow of consciousness and limit communication to the mental level. So, as information technology makes such advances today our need for silence increases proportionately. It is becoming increasingly evident that more words and images or merely faster transmission of information do not ensure better communication. In fact there seem to be limits to the speed and quantity of information we can absorb before the mind blocks communication altogether and insists on resting. The more we speak the more we thirst for silence. St Benedict said that in many words we cannot avoid sin. Silence heals. Silence is forgiving.

This does not mean that Spirit opposes the ordinary languages of communication. She is the silence within them, inherent in all truthful speech. Spirit is communion, communication perfected. To speak from silence is to speak truthfully. Business meetings, political summits, family gatherings benefit from an opening period of meditation in which silence is tasted both personally and collectively, interiorly and externally. It reveals the spiritual dimension of the moment of gathering.

Whenever we do manage to communicate successfully we feel hopeful and joyful, renewed and revitalised. Communication makes us more alive. When however we fail to communicate we feel the cold presence of death. Desperation at such failures can destroy relationships in marriages or between nations. Fear and anger, pride and prejudice, oppression and censorship, religious, political or psychological repression block the channels of communication. They sin against the Holy Spirit because they refuse to allow people the communication which is the breath of life. When denied communication, consciousness contracts. We become smaller beings, less than human. The denial of free speech under totalitarian regimes and the way this inhibits the individual's ability to come to self-knowledge may be the main cause for the eventual self-destruction of those tyrannies. When people cannot communicate they cannot breathe the air of the Spirit and life diminishes in intensity and colour, in meaning and attractiveness. The repressed lose creativity and eventually even the will to live.

Jesus is a supreme communicator. His very existence is meaningful as the communication to and through humanity of the nature of the God whom he felt and called 'Abba'. To see him, he says, *is* to see the Father. His communication used words and images and the other forms of language like touch, but his message was perfected in death, with its shocking silence. From the heart of that silence the Spirit, his Spirit, completes what he was communicating through life and death. Whatever facilitates communication within ourselves and with others is spiritual and enhances life.

> 'If anyone is thirsty let him come to me; whoever believes in me let him drink. As Scripture says, "Streams of living water shall flow out from within him"'. He was speaking of the Spirit which believers in him would receive later; for the Spirit had not yet been given, because Jesus had not yet been glorified.[15]

'Belief in him' begins with radical attention to his words and empowers us to drink the Spirit's waters of communion. The mission of Jesus is to make humanity better able to communicate, to love friend and foe and to tell each other the truth in love.

⟨◦⟩◦⟨◦⟩

The Spirit changes the way we see God. When Jesus told the Samaritan woman that henceforth worship of God must be 'in spirit and in truth' he indicated how we must eventually transcend any cultic relationship with God that turns Him into a *thing* or a being among other beings. In that kind of relationship, as we saw earlier, we tend to placate or flatter an idol of God whom we think of as being kind one moment and vengeful the next. A new sense of communion with God in the nonduality of the Spirit replaces this relationship of fear. Experiencing the Spirit often makes people talk of feeling God *within* them. But this only corrects the excessive emphasis previously placed on an external God. In the Spirit we live and move and have being in God like fish in water or birds in the air. Everything we think of as inner or outer is 'in God'.

As we enter an era of global spirituality (not the same as a global religion) the words of Jesus to the Samaritan woman resonate more deeply with modern experience. They affirm that the sending of the Spirit frees communication with God from dependence on language and ritual. Jesus thus severs with the sword of the Spirit the ancestral link between prayer and magic. Henceforth when we worship we are not constrained by words, hymns, chants, rituals or any of the religious theatrical spaces of humanity, their altars and pulpits, mosques and

[15] Jn 7:37-39.

synagogues, temples and zendos. We can now inhabit these traditions and sacred places in a quite new way. The Spirit within the worshippers in the sacred space is the authenticity of their worship. In the Spirit's silence all worshippers, from whatever mountain they have walked, can meet as one.

⟨ᴏ⋆ᴏ⋆ᴏ⟩

Spirit vitalises like breath, flows like water, purifies like fire, liberates like truth. And burns like fire. St John says that Jesus 'sends' this Spirit from the Father: the 'spirit of truth that issues from the Father.'[16] He also describes Jesus saying that the Father will send the Spirit, who is to be our advocate, 'in my name'.[17] There is a rich ambiguity here. The Spirit comes from the Father but also from Jesus who is one with the Father. The communion of Jesus with his Father *is* the Spirit. Spirit therefore sends Spirit. The giver and the gift are one and the same reality. This is the gift given in friendship, friendship with God.

The Holy Spirit whom Jesus and the Father send is an advocate, a *friend*. She is a friendly power unconditionally on our side. Like a true friend she may at times tell hard truths, out of love, but she is never condemnatory. She cannot reject. Her friendship never wears out. She does not take our self-responsibility out of our hands. But she helps to bear that responsibility in the most authentic way. She remains with us as an active guiding intelligence. Forgetful and inattentive as we are, she continually jogs our memory and nudges us awake. To live by the Spirit, making communion a priority, we are in for endless surprises:

> Your Advocate, the Holy Spirit whom the Father will send in my name will teach you everything, and will call to mind all that I have told you.[18]

The burden of truth, Jesus said, was too great for his disciples to carry at the time he spoke these words to them. So the spirit of truth would come later in order to 'guide (them) into all the truth'. Human beings, who cannot bear very much reality at once, need time to learn and understand. The Spirit's intelligence of love controls the flow of truth in the measure that suits our capacity. Communion is consum-

[16] Jn 15:26-27.
[17] Jn 14:26.
[18] Jn 14:26.

mated only through time when understanding, memory and insight are integrated in silence. What we find difficult to absorb all at once on our own is stored in the living transmission of spirit which we call tradition.

◦◦◦◦

The Spirit of truth, the Spirit *is* truth. But 'what is truth?' Pilate's cynical, desperate question exposed his inability to listen to the question of Jesus.

The truth is *what is*. Everything that *is*, is the truth. Truth is not merely the right answer to a question. The whole truth comprises the question, the working out of the answer and all the wrong answers, as well as the final solution. Truth includes all falsehood and illusion; it ultimately absorbs and makes even wasted time and absurdity meaningful. As forgiveness supremely shows, truth even redeems sad, lost, wasted time.

The joy of realising the truth is the bliss of the Spirit. It erases the shame of all previous failures. Aware that this Spirit of truth is with us as a friend, we are better able to tolerate in others and in ourselves what has not yet reached fullness of being and become fully truthful. Truth is tolerant because the Spirit is forgiving love. It allows the untrue to survive for the time being as a loving parent allows a child to make mistakes. Truth embraces rather than excommunicates its enemies. It is made manifest after much distillation of experience. It is not an object or an answer to be stared at and preserved. When there is no ego through which the truth has to pass, communication dilates into communion.

The Spirit is the egolessness, the boundless emptiness, of God. She therefore fills everything with her emptiness and contains 'all the truth'. Only emptiness can contain everything. Returning to us in the Spirit of truth, as friend and teacher, Jesus can therefore be both God and man, historical and cosmic, personal and universal. He is wave and particle, fully individuated, able to be his unique individual self and to be indivisible from everything. This makes his death, all death, meaningful and necessary.

In St John's gospel the Resurrection and the sending of the Spirit are seen as a single event. On the evening of Easter Day Jesus came and stood among his disciples while they were huddled fearfully in a locked room. His first word to them was *shalom*. The rich Hebrew word for peace invoked the blessing of the harmony of all orders of being. *Shalom* flows directly from the Divine harmony which is the Spirit. To receive it is to share in that peace beyond all understanding.

Jesus then breathed on them saying, 'Receive the Holy Spirit.' His breath, which carried his words into their minds and listening hearts, is a medium of the Spirit. Then he gave them the power to forgive sins. This power to forgive those whom we have wronged and who have wronged us is a charism of the Spirit because forgiveness removes the greatest of all obstacles to communication. It heals wounds, confesses the truth that sets us free, consoles pain, calms anger, dissolves resentment, achieves the reconciliation of enemies. Whoever knows the truth has the power to forgive. Jesus understood his enemies and so could forgive them.

Father forgive them for they know not what they do.[19]

We learn through her effect on ourselves what the Spirit is: a friend who has no favourites and who liberates the power to love, to forgive endlessly. She is beyond observation but we recognise her by the traces of her silent, guiding, healing, consoling passage through our lives.

<O*O*O>

Without the Holy Spirit there would be no story of Jesus to tell from one generation to another in ever-new and richer ways, no community to retell his story in word, art, song and dance. Without the Spirit the church would surely have crumbled long ago under the weight of its human imperfections. Since his Resurrection Jesus is recognised through the Holy Spirit.

He taught through the Spirit even before the Ascension, while he was still in the intermediate state the East calls the subtle body. After these appearances he moved into another state through the Ascension, into his spiritual body which was his 'glorification', his complete absorption into the ground of being that he knew as the *Father*. It is described symbolically in the Acts of the Apostles:

When they were all together, they asked him, 'Lord, is this the time at which you are to restore the sovereignty to Israel?' He answered, 'It is not for you to know about dates and times which the Father set within his own control. But you will receive power

[19] Lk 23:34.

when the Holy Spirit comes upon you ... ' After he had said this, he was lifted up before their very eyes, and a cloud took him from their sight.[20]

His disappearance from their material world brought him even closer to his disciples. Through the giving of the Spirit he was able now to connect with them directly from the Father, the ground of Being itself. In the account of Pentecost this Spirit conveyed the power of universal communication:

> They were all filled with the Holy Spirit and began to talk in other tongues as the Spirit gave them utterance ... At this sound a crowd gathered and were bewildered because each one heard his own language spoken.

For the first Christians the Spirit was not a sectarian possession but a gift bestowed on all humanity. This meant that those who wanted to receive baptism did not need to undergo the rites of Jewish initiation. Their faith had already 'purified' them:

> In fact God who can read everyone's hearts, showed his approval of them by giving the Holy Spirit to them just as he had to us. God made no distinction between them and us, since he purified their hearts by faith.[21]

It also had a wider remit than Gentiles wanting to join Christian communities with a Jewish culture. The gift of the Spirit touched every person who was willing to listen, to feel, its touch:

> Now there were devout people living in Jerusalem from every nation under heaven and at this sound they all assembled, each one bewildered to hear these men speaking his own language. They were amazed and astonished ... 'We hear them preaching in our own language about the marvels of God.' Everyone was amazed and unable to explain it; they asked one another what it all meant.[22]

What is easily overlooked in this description of the Pentecostal experience of the Spirit is the dominant reaction of 'amazement and wonder'. For some, the ineffability of this wondrousness of the Spirit just

[20] Acts 1:6-9.
[21] Acts 15:8-10.
[22] Acts 2:5-12.

showed how nonsensical it all was. They scoffed and dismissed the apostles as drunkards, acting and speaking irrationally. This quite predictable reaction, however, missed an essential aspect of the way we do express our knowledge of God. It can only be grasped by a letting-go. It can only be expressed in paradox and 'foolishness'. It can only be understood by living with it. It is best expounded in the form of questions. At the beginning of the gospel story the same point was illustrated in the response of Mary, the mother of Jesus, to what was happening to her and her son. When the angel announced her destiny

> She was deeply disturbed by these words and asked herself what this greeting could mean.[23]

When the adolescent Jesus showed her, as painfully for her as any mother, that his destiny would involve a separation from her, she and Joseph simply 'did not understand what he meant'.[24] Mary, a model of the church and paradigm of contemplation, cannot mentally grasp the meaning of the Spirit as it touches her at the deepest level. But precisely in accepting this unknowability—living in open-minded wonder, pondering these mysteries in her heart—she expands in a knowledge that is revealed most tragically at the foot of the Cross and, finally, most ecstatically on the day of Pentecost. The wonder is that what is unknowable to reason alone is perfectly understood by love.

The post-Resurrection sending of the Spirit was a sign of the Kingdom. It expresses a radical new equality existing between all human beings. In the Spirit people could dare to feel a love that recognised no boundaries. She created a revolutionary kind of historical community in which ancient distinctions of caste and class, even of gender, race and religion, lost their old sectarian meanings and their power to divide. Faith prepared the ground for this new *unity*. Faith—which is openness to the nondual and our inherent capacity for transcendent relationship—disposes us to receive the Spirit. Faith is proven by the way people live with others in equality, compassion and tolerance. The dualistic, divisive ego, of course, ever lies in wait, sometimes dormant, always easily aroused and reinstated. The innocence of the early church, like that of all beginnings, was soon compromised in its squab-

[23] Lk 1:29.
[24] Lk 2:50.

bles and mutual exclusions. But if we have only once, and however briefly, seen ourselves in the light of the Spirit, the ego's return can never regain its old tyranny.

We are told in Acts that the people who heard the Spirit-filled disciples speak were 'cut to the heart'.[25] Their words, like those of Jesus, were living forces. People were so deeply moved that they were impelled to ask, 'Friends what are we to do?' Peter's answer encapsulates the new Way: repent, be baptised 'in the name of Jesus' for the forgiveness of sins and receive the gift of the Holy Spirit. Turn around, let go, live.

◦◦◦◦◦

How can we today understand this gift of Jesus, the Holy Spirit? How do we receive his transmission of the Spirit which, above all, empowers people to a new degree of loving?

Firstly, we need to hear it spoken about. Ordinary human communication is necessary. Understanding and recognition at the mental and physical level is a preliminary if any relationship is to open spiritually. The more mundane ways in which we come to know someone are the soil in which fuller union develops. To understand and recognise Jesus as humanity's friend, the sender of the Spirit, we will first need to hear him described, however inadequately, by those who have recognised him in their own lives. We will need to be introduced to him if we are ever to say who he is for us. Communication of what is silent, beyond the power of thought and words, begins in language charged with the life of the Spirit.

Secondly, we must be prepared to receive a gift. We are not trying to crack a problem or even get an experience. 'All you need,' says the second step of Alcoholics Anonymous, 'is the open mind.'[26] The Spirit soon teaches us what a gift really means. Any relationship between two people is transformed by the giving and receiving of a gift. Think of any gift you have received recently, at Christmas or a birthday. If you had refused it the relationship in which it had been offered would have been damaged. Accepting the gift affirmed and deepened the relationship. In receiving it you were thereby giving something precious back to the giver. The giver received the gift of your acceptance. The roles of giver and receiver are thus subtly reversed or interwoven in

---

[25] Acts 2:37.
[26] *Twelve Steps and Twelve Traditions* (New York: AA Grapevine Inc., 1952), p. 26.

the ceremony of the gift. Their separate roles are transcended and united in a higher nondual relationship through the simple ritual by which one gives and the other receives a gift. A genuine gift thus given and received opens a space of freedom between giver and receiver in which they expand beyond the boundaries of their separate identities. The gift celebrates the freedom to love and to be loved simultaneously. Receiving a gift—as we do for example in meditation by 'accepting the gift of our being'—frees us to penetrate beyond all separateness, all forms of the dualistic mind and to be expanded by the liberty of the Spirit's unity.

Spirit can take any form and yet remain unbound by it. We do not receive the Spirit in a fixed form once and for all. To freeze the forms diminishes our capacity to receive the Spirit and to live by her power. It is at the risk of our spiritual life that we solidify the fluid, airy, fiery forms through which the Spirit communicates herself to us. All these forms—relationships, concepts, scripture, sacrament, experiences of baptism in the Spirit or mystical awakening, epiphanies of beauty and truth in nature or in art or literature, sex, song or dance,— are changeable. *Letting go* and giving is at the heart of the ritual of the gift. Spiritual growth, too, is about letting forms dissolve at the right moment.

We cannot live by form alone. Nor can we live without forms and structures. Human life is not abstraction but incarnation. Forms are needed as the benchmarks of truth. They can also be sacred. They give us some small stability in a world built on sand. But we cannot live spiritually if we do not renounce them even if doing so feels for all the world like death. In his death Jesus let go of his familiar way of being present to those he knew and loved. But in doing this he was embracing his life's mission. In their turn, his family and disciples had to let go of his form of presence once the Resurrection experience had shown them that he was still with them. Psychological habits and patterns as well as the absolute claim of all social structures must disappear, if not externally, at least interiorly before the Spirit can be experienced fully in the freedom-from-form which is its mystery. The interior renunciation of forms and structures, beliefs and desires is the work of prayer.

Very few of us can easily endure the disappearance of any of the patterns of life we inhabit, relationships, jobs, social titles or group membership, because all of them support what we call our 'identity'. Yet deep down we all know that the day is coming when everything *must* become formless, when death will devour everything in which we invested our dreams of immortality. There are many 'little deaths' which anticipate this great surrender of all form and possessions. Sex can offer one such temporary death of the ego; meditation leads to a more permanent state of ecstasy. Dedicated service to the well-being of others can be one way to let go. Solitude or social action, celibacy or family life are all ways of life appropriate for different people at particular times. One form is not inherently superior to another. People are different and ways of life have relative value. Any path followed in faith, guided by the friendship of the Spirit, can lead to the same, single, great self-emptying.

The dissolving of structures and the breaking of forms occurs both in the mind and in the relationships that bond people. It is this death of internal and external structures which we embrace each time we love, turning to another while taking the attention off ourselves. We pay attention also in the making of art or in that art of prayer and work of love which is meditation. In the silence and stillness of any act of generous attention, however hidden or mundane, the thought-forms and desires which bind us to the ego break open and fall away.

Death happens from moment to moment as the myriad little forms of things fall apart. Just as my fingers touch the keys of this word processor and the screen changes with each new letter, adding and deleting, so death is constantly dissolving forms, and life is constantly restoring them. As your mind's eye moves from line to line of this book you are making and unmaking forms. In daily life healthy maturity requires that we learn to let go of people and things, status and possessions, plans and desires. Every life, however uneventful it may seem, has its tragic and momentous transitions. And everyone lets go eventually when the body itself dissolves at the hour of death.

Jesus had to go away in order for the Spirit to be sent because Spirit is released through the breaking of forms. At the Last Supper Jesus took bread and *broke* it so that this ritual would be able to communicate his presence. Then having broken it, he *gave* it to them. We can only give what we have broken out of, what we have let go of. One of the ways we receive the gift of the Spirit, therefore, is through death: the countless little deaths of the ego as well as the 'second death' which sweeps away everything we know both of the body and its inseparable friend, the mind.

Another way of receiving the Spirit is solitude. Perhaps baptism in the Spirit means baptism into solitude.

God is met in the desert as well as in the garden. Merely withdrawing to a desolate or secluded place, however, does not guarantee solitude. Physical or psychological isolation no more creates solitude than candles and incense make prayer. The need for solitude means more than the psychological need for space and time alone. Solitude is much more than being alone. It is the discovery, the recognition and the acceptance of one's uniqueness.

This uniqueness should not be confused with what the ego thinks of as its specialness at the centre of the universe. All the ego's claims for special treatment are only a pale reflection of the radiant uniqueness inherent in the Self. Uniqueness is experienced rather than thought, felt rather than imagined or defined, received as gift rather than claimed as a right. It need not be desired because it is already present. It can only be experienced when the *separateness* of the individual has been dissolved and given way to *indivisibility*, in the non-duality of the Spirit. The true nature of solitude according to Ramana Maharshi is not determined by where you live or what you do, but by the absence of thought.

Solitude is realised by stilling the surface levels of consciousness. Sometimes this profound solitary uniqueness flashes upon meditators in the early days of their practice. For an instant they know themselves to be an utterly unique entity in the cosmos. Familiar perceptions of identity drop off to reveal the glittering diamond of being in a core of pure, unconditioned existence. Momentarily this insight can be a terrifying as well as exhilarating self-discovery. (That is why it should not be artificially induced by drugs or extreme asceticism.) It can often be overwhelming because we misinterpret it as a glimpse of the loneliness and isolation of existence. But as continued practice integrates the experience we come to see that solitude is nothing to be feared. Our uniqueness is the incontrovertible proof we are loved.

In love as in meditation we are continually moved along a spectrum of consciousness beyond judgement and thought to pure awareness. Meditation is not what we think. Love is not what we fantasise. All the material forms and the psychological patterns of life which we habitually cling to are surrendered in the nonpossessiveness, the 'poverty' of love. Thinking is stilled. The paradox—and this is the great arch we pass through to enter the kingdom of God—is that in the death of the 'I-thought', which is the source of all forms and patterns of mind, the Self rises. Only when the 'I' has gone can 'I' share the 'I AM' of God.

> Then he called the people to him, as well as his disciples, and said to them, 'Anyone who wishes to be a follower of mine must leave self behind. He must take up his cross and come with me. Whoever cares for his own safety is lost; but if a person will let himself be lost for my sake, he will find his true self.'[27]

---

[27] Mk 8:34-35, Mt 16:25.

❧ 10 ❧

Meditation

*T*here are privileged places in our lives where we feel there is nothing to explain and where the past can catch up with the present. Places of acceptance: geographical like islands, psychological like marriages or spiritual like the times of meditation every day. Because I speak too much about meditation I enjoy being in places where it does not need to be spoken of and Bere Island was one of these. Once my cousins asked me about it. (I had given them a book on an earlier visit and they received the quarterly newsletter from the World Community.) Perhaps they were simply curious or wanted to check the relationship of this phenomenon to the church as they understood it. I liked the intelligent objectivity of their questions and their level of comfort in their own style of religion. They were not asking for anything more from religion as they knew it. But they also knew there must be more because their religion had taught them about its own mystery. I only wished they could have been better persuaded that the more hidden in their faith was wholly their birthright. As I explained what meditation was and where it came from and how it related to the forms of prayer they knew best I suddenly felt I was speaking too much. Pleasantly, in Irish fashion, the topic of our conversation sailed off in another direction.

As I walked back to my cottage through the soft drizzle of the afternoon for my next meditation, trying to avoid the puddles and failing, I felt what a cow must feel like ambling its way to milking time. In fact it was milking time and the cows, going in the opposite direction from mine, threw me a tired look of sympathy as they followed each other past me down the hill. Meditation, which cows may understand better than we think, needs to be talked about—a little. I remembered vividly as I approached my cottage how I had first been introduced to the spiritual practice which has become so much part of my life now that my life is inseparable from it. John Main had initiated me in a few quiet words. I forget the words but not the communication. He did not say I had to meditate or even that I should. He did not check up on me to see if I had started. He did not ask me to describe what I experienced. Once, some years later, when I had had an 'experience' and was becoming attached to it, I mentioned it to him with suppressed self-gratification. Maybe I expected his approval. Instead I got a look and a sharp word which, like the second and louder alarm

195

clock bell in the morning, finally woke me up to see what foolishness I was
slipping into.

With many of his friends John Main did not speak about meditation unless
they first raised the subject with him. The wisdom of meditation includes the
wisdom of knowing when not to speak about it. John Main—and the island—
taught me how silence, after all, best communicates silence.

⟨◦⟩◦⟨◦⟩

To summarise: To be able to say who Jesus is we need to know who
we ourselves are. How well we can see and recognize him in his spiritual body depends upon the clarity and depth of our self-knowledge.

The goal of life—it can be called 'heaven', 'nirvana', 'liberation',
'salvation' or 'enlightenment'—is to know fully who we are. Self-
transcendence is the way to self-knowledge. Jesus helps to remove the
barriers that block self-knowledge by the way he communicates, in the
Spirit, his knowledge of who he is. Another's self-knowledge always
stimulates our own movement towards self-discovery and self-
acceptance that are the twin poles of the unified state of self-
knowledge. In this state the centre of consciousness no longer resides
in the ego. From the deeper centre of the true self we are conscious
of union with others within our uniqueness rather than separation.
There are not many gods but one God, not many selves but one Self,
one True 'I AM' in which all beings share in Being.

Whoever has found this in themselves helps to awaken it in others.
Individual identity is not lost when we know ourselves but it is transcended. We are freed of its inherent illusions of self-sufficiency and
self-centredness. This individuality is lost by letting go of it. The true
Self then becomes clear and, from the ego's point of view initially, is
seen as a stranger. There are not many individual enlightenments as
the ego may imagine but the one great enlightenment of the Self in
which all participate. And, because self-knowledge cannot be encap-
sulated in any mental concept or image or psychic or psychological
happening, there is *no* single, universal definition of the Self. No
definition can express the lightning flash of insight into the ordinary
which awakens self-knowledge. An ordinary, completely open-ended
question, not a dogmatic definition demanding assent, is how Jesus
invites us to share his self-knowledge. The question is borne on the
breeze of the Holy Spirit, not as the imposition of an idea, but as
an opportunity, an invitation, an opening to faith, a way to enter
the Kingdom.

I said above that the process through which self-knowledge arises embraces the whole spectrum of life-experience. All forms of love and all relationships, work and play, physical, mental and psychological growth, creativity and frustration, good and evil, vice and virtue, grief and joy, loss and gain—all invite the self-transcendence which leads to liberation from our habitual state of submersion in ego. To co-relate all these experiences and make them fully conscious, all religious traditions have recognised the essential value of meditation. This means the simplifying practice of silence and stillness, of non-action beyond thought and imagination, the stilling of the activities of the mind. Integrated into ordinary life, the practice of meditation harmonises and integrates in the spirit all that we think and feel and say and do.

The word 'meditation' has acquired a variety of meanings in western tradition. The 'meditatio' of the Desert monks meant simply a prayer of the heart, a kind of chewing or repetition of the Word. By the seventeenth century it had come to mean almost exclusively an organised method of cerebral prayer employing intellectual analysis and visual imagination. In the East there are also many kinds of meditation but they essentially refer to a nondiscursive, silent practice. Here I am using the word 'meditation' in its nondiscursive sense roughly synonymous with contemplation. One could say that meditation is the work we do to accept the gift of contemplation which is already given and present in the heart.

In both Western and Eastern traditions, meditation (or contemplation) is acknowledged as an essential work, an ongoing discipline of the pilgrimage of spiritual growth. In one sense it is both means and end. Meditation reconciles the contradictions and opposites which run across the spectrum of human wholeness. Prayer is the deepest, the primal therapy of the suffering human condition. Therefore meditation ('pure prayer') is not an elite practice for the spiritually advanced. It is the natural way to grow. Not only the *terminus ad quem* but the *terminus a quo*. Nor is meditation the get-away-from-it-all narcissistic indulgence which advertising posters trendily proclaim to the stressed and hyperactive commuters of the Western (and increasingly the Asian) world. The spiritual journey involves the need and desire to meditate. It is a universal practice although each individual, like each spiritual tradition, appropriates it in his or her own way. Meditation is not leisure activity—though it takes time and requires relaxation. From a spiritual perspective you relax in order to meditate rather than meditating just in order to relax. You *can* survive without it. But it is the wind in the sail of the soul. A work that harmonises the usually discordant dimensions of our consciousness. Its fruits are agreed by all traditions to be preferable to their opposites. They need little definition or defence: compassion and wisdom, generosity and tolerance, forgiveness and kindness, gentleness and peace, joy and creativity. In other words, happiness and simple, basic human goodness.

By liberating these potential qualities, meditation advances the cause of human wholeness. It illustrates in real life that holiness is not just about interiority. To be *good* means simply to have the inner and outer dimensions of ourselves in union, to be in harmony with our true nature. Because this wholeness *is* the spirit, meditation opens everything we do to the spiritual dimension. With regular practice meditation thus establishes a deeply satisfying and peaceful consistency within ourselves and between ourselves, others and all the activities of our lives.

⸱◦⸱◦⸱◦⸱

To conclude our listening to the question of Jesus, I want to turn now to meditation and to explore how it is the natural response to everything which that question asks us about him and ourselves. We will see that it is a way of silence and self-transcendence, a way of relationship and solitude, a way to read without words, to know without thought. Through self-knowledge the meditator is brought to the threshold of the knowledge of God within a relationship with Jesus that asks nothing of us except the total gift of self. This relationship begins to grow as soon as we seriously, silently attend to his question. Meditation, in the light of Christian faith, is a deepening encounter with the mind of Christ. We meet the Risen Jesus even if we do yet fully recognize or name him.[1]

Like Mary of Magdala each person probably has to make several turns before recognising clearly in whose presence we stand. Every turning will be a step towards conversion, not perhaps in formal religious terms, but towards a personal reality higher than we can imagine. Each stage of this recognition will have a negative and a positive

---

[1] Saying this is not, I believe, a Christian way of winning the competition for supremacy with other religions. It is the essence of Christian belief that Jesus embodies the Logos which is the normative principle of divine self-communication.

aspect, a turning away and a turning towards; each will be a unique death and a rising. Jesus warns those who follow his question into their own silence to be prepared for difficulties. To meditate is to *change direction* not merely in one's behaviour but in the fundamental processes of consciousness.

Meditation inaugurates a whole new way of being. It is less a technique than a way of life. It is initiated by the gradually emergent experience of communion, oneness with self and others that reaches beyond the boundaries of dualistic relationship. Although most people are passionately interested in their relationships and see them as the most sacred element of their lives, *relationships* as such are but a stage on the human journey. Beyond relationship—at the silent heart of every relationship, where the walls dividing us crumble—is union. In relationship we are always looking at a separate *other*. The looking at, the distance implied in that objectification of the other, creates the suffering inherent in all relationship. It is the suffering of conflict arising from the ego's desire to possess and control. It is the suffering too of the eventual and unavoidable loss of the one we love. In union, however, there can be no possessiveness because desire itself has been transcended. Egotistical boundaries are dissolved. Uniqueness embraces uniqueness and finds selfhood in otherness, sameness in difference. Fear and desire, domination and submission are ended. What is gained is more than desire ever fantasised. When human relationships, rarely and usually briefly, touch this degree of fullness they can truly be called spiritual friendship. They realise their destiny and potential as ways of sharing through the Spirit in the divine community of love. In union otherness is shared, entered into, absorbed rather than externalized. We are within the other and they are within us.

All this is the fruit of meditation. The seed of union lies in our nature waiting to be germinated. Meditation accepts the invitation of this potential and prepares us for the death which growth demands. All this is important to grasp before starting to meditate. It saves unnecessary false starts and moderates impatience. It helps us see that the place we should look for the fruits of meditation is not the meditation period itself—what 'happens' (or doesn't)—but in the manner and quality of our lives, particularly our relationships. We are not looking for anything extraordinary to *happen* in meditation. The point is to see the presence of God in the ordinary, to transform our perception of reality, not to recreate the world to conform to our plans. It is not an escape from life's problems. It is not easy. But it is—and this is the most important aspect of meditation to see clearly—utterly simple. The joy and the peace beyond understanding that results is what *happens*.

Meditation is concerned not so much with our relationship to God as with our union with God. This does not mean that all relationship with God (together with the ideas, images and dialogue involved in relationship) is thereby ended. The idea of relationship continues to be a necessary framework of coming to meaning and decisions. It remains an important language of life. Relationship endures as long as we continue to utter or think in terms of our own 'I', that is until the end of time. But relationship is also changed radically by meditation. The language of relationship is enhanced and rendered more meaningful. Our knowledge and love of God no longer stop short at the stage of relationship but, as all love wishes to do, pushes on towards complete union. The immediate consequence of this deepening of relationship in communion is felt in human relationships. It is perceptible too in the way we feel part of the natural world. The humanity of Jesus and his relationship to the universe come to be experienced from within. The change undergone in all these dimensions is often described as a *coming home*. Home to ourselves and to our innate capacity for transcendence.

These are some of the reasons that meditation is such an important source of hope and vision for the next millennium. The recovery of its contemplative tradition is the source of renewal for Christianity. Out of its crisis a contemplative Christianity will join other faiths as a mediator of compassionate action and healing wisdom to the world.

Through the recovery of the practice of meditation, religion and spirituality, which are moving apart rapidly at present, can be reharmonised. After all, they share a common goal of uplifting the human spirit. Deeper spirituality means deeper prayer. And the health of religion is the quality of its prayer life. To find depth we must return to the life-giving roots of the tradition. Something ancient must be embraced as something new so that a contemporary way of seeing Jesus, of listening to his question and of saying who he is can be born. His question is intrinsic to our culture's search for meaning, peace and justice, and the good life. It also speaks wisely to all that today we understand by the terms self-awareness, self-fulfilment, and transcendence. His question can help guide that search for modern people provided we can find the silence from which to listen to it.

The Christian tradition was born in the first experience of the risen Jesus. It is perennially renewed by its return to the roots of that experience. In its contemplative form the Christian tradition is focussed on this foundational experience even when it is not expressly describing it. The Christian contemplative journey always refers to the living word of the teaching of Jesus and to his presence within and among us in the Spirit. We may begin meditating at any point in our life and for a wide range of motives. Eventually, however, fidelity will lead to faith. Because meditation is as simple and as human as breathing we can learn much from what other traditions have to teach about it. But to understand the Christian meaning of meditation we need to see firstly how it is grounded in the teaching of Jesus. The essential elements of meditation are to be found in his great teaching on prayer in the Sermon on the Mount.

⋯⊙⋯⊙⋯⊙⋯

His disciples once asked Jesus to teach them to pray as John the Baptist had taught his disciples. In reply Jesus gave them a short collection of phrases similar to the Eighteen Benedictions and the Qaddish of the synagogue liturgy.[2]

> Our Father, who art in heaven. Holy is your Name. May your kingdom come and your will be done on earth as it is in heaven. Give us this day our daily bread and forgive us our transgressions as we forgive those who transgress against us. Lead us not into temptation and deliver us from evil.[3]

The Our Father sums up Jesus' advice that prayer should be sincere, direct and brief. He is adamant that the self-dramatising of the ego should be abandoned. Some scholars believe that, translated back into the original Aramaic, this prayer is a collection of short rhythmic phrases summarizing the content and style of the teaching of Jesus in a style typical of the rabbinical teachers of his day. The phrases would have been memorised and repeated frequently and interiorly. From the beginning of the Church innumerable commentaries on the Lord's Prayer have seen in it the key to his teaching about prayer and taken

---

[2] Raymond E. Brown, *New Jerome Biblical Commentary*, p. 645.
[3] Mt 6:9; Lk 11:2-4. These are two slightly different versions of a prayer that has been regarded as especially sacred by Christians as it was first given by Jesus to the apostles and commentary on it has formed the basis of many spiritual teachings on prayer.

it as a starting point for an ever-deepening theology of prayer.[4] To pray
the Our Father requires more than the mechanical repetition or chant-
ing of the words. It requires mindfulness. Some commentators have
suggested it should never take less than three minutes to recite it. As
we saw in Chapter Eight, Simone Weil discovered in her way of reciting
the Lord's Prayer that it requires *attention* through a faithful repetition
that leads to stillness and insight.

In Chapter Six of St Matthew's gospel, the setting in which Jesus
taught this formula also emphasises attention as the primary quality
of all prayer. His teaching distils the essential elements of meditation.
Firstly, he emphasises how prayer must be rooted in the sincerity of
the true Self rather than in the ego's self-consciousness:

> Be careful not to make a show of your religion before men; if you
> do, no reward awaits you in your Father's house in heaven.

Whenever we find security or take pleasure in the approval of others
the authenticity of prayer is compromised. Its motivation becomes
impure. Good deeds performed in the desire for public recognition lack
virtue. To purify the 'ground of our beseeching', as Mother Julian calls
it, Jesus recommends solitude and interiority, the silent intimacy and
the hidden mystery of prayer:

> When you pray, go into a room by yourself, shut the door and
> pray to your Father who is there in the secret place; and your
> Father who sees what is secret will reward you.

As a private room would have been a great luxury in Jesus' time, his
focus is not so much on domestic arrangements as on the orientation
of the mind and heart at the time of prayer. Even the ascetical practices of prayer, such as fasting, he taught, should be performed in a
discreet and modest way. They are not solemn ways of feeling holier
or bargaining positions in a struggle to get what we want out of God.
'I'll give up sweets for Lent if you help me get the job I want.' They
are not control techniques. They are not the ego's magic. The disciplines of the spiritual life, Jesus says, should be performed quietly and
cheerfully.

[4] John Cassian, *The Conferences*, trans. Boniface Ramsey; see Cassian's commentary
on the Lord's Prayer in his ninth Conference which prepares for the practical
instruction on meditation in Conference Ten.

Secondly, Jesus emphasises verbal economy in prayer. We should not go 'babbling on like the heathen who think the more they say the more likely they are to be heard'. Quantity and length, especially when we pray out of our heartfelt needs, do not authenticate prayer because

Your Father knows what you need before you ask him.

Prayer is not informing God of our needs or asking God to change 'his' mind. We are not setting up our will in opposition to God's will or telling God what he should be doing. Such egocentric prayer fosters many forms of neurotic religious behaviour, such as praying for victory over others or the fulfilling of egotistical desires. Absurdity of this kind begins by creating a God in our own ego- (or super-ego)image. It may then continue in the obsessive maintenance of a fantasy relationship with the false god of our making. Such a god can develop enough autonomous psychic life to close us to true divinity when it approaches. This can be just as dangerous spiritually as the way the demon of the ego weaves the illusion that we inhabit a personal reality separate and independent from God.

In the petitions of the Lord's Prayer we see how all prayer touches on human relationships no less than the root-relationship with God. The prayer shows the single web of consciousness that comprises knowledge of God, self-knowledge and relationship to others. If we have not forgiven those who sin against us we will never ourselves feel forgiven nor can we ever be free from the fear that God will punish us for our sins.

A third emphasis in Jesus' teaching on prayer concerns radical detachment from material anxieties. We cannot serve both the God who is Spirit and the god of materialism. And so, Jesus says, when you pray,

I bid you put away anxious thoughts about food and drink to keep you alive and clothes to cover your body.

In the Galilee of Jesus' time he was probably addressing not a band of starving peasants but an affluent and sophisticated audience. To tell the starving not to worry about food is not the same as telling it to the rich. Anxiety about material concerns does not mean a total disregard for the basic necessities of life. We need to eat and drink. Identifying the Self and true happiness with what goes extravagantly beyond basic needs is the problem.

Liberation from desire and fear and developing inner and outer trust are the conditions of prayer according to the teaching of Jesus. They are supported by the fourth great emphasis of his teaching: pure attention to the power of God at the heart of all reality:

> Set your mind on God's kingdom and his justice before everything else, and all the rest will come to you as well.

By this mindfulness we are led into the dynamic pilgrimage at the heart of prayer, to the threshold of continuous prayer, into the stillness of *here* and the peace of *now*.

> So do not be anxious about tomorrow; tomorrow will look after itself.

There are many other sayings and stories of Jesus which elaborate on the Sermon on the Mount's essential teaching on prayer. Often, for example, he emphasises the need for perseverance in prayer and its power to move the mountain of the ego and germinate the inner seed of the Kingdom. He spoke too about praying 'in my name', a phrase which means 'in my way', or 'in the way I do it'. The Sermon on the Mount summarises prayer as a spiritual practice transcending egotism and therefore dissolving fear and desire. It combines interiority, simplicity, trust, attention and being in the present moment.

How can we practice what he preached? How can we do all this simultaneously and naturally? There are many forms of prayer: petition, intercession, praise, scripture, liturgy and worship, discursive, devotional, charismatic. We can pray on a solitary walk in the country by contemplating nature or by attending a solemn cathedral service with choir, incense and sermons. We pray with thanks for a happy birth, in sorrow for a peaceful death, in perplexity over misfortune, in distraction much of the time. All ways of prayer are valid, all are effective in their own way. The ordinary prayer of Christians has however suffered from the loss of its contemplative dimension. Without it all these different forms tend to settle into an orbit around the ego of the person praying. This was my own experience and it led to a growing dissatisfaction with prayer in any form, a sense of being bored with God. Without the *contemplative* dimension any form of prayer risks becoming merely formal: ritualistic, neurotic, compulsive, self-indulgent. Such forms of prayer can degenerate into little more than ways for a group to relate to itself or for an individual to apply a little self-therapy in the stress of life. They lose their transcendent potential in the Spirit, and lose touch with that communion with the loving ground of being which Jesus called *his* Father and *our* Father. No one can judge another's prayer but the fruits of prayer are self-evident. If prayer does not make a difference—if it does not change the one praying first of all—something essential is missing.

◦»◦»◦›

The burning question today for Christian faith—no less perhaps for other believers and nonbelievers alike—is how can we recover the lost contemplative dimension of life? The way we pray is the way we live.

Many Westerners have sought for it in the East where the interiority of the spiritual life is more instinctive. But many Christians seek in a Christian tradition for a contemplative prayer *practice*, to help them apply the teaching of Jesus in daily life and to pray 'in his name'.

Such a practice has been tragically missing from Christian spiritual formation in modern times. Down the centuries, indeed, the deep roots of meditative practice have been marginalised in Christian life and largely forgotten. As a result, when they are recovered, they often create suspicion. The teachers of the religion were not taught how to meditate. Yet a Christian way of meditation, simple and capable of being practiced by all, is to be found in the teachings of the first Christian monks. A number of contemporary teachers have drawn attention to it. A modern Benedictine monk, John Main, recognised and recovered it from long practical neglect. His contemporary way of teaching it has helped a great many people of all ages and walks of life around the world to open up the contemplative dimension of their faith and their daily lives. Through his transmission of this tradition they have been enabled to play again the lost chord of Christian prayer. They have found, 'through their own experience' as John Main liked to say, that they could verify, deepen and *personalise* the mysteries of their faith. The seed of their faith germinated through a prayer of the heart which has been practiced by their fellow Christians from the beginning and has subtle links with the contemplative tradition in other faiths.

Over the past twenty years this dramatic rediscovery of Christian meditation has deepened the way many can understand their Christian identity. Until quite recently meditation was considered the preserve of cloistered specialists. Lay people and others in the 'active life' were considered either unsuitable or incapable of the greater depths of prayer. Today, however, through the influence of many Christian teachers, of whom the monks Henri le Saux, Thomas Merton, Bede Griffiths,

Thomas Keating and John Main are exemplars, contemplative practice has been reclaimed as a universal dimension of Christian spirituality. It has changed rapidly from being seen as a monastic or clerical privilege to become the daily practice of lay people in all walks of life. These are now also its principal teachers as is evident in a contemplative network, The World Community for Christian Meditation, that grew from John Main's teaching.

In the early fifth century John Cassian, who had settled in southern France after absorbing the teaching of the Desert Fathers, compiled the authoritative distillation of their practical wisdom in his *Conferences of the Fathers*.[5] In the late 1960s John Main was able to recognise in their teaching on prayer the Christian practice of the *mantra*. He saw it as a sublimely simple and appropriate method of nondiscursive meditation that allowed modern Christian to explore the full depths of their spirit in the unabashed light of their Christian faith and tradition.

> The formula for this discipline and prayer that you are seeking, then, shall be presented to you. Every monk who longs for the continual awareness of God should be in the habit of meditating on it ceaselessly in his heart, after having driven out every kind of thought, because he will be unable to hold fast to it in any other way than by being freed from all bodily cares and concerns. Just as this was handed down to us by a few of the oldest fathers who were left, so also we pass it on to none but the most exceptional, who truly desire it ... This verse should be poured out in unceasing prayer so that we may be delivered in adversity and preserved and not puffed up in prosperity. You should I say meditate constantly on this verse in your heart ... Let sleep overtake you as you meditate upon this verse until you are formed by having used it ceaselessly and are in the habit of repeating it even while asleep ... Let the mind hold ceaselessly to this formula above all until it has been strengthened by constantly using and continually meditating upon it and until it renounces and rejects the whole wealth and abundance of thoughts. Thus straitened by the poverty of this verse it will very easily attain to that gospel beatitude which holds the first place among the other beatitudes.[6]

In his youth Main had learned to meditate with the mantra from an Indian teacher whom he met and studied briefly with in Malaya. What he learned by word and example from his teacher enabled him to see

[5] Ibid.
[6] Ibid., pp. 379-383.

what Cassian actually meant in his tenth Conference when he emphasised so pointedly the 'continual repetition' in the heart of the *formula* drawn from scripture. The way that teaching had for so long been neglected, misinterpreted or dismissed showed Main how essentially *personal* is the handing on of the tradition of meditation—and how important it is that there be adequately experienced teachers. Neither Cassian nor Main claimed that this was the 'only' or even the best way to meditate, certainly not that it excluded other ways. They also both recognised the variety, mysteriousness and fluidity of prayer. Cassian introduces his magisterial Tenth Conference on the mantra with the brilliant Ninth Conference which describes the diversity as well as the unifying purpose. It has a direction. It is taking us somewhere. As a monk Main's own daily life, like Cassian's, was enriched by scripture, communal worship, Eucharistic liturgy and art. But both also saw, painfully clearly, that the great problem in prayer is the complex and distracted mind. Without solving this, the forms of prayer can remain tragically superficial and so, even when practiced with good intentions, effect no deep transformation. Cassian and Main knew that this problem called for a remedy that was absolutely radical in its simplicity. In the traditional practice of the *formula*, or *mantra*, they saw how attention leads to simplicity. This led them to see further: in poverty of spirit union with the prayer of Jesus, who is perfectly attentive to the Father and to us who are praying, is realised. Our prayer is therefore taken up into his.

John Main saw in Cassian's Christocentric teaching of the mantra a living transmission which addressed the modern hunger for authentically deeper spiritual knowledge. He clearly saw that what modern people needed was an alternative and antidote for their compulsive self-analysis and a healing for the personal woundedness afflicting so many in this society. The mantra is not magic. It is not an easy practice to follow. But it is simple. And so complex a mentality as our own demands nothing less than a discipline of complete simplicity. It requires commitment and perseverance which are not congenial to the modern personality. But an increasing number of people sense that it is what they need. Main, like Cassian and the fourteenth-century *Cloud of Unknowing* and many other teachers of this tradition, built their teaching on this insight into simplicity but without compromising its demanding authenticity. In a simple, direct and practical style he taught Christian meditation in a way that empowered others to discover the depth of the practice for themselves:

As I have suggested, prayer is not a matter of talking to God, but of listening to Him,[7] or being with Him. It is this simple understanding of prayer that lies behind John Cassian's advice that if we want to pray, to listen, we must become quiet and still, by reciting a short verse over and over again. Cassian received this method as something which was an old, established tradition in his own day and it is an enduring universal tradition...Let me repeat the basic technique of meditation. Sit down comfortably, relax. Make sure you are sitting upright. Breathe calmly and regularly. Close your eyes and then in your mind and heart begin to repeat the word that you have chosen as your meditation word...Choosing your word, or mantra, is of some importance. Ideally, you should choose your mantra in consultation with your teacher. But there are various mantras which are possible for a beginner...Some of these words were first taken over as mantras for Christian meditation by the Church in its earliest days. One of these is the word *maranatha*. This is the mantra I recommend to most beginners, the Aramaic phrase *maranatha*, which means, 'Come Lord. Come Lord Jesus.'[8]

⋅⌖⋅⌖⋅⌖⋅

Sitting down to meditate for the first time is a decisive moment in your spiritual path. It is similar to turning on the ignition at the beginning of a long car trip. What happens then? The journey simply begins. You pull away from the curb. Then like all journeys it proceeds by stages. There are delays, traffic jams, wrong turns, moments of exhaustion as well as the thrill of travel and the discovery of the new. These stages and their events could be described by means of a simple map of the levels of consciousness or as stages of self-knowledge unfolding through a gentle and steady discipline.

We begin at the beginning, on the surface. As soon as we begin to meditate we discover the first and superficial level of consciousness: restless, light-headed, undisciplined, distracted mental activity, rampant fantasy. It comes as something of a shock to realise just how uncontrolled and chaotic this level of mind actually is. In our culture

---

[7] John Main wrote before the widespread convention of inclusive language but this does not indicate any insensitivity in his thought to the equality of women and men in all fields including the spiritual.

[8] John Main, *Word into Silence* (London: Darton, Longman and Todd, 1980), pp. 10-11.

we so rarely practice any conscious attention that when we do it seems strange and straining. A recent survey estimated that for most people attention span becomes difficult after anything longer than a television commercial. Yet we rarely appreciate just how inattentive we are. Memorisation skills that from classical times were basic training in elementary education once developed a natural discipline of mental attention. A strong memory was seen as part of healthy mental life. Today when home computers can remember infinitely more than any individual human mind we have become lazy, depriving ourselves of the pleasure and benefit of developing the muscle of memory. We thrive on trivia. We crave ever-stronger stimulation. Our fixation on screens reduces consciousness to whatever image is momentarily flitting before our eyes.

Discovering our chronic distractedness can, at least initially, make meditation an upsetting and humiliating experience. Even if we think of ourselves as relatively calm and recollected, meditation soon disillusions us. The first step of self-knowledge clearly shows that our mind is neither stable nor clear. At this early stage the journey may seem to have ground to a halt before it has even begun. We have no choice but to accept that we are not nearly as capable of paying attention as we had thought. The shock of this discovery may undermine the will to persevere. It can be discouraging and it will certainly recur. But it helps to reflect that if we *can* see clearly that we are distracted then that very awareness is progress. Once recognized, confusion begins to clear. We begin to see the truly simple nature of meditation and to appreciate the challenge it presents.

The first level of self-knowledge is turbulent. We may also as high-level achievers be trying too hard, even giving ourselves headaches trying to meditate! Walter Hilton in the fourteenth century says, (today we might reverse the gender roles), 'It is like a man coming home from work to find a smoking fire and a nagging wife'. The early Desert Fathers and mothers did not have domestic problems. But they were shocked to discover that, even in their desert hermitages, they were unable to abandon the anxieties, temptations and erotic fantasies of their former lives. Sitting with no external distraction they found themselves, like us today, bombarded by unrestrained mental activity, thinking or fantasising compulsively about everything they thought they had abandoned. They seethed at their brethren, condemning the lazy, envying the holier. They obsessed about the trivia of their manual labour of weaving mats or work in the fields. They became compulsive about their few material possessions. They fantasised about sex and, even more, about food.

◦◦◦◦◦

Perhaps we are no more inherently distracted today than the monks of the desert or meditators in any time or culture. It just seems much more difficult for us to get to first base.

Distraction and the craving for variety are endemic to the human mind. The ego is by nature restless in its quest for pleasure and the evasion of pain. The human mind today, however, is bombarded by image and information bytes as never before. Print and electronic media and the speed of communication accelerate the volume and intensity of distractedness. The average office worker is stressed merely by the number of daily E-mails. The hungry consumer mentality contributes added stress on mind and body. Information technology has perhaps even developed a new level of human consciousness, the collective media-consciousness. This has potential for unifying humanity but as great a danger of reducing the individual mind to a clone in the mass-mind. Advertising, gossip, information, news, chat, erotica, entertainment, stimulate minds from Hyderabad to Harwich with the same material. Cyberspace saturates us daily and we cry for more. One of the fruits of meditation is the gift of discernment: about what the media is doing and saying to us, about when to switch off the screen. By creating the space of solitude through daily practice meditation protects the dignity of individual privacy. As a result of this it also develops the social values of personal liberty and responsible participation in society's decision-making. The passivity and fatalism that media-saturation can create is challenged by meditation, if only because people of wisdom are less easily misled.

We meditate in this world. Our decision to meditate represents a commitment to participate responsibly even in a world going mad. It trains discernment and limits intolerance. It teaches faithfulness to the community of the true Self thus protecting human dignity. Each time we sit to meditate we carry our own and the world's baggage into the work of attention. It is a way of loving the world we are part of and contributing to its well-being. Precisely because it is a way of letting go of ourselves meditation helps us to share the burden of humanity.

A capacity for wonder and a love of wisdom returns with contemplative practice. Imperceptibly, over the years, exposure to the media can erode our capacity for direct experience. Increasingly we experience events and emotions secondhand, through the views of others or the cult of celebrity. This alienation from personal experience can turn our gift for empathy into apathy. We are rendered too unreal to serve others. Yet the media can also make us aware of the need for peace of mind. Distraction, alienation, frustration can stimulate us to undertake the contemplative journey. 'Where sin is, grace abounds all the more,' according to St Paul. Noise awakens the thirst for silence and this thirst is the global spirituality of our time.

So, turning off phones, television, radio, computer and stereo we sit in silence and stillness to meditate. We take time to sit well, back straight, alert and relaxed. Breathing regularly. The door is closed. The kids are being looked after. The files on our desk can wait. We have a precious half hour *to be*. We have entered into our inner room. What happens next?

All hell breaks loose. The programming continues. Shreds of advertising jingles, subconsciously implanted images, fear-producing news stories, fantasies and nightmares all jumble around in the mind when we sit to meditate. In addition to what the media has delivered there are the zillion daily errands and transient problems of our personal lives. You sit to meditate and begin saying the mantra, then immediately you remember you should have taken the car to the garage—*is my next appointment at three or four?—should I do the washing today or tomorrow—wasn't that dinner guest's dress a beautiful colour last night? Hang on, I should be saying the mantra. Am I saying it properly? Is this really getting me anywhere? I wonder if you know when enlightenment happens. Is God really in this? Am I wasting time. Is there a better way of doing it? I must decide whether to take the morning or evening flight from Boston. Where's the mantra gone now? Come on, back to it. How much longer is this going to last? Did I set the alarm properly? I'll take a quick look. A cup of coffee would be nice, if I've got time. This will be better when I make a retreat. It will be lovely to be just quiet and away. Then I'll be able to meditate. Should I go for the full week I have off or keep a few days free for a holiday as well? What would John Main advise? Or the Gita? The* Bhagavad-Gita *is wonderful. Mortality is a great teacher. Say your mantra. You're wasting precious time. Why does my side hurt after meals? My father died of cancer. I am going to start a low-fat diet next week. There are special products now at the supermarket for that. Did I get the new supermarket credit card? There are so many things to remember. Jesus said one thing is necessary. I wonder what it is? The alarm will go off any second now. Let's say the mantra from now till then...Oh I forgot the...*

◦◦◦◦◦

In the Sermon on the Mount Jesus identified material concerns as our main source of anxiety. How can we make ourselves more comfortable and reduce personal suffering? This is the major preoccupation which obscures the present moment and disrupts true priorities.

> Therefore I bid you put away anxious thoughts about food and drink to keep you alive, and clothes to cover your body. Surely life is more than food, the body more than clothes.[9]

When he tells us not to worry Jesus is not denying the reality of daily problems. It is anxiety he is telling us to abandon, not reality. Learning not to worry is hard work. His teaching is that consciousness is more than the thoughts or feelings that occupy its concerns for the body. It is also soul and spirit. And so, despite its 'attention-deficiency disorder', even the modern mind has also its natural capacity to be still and to transcend its fixations. In depth it discovers its own clarity where it is at peace, free from anxiety. Most of us have half-a-dozen or so favourite anxieties, like bitter sweets we suck on endlessly. We would be frightened to be deprived of them. Jesus challenges us to go beyond the fear of letting go of anxiety, the fear we have of peace itself. The practice of meditation is a way of applying his teaching on prayer; it proves through experience that the human mind can indeed choose not to worry.

This is not to say we can easily blank the mind and dispel all thoughts at will. In meditation we remain distracted and yet are free from distraction. This is because—however minimally at first—we are free to choose where to place our attention. Gradually the discipline of daily practice strengthens this freedom. It would be childish to imagine that this is fully realised in a short time. We stay distracted for a long time. We soon get used to distractions as traveling companions on the path of meditation. But they do not have to dominate. Choosing to say the mantra faithfully and to keep returning to it whenever distractions intervene exercises the freedom we have to *pay attention*. It is not a choice in the sense in which we choose a particular

[9] Mt 6:25.

brand off the supermarket shelf. It is the choice to commit. The way of the mantra is an act of faith not a movement of the ego's power. Within every act of faith there is a declaration of love. Faith prepares the ground for the seed of the mantra to germinate in love. We do not create the miracle of life and growth by ourselves but we are responsible for its unfolding. Coming to peace of mind and heart—to silence, stillness and simplicity—requires not the will of a type-A high-achiever but the unconditional, sustained attention and fidelity of a disciple. It means learning to *wait* in hope, with heightened and certain expectancy but without demands and expectations:

> Hold yourselves ready then because the Son of Man will come at the time you least expect him.[10]

Perseverance in stillness is the dynamic of prayer. The teaching of Jesus on prayer is proven through our own experience. It becomes pertinent to us personally as soon as we begin to meditate and try to persevere. When we face the surface distractions and anxieties, the spirit of discipleship begins to mature. By this work of attention self-knowledge grows and we are already responding to the seminal question about who he—and we truly are.

Until you meditate, meditation may seem a mind-game, abstract and cerebral. Once experienced it shows itself to be the most incarnate and holistic path of prayer. Its effects are felt in the whole person as the words of the gospel take flesh in daily life. The teaching of Jesus permeates everything. What happens in and to us, our own experience, becomes the medium of seeing and recognising him. As John Main said, meditation *verifies* the truths of faith.

Meditation is a journey of awakening. Practiced in faith, we see that it is the journey hidden within the visible journey of life. To meditate is simply human. To meditate as a Christian is to see that by descending into the centre of our being we discover, in relationship and in the communion of the Spirit, who Jesus is.

What more can we say about the route taken by this journey beyond words?

[10] Lk 12:40.

❧ 11 ❧

The Labyrinth

My cottage was deliciously but painfully simple. When I first arrived from London looking forward to the simple life my initial reaction on entering the cottage was a mixture of fear and panic. It was simply too simple. Panic swept through me as I viewed the single cold water tap, the rusty gas cylinder stove, the bare light bulbs, the absence of sanitary plumbing without which civilisation is inconceivable to most of us. Everything was clean and what was there worked but there was so little and it was so unadorned. A discreet corner behind a wall in the field became my bathroom however and the cold water could be boiled for washing as well as cooking, the bed was warm once you were in it clutching the hot water bottle, the peat fire made the house a home, routines set in immediately. Like everyone else, I adapted surprisingly quickly.

The simplicity of the house then insisted on a simplification of mind and feeling. What I read and wrote and thought during those visits were continuously measured by the physical simplicity I inhabited. Returning to the city demanded an increasingly more difficult re-adaptation; more challenging than simplicity was having to accommodate to speed, consumerism and complexity again. I noticed, as I had once after spending a month in Africa, how many foolish obstacles to peace we construct and worship for the sake of comfort and conformity.

The simplicity of my hermitage, however, soon felt insufficient. An unexpected taste developed, a thirst for an absolute reduction to bare essentials, total and unconditional simplicity. Even if it seemed beyond my capacity, the mere thought of it was exhilarating, suspiciously like the very desire it sought to transcend. I could have gone all the way—naked, sleeping under the hedgerows and living off berries—and really worried my cousins about my sanity. But however solitary, I was not isolated; the island community taught me common sense and moderation. Once free from the labyrinth of urban complexity the important work unfolded on an interior plane. In fact there was even a point, I saw, where simplification needed to stop before it became fanatical. I had to remember that creation is good and like everyone else I was meant to enjoy the simple pleasures of life not to anticipate my extinction.

At that point what I needed was not more physical deprivation but the steadiness to confront the complexity of my desires, fears, memories and plans.

And to learn to be simple, where and how I was. This seemed the real meaning of simplicity: in the mind and not only in material things. Once glimpsed, this goal of purifying the heart informs and prioritises everything in life—freshly and disturbingly. Entering any labyrinth is exciting and frightening. All one needs is a place to belong, a path to follow and a few friends to keep you sane.

⋰⊙⋰⊙⋰⊙⋱

The gospels show that Jesus did not select his disciples because they were virtuous or wise. They are often seen squabbling over rank and status, misinterpreting what he said and misunderstanding who he was. Peter the 'rock' and prince of the apostles denied him. Judas betrayed him. All scattered when he was arrested. Initially most failed or refused to believe his resurrection. Jesus *chose* his disciples, they did not choose him, for reasons best known to himself; and he accepted them as they were. Discipleship is pragmatic as well as idealistic. In the same way we start meditating as we are. However great and inspirational the theory, faithful practice grounds us in humility. Both in meditation and discipleship the key to wisdom is the awareness not of choosing but of being chosen, not of proud achievement but fidelity.

Within a few seconds of starting each meditation the mantra slips away as we are carried off on a new wave of thought or feeling. At this first, highly distracted level of consciousness we are introduced to the central purpose of meditation: to unhook from thinking and to rest in the present moment, where we already are.

For many people this seems just too simple. For religious people as well meditation can seem totally bizarre, 'not like prayer at all'. How can it be prayer if you are not thinking about God? They wonder where is faith in this void of silence and stillness? We have positively to *want* to learn that the basic aim of prayer is to move away from *thinking* about God or *imagining* anything. 'If you can understand it," said St Augustine, 'it isn't God.' The overly cerebral Western meditator will at first have to take it on trust that while thought and imagination are natural and continuous activities of the mind there is a still-deeper mind that rests in wakeful stillness. Meditation teaches us to accept that underlying all mental activity is consciousness itself. The invitation inherent in human existence is to go deeper than all levels of the mind into the pure *consciousness* which pervades all reality and which is called *spirit*. With regular practice meditation gradually calms the hyperactivity of mental processes. A path is cleared into the silence

that is the Spirit's self-communication, the crystal clarity of wakeful
love at the deepest level of consciousness.

The deeper we go the clearer is the stillness we find. The stillness
is the present moment, which is the only moment where knowing God
is possible. God in the biblical revelation says simply 'I AM'. This is
why Thomas Aquinas said, we can accurately say only *that* God is but
never *what* God is. The only moment when we can meet God is now,
the only place is here. Meditation is the process of coming home to
the here and now. As soon as we sit to meditate we discover how
little of us is actually here and now. Our own absent-mindedness explains our weak sense of God. But if God seems absent, distant or nonexistent it is actually because *we* are.

Feelings of guilt or discouragement at our degree of distraction are
irrelevant. Accepting the fact of distraction is simply a stage in self-
knowledge, self-acceptance and integration: the very process which
constitutes the spiritual path. In its early stages we call it repentance—
seeing and accepting ourselves as we are. This is by nature humbling
to our self-esteem. Meditation quickly brings us to humility. Again and
again we return to the mantra, learning as we do so the meaning of
humility and fidelity. Like the prodigal son, after frequent bouts of
self-indulgence, we 'come to our senses' not once but as many times
as necessary. We turn round again and return home. We also have to
deal with the condemnatory elder brother syndrome in our own psyche. Above all, like both sons, we have to learn who the *Father* really
is who welcomes us back so humbly and so often and calls us to join
the feast of life he has put on for us.

◦⊷◦⊷◦

Coming into the present moment means detaching ourselves from the
mental web of past and future that enmeshes us. It seems a tight web
while we are caught in it but as soon as we start saying the mantra
we realize how fragile it is. The distractions harassing us like a plague
of locusts, especially in the early stages of learning to meditate, arise
from the hundred thousand thoughts of past and future where our
sadnesses, guilts, fears and fantasies reside. Only stop thinking of the
past and future, only begin to let go the thoughts, and a 'peace beyond
understanding', which has always been present, emerges.

At the time of meditation all mental activity whether secular or
religious can be regarded as distraction. Literally, the word *distraction*
means to be drawn or dragged away from a true direction. Beset by

our involuntary thoughts, desires, fears, anxieties and fantasies, we lose the *traction* needed to keep us on the road. Sustaining a sense of direction requires constant alert attention. The mantra is the *tractor*, that which gives traction to the distracted. It ploughs the field in fertile lines, clearing hard ground and preparing it for the seed of the Word. During the meditation period itself, however, all spiritual insights should be generously ploughed into the field of silence along with every other thought or feeling. Christians sometimes fear this means they are blocking the Spirit. It is in fact embracing poverty of spirit, the first beatitude—the state in which we are most open to the Spirit.

Of course not all thoughts are of equal value. There is a difference between thinking of the Resurrection appearances of Jesus and planning how to get your revenge on an enemy at work. Some thoughts are better suited than others to prepare us to move beyond thought. But at the times of meditation, what *The Cloud of Unknowing* calls the time of 'the work', all thought, sacred and secular, sublime and ridiculous, is surrendered as grist for the mill of silence. Even every thought of God, which as Gregory of Nyssa said, tends to become an idol. No force or violence, however, should be used in letting go of the seemingly endless flood of distraction. Saying the mantra is an act of love, of non-violence. We are not even trying aggressively to suppress thought in order to concentrate on the mantra. But we are turning away from mere thought by paying attention to the mantra.

These are essential distinctions for the meditator to understand at an early stage. They help one to start the journey with a clear understanding of its goal-less purpose. Practicing nonviolence towards one's self in the discipline of the mantra illuminates the teaching of Jesus which applies in all human relationships.

> Do not set yourself against the person who wrongs you. If someone slaps you on the right cheek, turn and offer him your left. If someone wants to sue you for your shirt, let him have your coat as well.[1]

‹◦»◦«◦›

Detachment is another term for poverty of spirit. Meditation teaches us that this is an affirmative and liberating state even when it is most difficult. What do we find when we let go?

[1] Mt 5:39-41.

At Christmas the giving and receiving of presents is a joyful ritual. Within a short time the gifts, or most of them, have lost their gift-edness and become possessions which clutter up our homes and lives. This is when the letting go of what we have received must begin. Poverty of spirit is such a key virtue in the teaching of Jesus for this reason. It connects our personal spiritual practice with the great truth of the Kingdom. Jesus shows us that the Kingdom belongs to those who *possess* nothing. We should not miss the humour in that teaching. It does not mean we are trying to possess a thing called 'nothing'. St John of the Cross expressed it when he said the only thing we possess is what we do not possess.

Letting go *is* the practice of meditation; it is simple but not easy. When we do manage it, however, and our desires, fears, anxieties and fantasies subside, the Kingdom *happens* naturally and without effort. For John Main it is as natural as the opening of a flower. But how difficult and frustrating it is when we try to make a flower open or a kettle boil faster. We are like young children impatient to be older and bigger or old people desperately trying to be younger and less wrinkled.

We are not talking here about destroying the distractions, simply about letting them go. So a familiar fear or anxiety may remain in the field of consciousness but it has been temporarily shelved, asked to wait outside while a more important meeting takes place. In this way we reclaim the power we have unconsciously given to these mental patterns and as we become more empowered with that alienated con-sciousness we experience a growth in freedom and well-being. The letting go may be for brief moments only. Then the thought returns, slips back into the room and starts to pester us again. At worst we lose our freedom entirely and become dominated again by the old fixated pattern of thought.

In the brief freedom of poverty, however, we have tasted peace. If we try to capture that taste, to preserve it for later use, we are at-tempting to turn gift into possession. Even to think about it concep-tually is to try to possess it and this drives it away. Yet the *taste* of reality, very different from the *thought* of it, changes us. Liberty, joy, peace are aspects of the same reality but each has its particular flavour. We do not forget a taste even if at first it seems strange and we have to acquire a more refined appreciation of it. Slowly it dawns on us that this brief glimpse is a peek into our essential and true nature. Our normal and natural state is to be filled with thankful wonder for the gift of being, not the fear and desire associated with trying to possess and manipulate it. How can we face this subtle reality? *The Cloud* reminds us that God can be known by love but not by thought. When we arrive at the threshold of contemplation, therefore, we learn not to think about what we see but to love it. We love it when we experience that it is loving us.

The work of poverty is endless. Contemplation is more than an experience in life: it is a way of life. Progressively we learn to do the work better, with more patience and gentleness. We learn to meditate for the right reasons. Above all, we learn to *do* it and that we are fooling ourselves if we prefer to think about it rather than do it. If such a simple thing seems so difficult to learn it is only because the mind is so strongly attached to its patterns of desire, fear, fantasy and anxiety. These are the mind's possessions and to renounce all possessions, as the rich young man who met Jesus discovered, is a big demand. We fear possessing nothing because we fear having nothing: nothing to think about, nothing to desire, nothing to love, nothing to do. Is not this the worst state of depression and lifelessness? What would happen, we ask on the threshold of poverty of spirit, if we were stuck here in poverty forever? Would my mind survive? Who would I be afterwards?

The poverty of meditation makes us aware of how much the ego fears God, the one reality we need have no fear of. God is love and, as St John tells us, perfect love casts out all fear. By returning to the same threshold over and over again in the daily practice of meditation we learn to allow this love to exorcise fear and to educate us about the real meaning of union with God. The poverty of the mantra teaches us that in this nothingness is everything we want. In this nowhere we are in the centre of reality and so we are everywhere. Poverty exposes the central paradox of the spiritual journey and the mantra grounds this paradox in personal experience. The mantra itself participates in this paradox because it is by hanging on to the mantra that we let go, and by making it our only possession we become wholly poor. All that it needs is fidelity.

◦⟡◦⟡◦

Because fidelity is always demanding we will frequently feel we have failed. At their first encounter with the frenetic activity that is our usual mental state—like a tree full of chattering monkeys—many people become so discouraged that they decide meditation is not for them and give up. They imagine they are the only ones who are so distracted and that everyone else has achieved perfect attention and profound peace. Their distractedness reinforces their habitual, depressing sense of inadequacy. It is just one more thing they have failed at. Perhaps they give up for a day, a week or for years. Everyone has the right to give up. But it would be a pity to give up too soon or for the wrong reason. Furthermore, counterbalancing the right to give up there is the duty inherent in human nature to keep on the pilgrimage towards the centre and ground of our being. It is a duty that cannot be lightly shirked.

Failure and success are in fact equally egotistical notions. They conflict with meditation which is an ego-transcending discipline. But they are also unavoidable. At times we will feel total failures. At other times (and far more dangerously) we may feel we have succeeded. These feelings must be seen for what they are: judgements by the ego about what the ego is not qualified to judge; measurements of something that cannot be measured. Jesus' injunction not to judge so that we will not be judged has relevance here too.

The feeling of failure is inherent in the ego's clinging sense of individuality. To feel *separately other* bears an existential sense of shame that is painfully connected to loneliness. Meditation confronts the pain of separateness and leads us through it. Once we know that we can deal with it, the feeling of sinfulness and failure is robbed of its power to block the manifestation of the Kingdom. As a result we experience the growth of happiness and authentic self-confidence.

If, during the first experiences of meditation, there was a taste, however fleeting, of stillness, if there was a single insight-experience of the present moment, and if true silence was known for a timeless instant in the still point between two waves of thought, that experience of grace can open a way which we can follow for many years without childishly demanding any rewards. Once seen, it is never forgotten. Once it is awake, the heart never sleeps again.

◦◦◦◦

Cassian compares the first level of consciousness to the fickleness of a feather blown every which way by every breeze of thought. Indian tradition calls this ever-busy operational mind *manas*. We will still be far from restoring it to full harmony when the focus of consciousness begins to move deeper, to the next level.

This is the world of stored memory (which Freud called the unconscious and which covers some of the meaning of the Sanskrit *citta*).

Literally everything that has ever happened to us and which makes up our uniqueness is filed here. The filing system of experience does not follow rational mental logic but has its own rules often governed by symbol and myth. All that we have ever thought, imagined, dreamed and done or left undone, with all the attendant motives and unconscious drives, has its proper place somewhere in this universe of individual memory.

The second level of consciousness, then, is not restricted to cerebral consciousness. As meditation begins its work on this level we realize, better than on the surface of consciousness, how thoroughly interwoven body and mind actually are. Memory does not live only in the chemical transactions of the brain's neurons, but in the joints, muscles and marrow of the body. How we sit at meditation is not a trivial consideration therefore. Posture reveals mental attitude and also corrects mental habits. It is important to prepare physically for meditation because the whole person we are is involved in the work and affected by it.

As happens in all relationships, meditation initiates a new understanding of time. A sustained friendship over many years possesses a quality of awareness that the short-lived relationship, however intense, must lack and aspires to. Musicians speak in the same way of a dimension of relationship which only time bestows on works they play throughout their lives. It is a feeling of familiarity and interwoven identity, or connaturality, continuously pierced by wonder at the newness of what is loved. So, too, the daily periods of meditation that may appear from the outside to be mere repetition actually unveil over time the reality of a relationship between self and others that stretches forwards and backwards in time.

Patience brings us to the stillness of the present moment. With time the poverty of the mantra takes the meditator deeper into our relationship with *all*, into universal love. Over time it sinks from the surface mind into the deeper heart-consciousness. Poverty of spirit never loses its freshness. Letting-go is a continuous practice. But it becomes a familiar presence and so awakens a quality of prayerfulness which colours all the experiences of life day after day.

Rooting the mantra in the heart also takes time. First, the mantra is *said* 'in the head', with many interruptions and distractions. It moves imperceptibly from the head to the boundless space of the heart where it is *sounded*, with deeper attention and less and less effort. As it becomes deeply rooted in the heart you come to *listen* to it. You know that it is there at all times whatever the emotional or intellectual activity on the other levels of consciousness. In the supermarket line or in the middle of a tense interview the mantra reminds you that you are in the present moment simply as you are.

It takes time to enter the present moment and to remain there. As T.S. Eliot said, only through time is time conquered. John Main described the way we say the mantra over time:

> We usually begin by saying the mantra, that is it seems as though we are speaking it with our mind silently, somewhere in our head. But as we make progress the mantra becomes more familiar, less of a stranger, less of an intruder in our consciousness. We find that less effort is required to persevere in saying it throughout the time of our meditation. Then it seems that we are not so much speaking it in our minds as sounding it in our heart, and this is the stage that we describe as the mantra becoming rooted in our hearts . . . When he described this stage of meditation, my teacher used to say that from this moment on it is as though the mantra is sounding in the valley below us while we are toiling up the side of a mountain. Meditation is in essence the art of concentration precisely because, the higher we toil up the mountain side, the fainter becomes the mantra sounding in the valley below us, and so the more attentively and seriously we have to listen to it. There then comes the day when we enter that 'cloud of unknowing' in which there is silence, absolute silence, and we can no longer hear the mantra.[2]

As the relationship in meditation grows we become more conscious of the different time-zones that human consciousness inhabits simultaneously. Not surprisingly, for this reason, patience and emotional stability are fruits of meditation. This grows without the loss of emotional intensity, concern for others or the childlike curiosity at the wonder of existence which makes life worth living. We learn from this that there is chronological time, the timer timing the thirty minutes of meditation morning and evening; the time needed to get through today's to-do list. There is also bodily time that controls the daily and longer-term cycles of somatic consciousness: our cycles of sexuality, digestion and excretion, menstruation and aging. And there is psychological time: the time it takes to remember, process and integrate all that we have done and had done to us. Also, if it means anything to

[2] John Main, *Word into Silence*, pp. 54-55.

call it this, there is spiritual time: the ever-present which is usually forgotten and can never be remembered.

◦•◦•◦•

In the world of the psyche what we think the past has done to us and what we project on to others has as much reality as what we have actually done or suffered. Discrimination in assessing our world and the path we are on is all-important and extremely difficult without the practice of letting go of our judgements and opinions. The psyche is a world where, if we are not to remain trapped in the pain of the past, judgement must continually give way to the knowing that comes as pure gift in insight. In meditation we see how the past can be judged rightly only if it is let go. So we choose not to judge, remember, relive or rewrite history in meditation. If we cling to the past until every detail has been examined and all the evidence heard we get stuck in endless court proceedings. Insight brings the power of for giveness. Forgiveness—rather than judgement, revenge or punishment— is what heals and transforms the turbulent and hurting memories of the unconscious.

Unhealed and unchecked, this deep unconscious level of the mind where experience is stored in memory can become a major obstacle to growth. It can destroy personal liberty more drastically than the worst kinds of external repression. As it is aroused, unloaded and eventually integrated, the long-forgotten or repressed suffering in the unconscious psyche can be hard to bear and frightening to face. We may prefer anything, even being imprisoned in pain and compulsion, rather than face these powerful hidden forces. Once accepted, however, they can no longer control us from behind their hidden depths and we are freed to fully participate in life.

Western psychology and Eastern mysticism share many crucial insights into the dynamics, blissful and agonising, of this level of mind. Like its counterparts in the Western contemplative traditions Asian wisdom takes seriously the imprinted effects (*vasanas*) of past action which become the set-patterns of mind and personal character. The lives of our ancestors as well as our own experience shape our personality. Countless *vasanas* caused by past *karma*—whatever has been thought, said and done—reside in the mind. The waves of thought and action make patterns deep in the mind just as the waves of the sea seem to furrow the ridges on the ocean floor. Deeply etched as these impressions or *vasanas* may be in us, the spiritual wisdom of East and

West insists that they can be changed. All patterns, even the most deep-set, are impermanent. In time meditation transforms every pattern of our conditioning by restoring us to the freedom of our true nature. *Though your sins be as scarlet they shall become as white as snow.* However much life might wear us down one day we shall, as the Zen masters say, see the face we had before our parents were born.

The work of silence in a regular practice of meditation transforms this second level of body-mind consciousness. Analysis is not its way of doing this nor can it be reduced to a technique of self-therapy. The interaction of grace and human frailty is too evident for that. Normally, most of the conflicts and blocks, the fears and rages of the unconscious resolve without our being fully aware of what is happening. In pain or relief, we may feel, without fully understanding how, that a profound healing is happening. Sometimes faded memories or long-forgotten feelings, an unexpected emotional surge linked to a relationship we thought long-buried, or apparently trivial incidents from the past may unexpectedly surface into consciousness. At times this may happen during the meditation period. For a while afterwards they may remain in the back of our mind during the day.

On the ship's bridge of consciousness, however, we are often only dimly aware of the work being done in the engine room of the unconscious psyche. Feelings of fear, anxiety, dullness, sadness, grief, unfulfilled longings and also of lightness, joy, skittishness, or the raw energy of libido may rise and fall in any sustained daily practice of meditation. No one experiences this with textbook predictability. Some are more self-analytical by temperament and others have already tried to unravel the mysteries of their unconscious through therapy. Maps can be drawn and the great teachers of West and East have given us many kinds. Teresa of Avila spoke of the mansions of the soul, St John of the Cross of the alternation of day and night, the Desert Fathers of the cycle of dryness and joy. The different levels of the psyche are graphically described in the Tibetan Book of the Dead as *bardo* realms. The dying person arrives at the third *bardo* realm where he encounters powerful, persuasive fantasies and many karmic images of fear and paranoia. Here the dying person is warned not to fear these mental emanations but to recognize them for what they are: forms of his own mind.

Jesus urges inner calm in facing the daily fears of life in which experiences of dying and rebirth are continuous. Indeed throughout the gospel story, from the Annunciation to the Ascension, fear is identified as the great obstacle to the Kingdom, the obverse of love, the enemy within:

Set your troubled hearts at rest and banish your fears.[3]

Whatever we face in this turbulent second level of consciousness, in the stored memory of our lives, there is nothing to fear—even nothingness.

◦◦◦◦◦◦

At the first level of consciousness the danger is that we become discouraged in the face of distraction and turn back. At the second level there is a more subtle danger. We will inevitably go through the *night of the senses* or the *dark night of the soul* described by the mystics as the process of purification which accompanies self-knowledge. These phases are far more disturbing than the mind's surface distractedness. But the danger to the spiritual journey that accompanies them is that we become entranced with ourselves. Like Narcissus looking into the mirror-pool we can collapse into the reflection of the ego and be drawn into self-pity or self-absorption. Infatuation with our own story at this level is an ever-present stumbling block in the path of integration. The ego defies the Self and tries to substitute for it. What is more fascinating than ourselves and the complex soap operas of our thoughts and feelings? What more appreciative and attentive an audience could there be than ourselves?

To avoid these pitfalls we need hope, faith and love. Jesus reassures his disciples that to ask is to receive, to seek is to find, to knock is to have the door opened.[4] Simple perseverance in the discipline of meditation leads to progress. Among other things we need in order to persevere is good company, the best antidote to narcissism. The fellowship of others who are making the same solitary journey as ourselves is a form of the Spirit's grace accompanying us on the pilgrimage. In solitude we need to be strengthened by the warmth and affirmation of a spiritual family. We need only remember not to confuse it with a blood family and not to project the problems we have had with our relatives onto our spiritual sisters and brothers.

Families remind us that no two people, however deeply united, are identical. Their personal experience will always be a commentary on

[3] Jn 14:27.
[4] Mt 7:7-8.

the other's. Precisely because two people are never at the same point in the journey, friendship, mutual inspiration and encouragement, are among the principal means by which the Spirit guides each one of us. Weekly meditation groups as well as the other forms of community which meditation creates and nurtures are essential in encouraging us to persevere when faith fails or anxiety strikes us down.

As on the first level on the spiral of consciousness the mantra, at this second level, is recited continuously whatever we may be feeling: 'in times of war and times of peace', as *The Cloud of Unknowing* puts it; 'in times of prosperity and adversity', as John Cassian puts it; 'from the beginning to the end of each meditation', as John Main said in his turn. With practice the mantra pushes its roots deeper into our being establishing harmony between the conscious and unconscious. Imperceptibly and gradually it sinks from the head to the heart. Over time we *say* the mantra, then *sound* it, then *listen* to it with less effort and more attention. Naturally, there are stormy days or dry periods of meditation when it seems next to impossible to say the mantra. We look for every justification not to sit and meditate. When we do, the mantra is immediately washed away by waves of thought and emotion. But if we do persevere or start again then, like the seed in the parable, which grows in the dark womb of the earth *(how we do not know*, Jesus said), the mantra faithfully guides us ever deeper. With depth comes clarity, stillness, self-knowledge, the great gift of compassion and the inner stillness needed for ever-more complete attention, more generous self-transcendence. The mantra imperceptibly progresses through the interspace of stillness, between the waves of thought and of the inner life.

> For the word of God is alive and active. It cuts more keenly than any two-edged sword, piercing as far as the place where life and spirit, joints and marrow divide. It sifts the purposes and thoughts of the heart. There is nothing in creation that can hide from him; everything lies naked and exposed to the eyes of the One to whom we must render account.[5]

For the Christian meditator the mantra is an icon of the living Word of God recited in a Christ-centred faith and in humanly devotion to Jesus the teacher. The journey to the place of meeting with him takes

[5] Heb 4:12-13.

time. There are several kinds of time. With time it brings us to the authentic poverty where we learn simply to be. Experiencing this lovely reality from time to time empowers us to endure many setbacks and disappointments along the way. There will be times of defeat and disappointment. But even when we seem to be regressing growth is happening if there is faith at work. In the darkest night an invisible light still shines. An attitude of nonpossessiveness and trust develops to replace greed and fear. With this comes a more and more unshakeable peace. Underlying all the turbulence peace flows from the knowledge that we are known and, once acknowledged, it becomes the condition of all further growth.

◦»◦»◦»

The work of psychological integration and so of self-knowledge continues to the end of our life.

I have roughly outlined the first two 'levels' of consciousness. First, the surface mind filled prominently with daily distraction. Second, the 'deeper' level of the unconscious. Naturally we should not assume these are merely sequential. One is not closed down when the other opens up. We are with them both for life. In varying degrees of intensity we can pass across them both in a single sitting. We move along their trajectories as if on a spiral, or walking a labyrinth, seemingly covering much of the same ground but with stronger awareness and less self-consciousness. Some reach the deeper levels sooner than others. Ultimately, because of the Spirit's guidance, the timing turns out to be perfect for everyone. But the surface monkey-mind will not quieten down totally before we have begun to move into the memory banks of our identity. Nor are all the accounts of these vaults balanced before we awaken to a third level of consciousness which *The Cloud of Unknowing* calls the 'naked awareness of our (ego) self'. India calls it the *ahamkara*, the 'one who drives the chariot', the 'I' that is not the Self. It is the ego's sense of individual existence whose meaning is not to develop an isolated existence but only to serve as a medium for the life of the Self.

Descent into this third level is a mixed bag of blessings. Gone is the burning feeling of 'hell' we had to work through at times on earlier levels. It gives way by degrees to a more hopeful sense of *purgatory*. Here we are purged, purified, straightened out and polished up. It is painful but it is different from hell's pains which at times felt eternal.

Now, even while suffering, we are conscious of growth. Julian of Norwich said we also know it is purgatory not hell because as time passes the pain gets less and heaven feels closer.

We sense as *The Cloud* says that here in the 'naked awareness' of our ego 'many of (our) past sins are, by grace, in the process of being rubbed away'. If sin means to miss the mark, the rubbing away of past sins improves future accuracy. We will still not always hit the mark. But we will see that we are aiming better and we will become more forgiving of our mistakes. *The Cloud* insists that meditation does not merely work on symptom-control but gets to the heart of the matter. It 'dries up' the actual root of sin even as it 'rubs away' the effects of earlier sin. Karma is being burned up and we are being freed from the compulsion to repeat patterns. At the third level of consciousness, then, we are not so much dealing with individual events, sins committed by or against us. We are confronting what the Christian tradition calls 'original sin', or our tendency, as the Buddhists would say, to 'afflictive emotions'. Yet as *The Cloud* says 'sinners make the best contemplatives'.

Our arrival on the third level means we become sharply aware of the ego-barrier. If this were the final stage of the journey we would be the unhappiest of creatures. The journey would have cheated us. Many people are in fact encouraged not to go beyond this barrier and conclude that it is the disappointing end of the road at least in this life. Sometimes they give up altogether or float back and settle where they have been earlier. Everyone hopes for a way around the wall of the naked ego rather than having to go through it. But the only way beyond it is the way through. If we do not sit and wait, the pain of separateness is prolonged and the opportunity of transcendence is missed.

The 'naked awareness of your own existence,'[6] as *The Cloud* calls it, reveals existential sorrow. It is not depression, guilt, grief or low spirits but something more ancestral, closer to the shame of Eden after the Fall. We are afflicted by a sense of personal need and incompleteness. This sorrow brings what the Desert Fathers called 'compunction of heart' (literally, the piercing or breaking of the heart). It is sometimes accompanied by what the desert monks called the 'gift of tears'. We weep when we are no longer in control and tears bring a feeling of

---

[6] *The Cloud of Unknowing and Other Works*, Ch. 43.

release and purging of the 'sorrow of existence'. Uncovering this deep, clinging sadness people will often painfully see the shadow cast by the ego across all their most precious and sacred relationships and ideals. They will ask themselves if they have ever really loved, if they have ever known transcendence, if even what they once thought their best deeds were really good. The ego's kingdom of separateness shows its resilience and defies even the most powerful of loves.

Painful as this feeling is it is pure grace. This stark sorrow is precisely what we should be seeking in meditation as the precondition for authentic joy. That is why the early monks prayed for compunction of heart and the gift of tears. *The Cloud* says that all will go well,

> if you can achieve this sorrow to this degree. Such sorrow cleanses the soul not only of sin but also of the suffering its sin has deserved. And it makes the soul ready to receive joy.[7]

Existential sorrow is not depression or anxiety although to a psychological eye alone it may seem to be. This is one of the areas where the distinction between therapist and spiritual teacher is all-important. It is a natural work in which human suffering becomes conscious of its meaning: like the friction of polishing, the labour of threshing, the patience of weeding. Karma is being destroyed by grace. Sin is being 'taken away' by this work. If Lucy in the "Peanuts" cartoon trying to understand her new philosophy can understand this she will know why *all will be well*. If karma can be eradicated and sin forgiven in this way, by the deepest sorrow, then all suffering has the potential of being redemptive, for oneself and others. The gates of hell are opened. A favourite theme of icon painters in the Eastern church and an article of the Creed is that Jesus 'descended into hell' after his death and released those imprisoned there.

This sorrow makes all the difference to how we respond to Jesus' question. The faith within the Christian community by which the question is listened to reminds us that there is nowhere we can go where we will not find he has been. Where he has been his presence always is. And so even in our deepest and darkest night of the soul, in the depth of hell, or in the shame of our ego's hurt pride and rejection of God, he is there knowing what we are suffering and extending compassion to us. Hope is not false consolation. *The Cloud* says

[7] Ibid.

that sorrow and separateness will eventually pass and then 'you ex-perience contemplation in its perfection'. We must pass through the sadness of existence before entering the joy of being.

⋅◦⋇◦⋇◦⋅

How do we do that? There are no techniques to transcend the brick wall of individual, separate identity. All we have are the disciplines of the spiritual journey: what the Buddha calls 'skillful means' and St Benedict the 'tools of the spiritual craft'. They are the qualities of fidelity and humility, perseverance and simplicity, which meditation both demands and develops.

Even when superficial or deeper distractions are calmed and we rest in meditation with little or no mental activity there still remains the root distraction of self-consciousness. As long as we can say or think to ourselves, 'I am silent,' clearly we are not. And until we are quite silent we have not arrived. Silence is the death of the separate-ness of the I-thought and its resurrection in the true Self of the Spirit.

If we are able to observe our states of prayer we are still thinking of our destination. We do not yet fully *know*, in a consciousness that absorbs and transcends what we think of as thought, that the Kingdom is within and we are already in the Kingdom. By the time we reach this naked awareness, however, the *faith* with which we have been saying the mantra is also coming to maturity. It has become an anti-dote to despair and depression. We know to keep listening to it as it sounds with ever-more subtlety in ever greater depths. We learn to live into deeper levels of being—both joy and suffering—without false con-solation. We transcend the ego's shallow judgement that suffering is something always to be avoided at any cost. We don't waste the op-portunities of growth even when they are painful.

> How we squander our hours of pain, how we gaze beyond them
> into the bitter duration to see if they have an end—tho' they are
> really seasons of us, our inborn landscapes.[8]

Now we are ready to face the great test. Are we prepared to practise detachment from what we instinctively know is our most precious possession, our separate identity? Relationship with the teacher at this point is of supreme importance. It allows us to risk our own death. By now the *discipline* of the mantra has led to the fortifying sense of

---

[8] R. M. Rilke, *Duino Elegies*, trans. Robert Hunter (Eugene: Hulogosi, 1993).

discipleship which empowers us to let ourselves go. We can leave self behind precisely because we know we are in union and that we are never alone. The words of Jesus become true in our own experience:

> So also none of you can be a disciple of mine without parting with all your possessions.[9]

If we are to embrace the eternity of the fullness of being (the 'I AM' of God), we must first face the stark reality of impermanence and emptiness. The temptation is always to reduce the intensity, to sink to a lesser degree of consciousness, even to fall asleep. The Buddha warned against clouding the mind at this or indeed any stage of the journey with intoxicants or sedatives, uppers or downers. Jesus urged everyone to stay fully conscious:

> Be alert, be wakeful. You do not know when the moment comes ... Keep awake then for you do not know when the master of the house is coming. Evening or midnight, cock-crow or early dawn—if he comes suddenly, he must—not find you asleep. And what I say to you, I say to everyone: Keep awake.[10]

> Keep a watch on yourselves; do not let your minds be dulled by dissipation and drunkenness and worldly cares so that the great Day closes upon you suddenly like a trap; for that day will come on all people, wherever they are, the whole world over. Be on the alert, praying at all times for the strength to pass safely through all these imminent troubles and to stand in the presence of the Son of Man.[11]

In the Letter to the Ephesians Paul says that this state of wakefulness leads to the 'spiritual powers of wisdom and vision' and on to *gnosis*, or spiritual knowledge. But even with the strongest faith, the sorrowful sense of separateness is not immediately dissipated even when wisdom begins to shine. The wall of the ego can feel like an insuperable obstacle, a dead end leaving us nowhere to run to. But, as the Resurrection reminds us, what seems and feels like the end is not. By facing our entrenched egoism and recognising its slow dying, meditation helps us to verify our own resurrection in our own experience.

The law of lower nature, of karma, and the domination of the limiting ego reign until...

[9] Lk 14:33.
[10] Mk 13:33-37.
[11] Lk 21:34-36.

...until a hole in the wall appears. First one brick is removed, as if by an unseen hand, and we glimpse a perspective beyond anything we had previously thought we were or were capable of knowing. It is an experience and yet it is known in a way unlike anything we have experienced before. We are no longer the merely individual person we thought we were. Life is changed irreversibly. We live and yet, like St Paul, we live no longer.

I am because I am not.

·◦·◦·◦·

'I' is always an individual. But the word 'individual' has totally changed its meaning in the last century. Originally it meant indivisible. *Individuus* was the translation of the Greek *atomos* which meant 'not cuttable, not divisible'. In medieval theology *individual* could even describe the indivisible unity of the Trinity. Husband and wife were also *individual* in this sense. Once an 'individual' was a person or thing seen in relation to the whole it belonged to. The whole defined the individual because the individual was indivisible from it. Until the eighteenth century the word was rarely used except in relation to the group of which it was part. Then by the mid-nineteenth century Darwin in *The Origin of Species* could use it in a quite different sense: 'no one supposes that all individuals of the same species are cast in the same actual mould'. Philosophy took this individualism further by seeing the individual as the 'substantial entity' from which the whole was derived. The tail had begun to wag the dog.

This somersault of meaning illustrates the huge shift in cultural understanding of personal identity (the 'self'). Much of our spiritual confusion arises from this. The *indivisible* part of a whole became no more than a separate part, merely a building block. Individualism and individuality became the modern attitudes towards the 'self', meaning now the autonomous, completely self-determining subject, not the person intrinsically united to God or the Whole. Differing approaches to individualism and individual rights continue to fuel the conflicts about what laws are just and how human rights relate to a citizen's duties. Notions of individual identity, 'what is a self?', may even underlie the turbulent and dangerous shift today from economic cooperation with our neighbours to the unbridled competitiveness of market forces. *Who I am* determines whether I exploit the environment for my individual benefit or steward it for humanity and the next generation with whom I am linked. The way we understand our selves and the Self explicates the unprecedented social shift from extended to single-parent families, from local and communal interdependence to the ideal of privacy and independence. The notorious claim of modern capitalism that 'society' does not exist threatens the weak and marginalised who cannot defend themselves, just as it enthrones the successful individual in a pleasure palace of consumption.[12]

The predominantly individualistic sense of selfhood affects models of spirituality as well. Prayer is seen as an individual attempt to relate to or control God. Contemplative experience is seen as merely 'personally fulfilling'. Spiritual individualism arrests the pilgrim soul at the ego stage of its personal development. Religious as well as legal, social, moral and economic values and practices all take a quite different direction when the individual ego is deceived by the illusion of self-sufficiency. It gallops on unchallenged by the liberating influence of discipline, moderation, self-restraint and personal sacrifice for the common good. Eventually spirituality itself is absorbed into the ego's 'programs for happiness' and can become just another consumer item advertising little effort and instant results.

Hyper-individualism is a modern, Western phenomenon spreading rapidly. Egoism in itself, however, is perennial and universal. Essentially it is the Fall of Man, the separation of the higher and lower levels of consciousness. The conclusion that we are essentially separate in our identity and in the pain of separation is ultimately a delusion. But, like the eating of the forbidden fruit, it is a 'happy fault'. Egoism is a stage in the way a human being emerges from total, unconscious absorption in the whole of which we are a part—but a whole, integral part. If we did not separate from the mother's womb with the painful cry of joy at birth we would not live. If we did not separate from parental love we could not make relationships of our own. If we did not learn to be detached from those we love we would smother them or be smothered. If we did not act maturely as members of the church or society we would not attain the dignity of a Christian or a free citizen. If we did not go through the phase of feeling separate from God we could never realise how indivisible from God we are.

Individuation is part of the process of our creation. We cannot learn to love or to be loved except as individuals. Yet love transforms individuality. That is love's terrible beauty and challenge. Especially when we are in love, we learn how we belong to a reality greater than

[12] Raymond Williams, *Keywords* (London: Fontana Paperbacks, 1983).

our separate selves. It is the alchemy of love to redefine our sense of who we are. The courage to love is to pay attention to the unique identity of the other, to let them be and to contemplate their existence as they do ours. So our individuality, cause of so much suffering, is also precious. It must be defended up to a certain point and only then surrendered. It has its social merits too. Without it a code of human rights could give little protection from tyranny, in the home, market place or court of law. Amnesty International highlights the plight of *individual* prisoners of conscience; it does not just discuss political theory. Jesus taught how the Good Shepherd puts the individual before the group, leaving the ninety-nine good sheep to look after themselves while he goes in search of the lost one. Most people learn most about love, and how to love, through one other person.

⋅◌⋅◌⋅◌⋅

Unless we pass through the shadow of the valley of separation we cannot rest in the green pastures of union. At some point in the journey the wall of individuality that seems to cut us off from the whole simply opens. The sorrow of existence that held it together dissolves and the wall collapses. At what point does this happen, we want to know. A mathematical point has position but no magnitude. In other words it happens but cannot be measured or located. It is the same with spiritual events. We know we are getting there as we see that we are asking 'How long now?', less often. Up against the wall of the ego we face several realities that arouse profound emotions: the present moment, death and the anxiety of living within fixed limits. When the wall opens all time is absorbed into the present moment, the eternal now of God's individual 'I AM.' Only God, as Simone Weil said, has the right to say 'I'.

(Was the wall ever really there at all?)

The opening of the wall allows the spiritual. Beyond the limitations of thought and psyche, beyond the temporal and spatial patterns of the levels of mind, there is the boundless liberty of spirit. Jesus told the Samaritan woman at Jacob's well that 'God is spirit'.[13] The Kingdom which Jesus taught and embodies in his relationship with us liberates us from individuality-as-separateness into individuality-as-indivisibility. In the Kingdom we pass from psychological isolation to

[13] Jn 4:24.

spiritual union. It is the end of individual history as we imagine it. The breaching of the wall of the ego is an eschatological moment, an end of time. But we experience it in time and therefore it changes the way we live in time. The sorrow inherent in knowing myself as being only and forever just *me* yields to welcoming a new identity gained in a sharing of being. On one side of the wall of the ego individuality means merely separateness. On the other side the meaning changes to union.

All relationships from the most intimate to the most impersonal are transformed by breaking through the wall of the ego. Listening to the question of Jesus throughout this transformation process will change the way we view the multiplicity of human relationships. Now they can be seen in a new light of a risen Self whom we meet at the frontier of our own identity. Here, through this aperture in our egoism, at this frontier of our identity where the question *Who am I?* becomes a pure experience of reality, we recognise the presence of the risen Jesus.

You are all one person in Christ Jesus.[14]

'He is the same yesterday, today and forever.' In relation to the journey of meditation this means that he is the same at all levels of consciousness: at the surface level of endless distraction, at the second level of stored memory and at the third level where we face the brick wall of our separated egoism. Our ability to see and recognize him is limited only by the level of consciousness where we are centred. But because he is, was and will be always the same his reality is not determined by our capacity to be conscious of him. He accompanies us whether we know him or not. The love St John speaks of is not our love for God but God's love for us. God is always the first to love.

Meeting Jesus in the Spirit, on the other side of the wall, does not mean that we did not also meet him at the earlier levels: even in the mind full of monkey-chatter, as we dashed from one thing to the next in stressful lives; or, in the solitary interior spaces of pain where hurt and shame struggle for resolution. And even as we sat before the wall of our naked egoism with all costumes abandoned, with nothing to cling to except the sorrow of individuality, he was present to us in our crucifixion as he was to us during his own.

[14] Gal 3:29.

The absence and presence of Jesus is the joyful mystery of Christian discipleship. Meditation teaches us how to see and live it at all levels of consciousness.

> In truth, in very truth, I tell you, I am the door of the sheepfold; anyone who comes into the fold through me shall be safe. He shall go in and come out and shall find pasturage.[15]

Here, at the *door* of the true Self, Jesus is known in the Resurrection. We primarily know him most intimately through the silent medium of the Spirit rather than through words, images, icons or even our deepest desire. Although the Spirit fills these as well. The light of divine consciousness that flashed into human nature in the Resurrection, transforming its nature backwards and forwards in time, has charged all forms of communication with power. The names by which Jesus describes himself are symbols of his meaning. They sacramentalise ordinary life. They are the forms of his epiphanies: Bread of life, Vine, Door of the Sheepfold, Good Shepherd, Way Truth and Life, Resurrection and Life, Light of the World—or simply Son of Man, a human being like us. Like Russian icons, incarnate forms of presence and prayer or like Mark Rothko's consciousness-flooding fields of colour the names which Jesus uses for himself help us to recognise him in ways that are at once intimate and universal.

◦⚬◦⚬◦

In front of this wall of egoism liberation dawns, salvation is realised. The question of Jesus is experienced and responded to most personally. Here also the Resurrection appearances in the Gospel can be wordlessly *read* in a way that prepares us to recognise him in our lives. This is where we understand that the purpose of revelation is not to explain or even to describe the mystery, but to liberate.

At what John Main called this 'frontier of our identity' we meet the guide who takes us over a crucial checkpoint in personal evolution. But this is not the end of the journey. In fact it is now only just beginning. It expands infinitely in the Spirit as it becomes a journey across the ocean of God. Touching the Ground of Being who is love, the journey unfolds with, in, but also *through* the person of Jesus. He can disappear at the moment we see him or think we have grasped

[15] Jn 10:7.

him; we go through him as well as with him because he has found the other, unlimited side of his own individuality. This is why we also call Jesus the *Christ*. He is Jesus, the historic individual and he is Christ the incarnation of the timeless archetype, the Son, the Logos, the Tao, the Dharma, the Atman who is Brahman. As Word, as Christ, as Way, as Wisdom, Jesus is to all people the truth (as they have discovered it) made flesh.

To know him we must know the truth of our selves. To know ourselves we must, as he showed us, die to egoism. Self-transcendence then leads to self-discovery in God. It is the Christian insight to understand the human journey to God as taking place through the Self (and selflessness) of Jesus in his fullness (and emptiness). Embracing this paradox allows us to see Jesus simultaneously as the Jewish teacher from Nazareth and as the Word: the Logos which, long before Bethlehem, Heraclitus said, 'pervades and governs all things'.

After this awakening has begun life goes on, apparently as before although everything is changed. Rather than being zapped out of our humdrum lives the surface and unconscious levels of mind are progressively harmonised and integrated. They function much as before, but better. We still peel vegetables and run to catch trains. But the ordinary mind now serves the goal of life differently. We no longer feel trapped in the routines of life and its unsatisfactoriness. Boredom gives way to wonder in the daily. There are no trivial pursuits. A Zen saying reminds us of this: Before enlightenment, chopping wood and drawing water; after enlightenment, chopping wood and drawing water. Before enlightenment, getting up, meditating, work, coming home, meditating, recreation, going to bed. After enlightenment . . .

Like St Paul we still carry a thorn in our flesh, sinful, accident-prone and incomplete. But we are now irreversibly conscious of the boundlessness of the Spirit. With the mind of Christ, we have seen through the hole in the wall and been there in the Spirit. Being boundless means that the Spirit makes every moment a new starting point and every event an arrival. The journey which continues because to seek is to find and to find is to seek. Now we can see that everything so far has been of spiritual significance. Its meaning is as part of the whole. Each time the process of self-integration makes us give a backward glance we see a new pattern. We review differently our sins and our tragedies. Compassion rather than regret or rebuke becomes the norm.

·◦»◦«◦·

Eventually, so the great pilgrims of the spirit assure us, all the bricks in the wall fall away and crumble. Transformation is gradual but every stage is irreversible. The hole which opens onto reality becomes the whole of reality. When reality is wholly open to us and we are wholly open to it where is the boundary? There is only the holy hole of wholeness!

Progressively the surface and psychological levels of consciousness are transformed in spirit. Gradually the fruits of the Spirit appear in every aspect of our personality. The individual ego—through which of course we continue to function in the world—becomes less inflamed, less itchy and neurotic, more fearless, more modest. It diminishes in hubris and self-protecting separateness. People surprise us when they say they think that we are becoming nicer and one day we will agree with them. The fruits of the spirit appearing in our human nature are both nice *and* good. They make life easier and they are qualities of the divine nature. Being divine each of these fruits of meditation affects the whole person, the whole picture of our lives. Our transformation is not less than *theosis*, divinisation:

> The harvest of the spirit is love, joy, peace, patience, kindness, goodness, fidelity, gentleness and self-control.[16]

Because we encounter the Risen Jesus in the Spirit, our individuality is lifted up by this meeting beyond its egotistical limits into union. Jesus does this work in us simply by being himself in relationship to us, individually and collectively. It is not in his nature to compel. The sheer power of his presence, the dynamism of his stillness, the meaningfulness of his silence, these are what bring us to the vision of God which is our common destiny.

> He will dwell with them and they shall be his people and God himself will be with them. He will wipe every tear from their eyes; there shall be an end to death and to mourning and crying and pain; for the old order has 'passed away. They shall see him face to face and bear his name on their foreheads. There shall be no more night, nor will they need the light of lamp or sun, for the Lord God will give them light.[17]

[16] Gal 5:5.
[17] Rev 21:3-4; 22:4-5.

❧ 12 ❧

Steps in Relationship

One soft day—a soft Irish day means one when it is drizzling rather than pouring—I ventured away from my peat fire into the fine mist outside. Following my nose, I found myself on the wild side of the island across the mushy bogs. The Atlantic was smashing itself against the rocks and cliffs, doing its work of erosion with infinite patience. The wind here on the exposed flank was wild and mighty. As I walked it was at my back, pushing me forwards and creating an unexpected silence in the midst of the storm. If it had come from another direction its force would have been dangerous, pushing me towards the edge of the cliff and its sheer enticing drop. Instead it pinned me closer to the side of the hill and the thin cut of the sheep track whose direction I was simply obeying. As if to show how indifferent nature is to the human notion of good or bad weather the sun on a whim decided to appear and suffuse the fury in the glorious gold of its light. Immediately the rising temperature raised my spirits and all the subtle colours of the cliff-face and the gorse returned, the soft pinks and purples and the ever-unclassifiable shades of Irish green for which there should be more words than the Eskimos have for snow. The curving path now directed me against the wind so that it blew hard into my face and body. Suddenly as I turned around a twist in the track I stopped a couple of feet away from a soundly sleeping young fox. Rust-coated, its white tipped tail curled contentedly around itself, it lay snuggled in its solitude in a sunbathed cleft of the cliff. The wind, betraying it, prevented my scent from alerting it to my presence.

I stood still, not knowing what to do, filled with a strange strong gratitude for this gift, wondering how long it would last. Time slowed and maybe even stopped for a moment. My silly thoughts shut up and for an instant or two the space in which I and this other creature, so beautiful in its unambiguous foxiness, were united was filled with a tenderness that embraced us both equally. Perhaps I was just beginning to sense that this tenderness, so precise and specific here and now, was not limited to this point and to these two creatures inhabiting the same creation. That without losing its omnipotent, heartbreaking intimacy, this same tenderness which filled this moment also touched the edges of our great home, the expanding universe. Might it be inviting even Mr Fox and me to gradually let go of what separated us, our clinging to ourselves, and become what

239

it is not just here but everywhere, not just now but always? Before this feeling could form as much as a thought Mr Fox opened his eyes and looked unblinkingly at me. Into me. I think that for an instant we may even have communicated.

These were brief, silent, immeasurable moments. I did not move. We simply looked without fear or desire at each other in the sun and unstopping wind. Maybe a flash of desire crossed my mind, the thought of touching, stroking, even possessing, and maybe this ended the perfect balance of our mutual contemplation. Maybe he forgot his trust and yielded to instinctual fear of a natural enemy. As if it were as perfectly alone as usual the fox calmly uncurled, got up and turned and trotted away without a backward look. It returned to the completeness it never left, to longings that could be fulfilled in the course of nature, to its work only of being itself. I, left behind, walked on feeling the comfortable disturbance of having seen the peace we seek so anxiously and can never cling to.

'Rabbuni, my master.'

'Do not cling to me.'

⋰⊙⋰⊙⋰⊙⋰

The question of who *we* say Jesus is has been the pole star of this book. Essential to our response to it is how well we know ourselves. There are of course many questions that Jesus raises for humanity. Questions concerning God, truth, life's meaning, peace, justice, compassion, forgiveness, religion, community, love. To those who want to listen, however, they are all constellated by his redemptive question as what leads us on the way of self-knowledge. It is self-knowledge that underpins the whole quest of this question.

Perhaps self-knowledge is the best way we have today to understand what 'salvation' means. Listening deeply to his question about who we say he is, we ask who we are. The truly redemptive question withdraws all projections and accepts full responsibility for the fact of the gift of our existence. Humility, the only wisdom, requires that we ask. When we ask we find, when we knock the door is opened. In finding the Self in ourselves we find ourselves in the Self. This is the freeing and enlightening *gnosi* of the gospel: liberation *from* the addiction of illusion and the fear of punishment; enlightenment *into* the love of the divinising light.

The question of Jesus is addressed to all, not just to baptised and practising Christians, because it is humbly posed by one of the human family's universal teachers, one of our great mutual friends. If in our madness for distraction and luxury we can afford no time to listen to it we have become dangerously mad. The churches that together make up the 'one true church' of Christianity which is his mystical body must constantly remember and teach the redemptive question. They must always learn how to teach what listening to it means. Christianity's work for humanity and for Christ is to reveal the power of the question which Jesus himself is to humanity. Its work is not to condemn, convert or debate, but to teach the value of simply listening to the master's question in prayer deeper than thought.

It is urgently important today for Westerners to learn to listen. Jesus so pervades the Western mind and culture that to ignore what he can teach us about listening creates a massive obstacle to self-knowledge. To ignore Jesus because of the imperfections of the churches is a foolishness of tragic dimension. Hence the Dalai Lama's and other Eastern teachers' advice to Westerners not to abandon their own religion. Jesus cannot be erased or post-modernised from the Western mind. His place in the human journey towards God cannot be superimposed by an image of Buddha or Krishna or any composite archetype or divinity. Christianity in the coming millennium, on the other hand, must be transformed. It will be very different from the Euro-American imperialist Christianity of the last millennium. By accepting the best of modern pluralism and questioning the worst of mere relativism and syncretism, Christianity will define itself both more specifically and more universally as its idea of sanctity, the goal of life, is expanded beyond the limits of a God who has favourite children. Listening to the question of Jesus does not necessarily lead to one's becoming a churchgoer but it broadens the idea of what the church is. Buddhists, Jews, Sikhs, Hindus, Jains, Muslims and all others need to listen to the question posed them by a teacher of such rare stature. Just as Christians need to listen to the questions the eternal Word raises through other religions. Listening requires the art of silence learned in meditation. But to listen with this attitude to the specific question that defines Christianity is to arrive at a new picture of what it means to be a disciple of Jesus, a Christian.

In this book I have said, and it is something which guides me daily, that one's personal spiritual journey needs a passionate love of the tradition. We also need to feel we are a contributing part of the evolving tradition as well as a recipient of what others have discovered and communicated. As in all relationship the giving and receiving must be balanced. His question, at the centre of gravity of the gospel and of his relationship to humanity, is the balancing force. As with any human relationship, there are stages, milestones in our response to his

question. Who *we* say he is will change over the lifetime of our relationship with him and the tradition that bears his name. Every person's
relationship, like the journey of faith, is unique. But there are also
universal patterns of growth that each person, in their uniqueness,
must recognise.

⊸⊙⊸⊙⊸⊙⊷

The first stage of relationship with Jesus is to meet him at the level
of our common humanity—simply, say, as a fellow meditator. By meditation here I mean not just the work of pure prayer but the whole
life-field of self-knowledge which it drives. Like any other normal
human being Jesus grew in this field of self-awareness. The gospel tells
us that 'the child grew big and strong...and as Jesus grew up he
advanced in wisdom and in favour with God and men'.[1] The first
Christian thinkers strongly asserted that Jesus was really and fully
human. His 'divinity' did not reduce the fullness of his humanity. Even
his being 'like us in all things except sin' does not imply that he was
more than human. Being without sin is another way of saying 'fully
human' because sin is what diminishes our human potential. His humanity shows us what we are capable of, what we essentially are.

Jesus had an ego. So it is not that the ego in itself is sinful. It is
egotism, fixation in the ego, that leads to the forgetting and betrayal
of our true Selves. Sin happens whenever the ego is mistaken for the
true Self. The temptation of Jesus in the wilderness, like his anguish
on the eve of his death, shows how like all human beings his ego
made him suffer. However he also demonstrates the human capacity
to live in a healthy balance between the ego and the Self, and not just
intermittently but continuously. Jesus was not superhuman but he did
not think or act as if his ego was his true Self. It was his individual
identity that permitted him to make friendships, to love his friends,
to express compassion for the forgotten and the suffering, to speak
out his anger against the unjust and the hypocritical. There is no fuller
expression of what it means to be human than the humanity of Jesus.
When egotism makes us believe that the only purpose of life is to seek
happiness and avoid pain, the Jesus of the gospels exposes the fallacy.
His compassion for others, even in the midst of his own suffering,
teaches that our pursuit of happiness is doomed unless we are primarily concerned about the well-being of others.

[1] Lk 2:40, 52.

St Luke tells us that as a child Jesus grew in wisdom and in depth of relationship with God and others. This points to how self-knowledge determines the quality of all relationship. The greatest gift we can make to others is this treasure of self-knowledge: not *what* we know about ourselves but *how* and *that* we know ourselves. The giving of self-knowledge is the highest of human achievements, the essential art of being human. No love is greater, or more costly, than the gift of our self-knowledge to another. It is what is meant by 'laying down your life for your friends'. The gospel of John, which gives both the most cosmic and most human of all the portraits of Jesus, revolves around this truth. It shows how the gift of his self-knowledge to his friends was the foundational step in his universal relationship with humanity through the Holy Spirit. The Spirit was needed to make this individuality universal. His self-knowledge did not flow from self-centredness, self-analysis and self-obsession: these are states of mind that preclude the self-transcendence that generates self-knowledge. It flowed from other-centredness, the noble and humble grace where we know ourselves by losing and finding ourselves in others.

The scribes and Pharisees were amazed at the wisdom of 'this untrained man', the carpenter's son from Nazareth when he told them that,

> The teaching that I give is not my own; it is the teaching of the one who sent me . . . Anyone whose teaching is merely his own, aims at honour for himself. But if someone aims at the honour of the one who sent him, he is sincere, and there is nothing false in him.[2]

Apart from the temptation in the desert or his agony in Gethsemane the gospels tell us little about the ways by which Jesus came to his physical and psychological maturity. Yet, despite this lack of bio-psychological information, it is hard when we read the gospels not to feel we are encountering a human being who knew fully what his humanity meant. He was human enough to weep at the death of a friend and to enjoy the company of particular friends, to need at times to be alone or with one or two close confidants, to get angry with hypocrisy and injustice and to be joyful at mealtimes, to fear death and to be concerned about who would care for his mother after his death. Yet every reading of the gospel strengthens the

[2] Jn 7:16, 18.

impression that he was fully human because his self-knowledge derived from consciousness of union with his Father. From this transcendent centre of self-awareness he knew himself in a way that was
historically unprecedented. His experience, furthermore, while personal and unique, was not private or exclusive. It was not just for
himself because it changed the quality of human consciousness universally. The way we know who we are in relationship to God and
each other is radically altered by the consciousness of Jesus. As the
Word made flesh his self-knowledge permeates every awakening of
consciousness.

To talk of 'meeting Jesus' may sound like a typical syllogism of religious language which makes people today so suspicious of religion.
Are we actually meeting Jesus or a figment of our imagination? Are
we only conversing with a subtle emanation of our own mind?
Shouldn't we, like the Buddhists, use the emanation but not get
drawn into taking it for real? How can you meet the dead? Does not
the Resurrection describe, not the literal return from the dead of one
person, but the universal experience of life renewing itself and light
emerging unvanquished and transformed from the darkest places of
human experience? These are not bad ways of understanding the gospels. For many they are adequate. But they do not represent the complete and embarrassing challenge of the Christian reading.

Every Christian also needs to ask these questions. Daily. However,
the logic pertaining to faith *is* in a sense circular: its starting point
and ending point are the same. We would not seek the goal unless we
had been impelled to seek it by having met it. To seek is to find, to
find is to seek. All forms of love teach this by the mystery of personal
identity they reveal. We love because we love. To love Jesus is to
believe in him, as St Augustine said. The difference between the beginning and the end of the journey is simply that we are fully conscious at the end.

In all relationship growth happens through the creative repetition
of a single but many-levelled act of faith. Reading and rereading the
gospels is one of the ways to nurture the relationship with Jesus.
Meditating deepens this faith and improves the quality of our spiritual
lectio. They are both faith-filled ways of listening to his question. The
basis of all relationship is faith and fidelity requires the applied self-
knowledge of those in the relationship. The betrayal of friendship, the
breaking up of a marriage, the tragic and foolish mistakes we make in
pursuit of happiness at others' expense, occur when faith fails, when

self-knowledge has been too weak to sustain the life of the relation-ship, too self-centred for self-transcendence.

Anyone's relationship with Jesus is subject to all these human laws. Knowing who Jesus is is not a once-for-all answer to a question but grows as an ever-changing relationship. We know Jesus humanly in a way that demands fidelity both to him and to our own growth in self-knowledge. St Paul's understanding of the cosmic Christ being built up in his mystical body suggests that even Jesus risen is still growing. We become fully human and share in the fully divine through union with his humanity. In the Spirit, the nonduality of God, Jesus can at the human level share with us everything that he is. This sharing is deeper than the expressive power of any image or concept. Like any relationship it grows through giving and receiving. He gives, we take, we give, he takes: until eventually giver and receiver dance into an ecstacie in which we, I and Thou, are freed to be each other.

Mystical jargon? If so, let it be tested at the level of common experience undertaken with the openness of faith. *Humanly* we can relate to the sense of life as crisis which drove Jesus to his Cross. Life judges us moment by moment and calls for a final verdict: good or bad, worth it or not worth it. To be in relationship with Jesus, like being in love, keeps us constantly open to ultimate meaning. What he condemns is what belittles humanity—triviality, hypocrisy or hatred. His question maintains us in a constant state of change which prefers even suffering to complacency. No plateau of religious domesticity or compromise is available in a relationship with him. It offers peace but at a high cost. His disciples, he warns, will, like him, have nowhere to lay their heads. It will not be an easy life but a worthwhile one.

We also relate *humanly* to his perception that the mystery of life is moral not mechanistic. Forgiveness not punishment expresses in human terms the nature of the Godhead. To err is human, to forgive is divine. Jesus leads us to see that no law, scientific or religious, can explain or control life because love is the supreme law, the beginning, end and meaning of it all. *Humanly* he communicates to us how even within the limits of his humanity he enjoyed the vision of God. He knew what prayer really is. To learn to pray under his guidance is to share his experience. He offers, not imposes, a new *human* way of seeing ourselves and the world.

Jesus prayed as a Jew. He meditated as a human being. He knew the divine presence which is at the heart of prayer. He grew in self-knowledge, above all, through his prayer:

> During this time he went out one day into the hill-country to pray, and spent the night in prayer to God.[3]

His prayer, as a normal part of his daily routine, is an aspect of his humanity we can easily identify with. He not only suffered like us. He prayed like us. In contemporary films and novels, like *Jesus of Montreal* or *The Last Temptation of Christ* or *Jesus Christ Superstar*, Jesus is portrayed as a spiritual man, prayerful but subject to the normal limitations of humanity. A great cinematic portrait of Jesus, like Pasolini's *The Gospel according to St Matthew*, can further evoke the charism of his human greatness that is both approachable and touchable, not like that of the rich or famous. Because of his humanity, approachable *and* alight with divinity, he can open the minds of those who truly listen to him.

To be human means to belong: to a family, a culture, to other human beings. Despite his own specific culture and religion, however, Jesus' humanity also has a universal constituency. He has not been transferred like a football star from the Jewish to the Christian team. Without losing touch with his human origins he belongs to all humanity. People of any culture can feel he is one of them as well as a model of what humanity is called to be. Jung said this was because he embodied the archetype of the Self at least for the Western psyche. His life and teaching combine in one individual so many of the great myths of humanity: teacher, seeker, sacrificial hero, monk, priest, prophet and friend. Son of Man and Son of God.

By all races and creeds he is loved, even worshipped. In many Hindu shrines an Irish print of the Sacred Heart of Jesus nestles next to Ganesh, the elephant-headed god of prophecy and family. Buddhists, Jews, Muslims and many religious Westerners who would not call themselves Christians revere Jesus of Nazareth, son of Mary, man of truth, man of sorrows, man of compassion, man of wisdom, authentic embodiment of the human mystery. Without needing to define the title technically (*a* or *the*) most people would pass the term 'Son of God'. Jesus, the meditator, arrived at this universality by human means,

[3] Lk 6:12.

through self-knowledge. And his self-knowledge was rooted in prayer, the struggle to be human and the holiness of human love.

⌒⌒⌒

There is an Hasidic saying that angels stand but a holy person moves on. Self-knowledge is dynamic. When we know ourselves we are changed from what we were. If relationship is to stimulate the growth of self-knowledge we need to listen to the other person, to keep pace with them, rather than fix and judge them.

If we are merely observing Jesus critically from the safe distance of modern scepticism we are evaluating him as we might judge a performance of Shakespeare or our own performance at work. Our friendship with him will not move far beyond the first stage of relationship. When however our 'meeting' with Jesus the meditator, an historical human being, interacts with our own journey of self-knowledge then the ensuing friendship pulls us into deeper relationship. This evolving friendship is the life of the spirit. As with many friendships it may be difficult to say in retrospect exactly when the decisive turn to intimacy happened.

The next phase of relationship opens in a movement of wonder. If philosophy, according to Aristotle, begins in wonder, so too, as Gregory of Nyssa claimed, God is better known by wonder than thought. Friendship deepens into the being of 'another myself' when the sheer amazing existence of another in our life hits us. With Jesus it is like, after admiring someone at a distance, we realise that we have really fallen in love with them. For many cradle Christians entering the second stage of relationship with Jesus is similar to a couple in an arranged marriage who come to realise that now and to their mutual surprise they love each other. The baptism of water has turned into the baptism of spirit.

Wonder, Coleridge said, is the suspension of the faculty of comparison. When our breath is taken away by a person, by art or by an act of selfless generosity we do not immediately compare it with similar experiences. In the moment of wonder the unique freshness of the experience is complete and sufficient. When a child explores the world everything is new and uniquely wonderful. This is what happens in love, too, when the singularity and uniqueness of the other person achieves a personal universality. The other's separateness has become inseparable from mine. We move together to the other side of the wall.

The second stage of relationship with Jesus is, like this, a movement of wonder. For some it can be a romance, a rush of emotional sweetness in which Jesus is sensed as intimately present now and in a special way *for me*. This is the warmth of new conversion. It brings a felt conviction of religious love: in my affair with Jesus I have found my saviour, the person with whom I am emotionally certain that I want to settle down for the rest of my life. As in all romanticism there can be a mixture of true love and possessive egotism in the devotional stage of the relationship with Jesus. It is bonding but eventually, like all feelings, proves changeable. It is the kind of romantic devotion that eventually matures only as it falls through the successive trap-doors of love. Like all romance it is tested and undergoes change. If it is artificially prolonged it becomes sentimental and sentimentality eventually degenerates into intolerance as the real person is exchanged for an imaginary fulfilment of emotional need. By living through this second stage of relationship we learn the important distinctions of the meaning of a 'saviour'.

⋅◦⋆◦⋆◦⋅

The word 'saviour' has been much abused. The fundamentalist warns that only *his* saviour can save and threatens damnation to those who deny this. Nevertheless, saviours are of concern to everyone as everyone is looking for salvation. This is the problem: our need for salvation is so intense that we too easily fall for the wrong kind of saviour. Jesus cannot be understood fully unless we can see in what sense he truly is a universal saviour.

We are on the lookout for a saviour but often without realising it. We project our need for a saviour onto hopeful-looking candidates: a person we think has been sent into our life to help us personally, or to our organisation to make us more efficient, to our office to improve the atmosphere or to our country to make it great again, to fulfil our personal needs or save us all from ruin and lead us to a glorious destiny. Socially, politically, even economically, we search for visionary leaders who will 'get us out of the mess we are in' and solve all our problems at a stroke. Today with the help of the media we get through saviours at quite a rate. Unrealistic expectations are wrecked in failures, scandals or the loss of media appeal. In the religious dimension the guru cult has swept into the spiritual vacuum of Western society. It often offers the enticing promise of shedding personal responsibility for one's spiritual journey by devotion to a master with a strong personality. Repeated disappointment soon breeds cynicism. We begin to doubt the meaning of salvation itself after so many failed messiahs and false saviours.

Salvation, however, is not only sought through charismatic individuals. Ignore the media focus on celebrity and many social movements can be seen as salvific: the ecological movement, peace and justice organisations, action groups for the abused, the aged, the oppressed or wrongfully imprisoned, movements to humanise medical science and treatment, some of the holistic and new age movements, the movement for homosexual equality, movements to end racial and gender injustice, contemplative communities and networks, interreligious ecumenism. These are *healing* and *prophetic* movements that seek to raise consciousness and enhance the quality of life globally. Working often on parallel lines or cooperatively they try to heal the wounds human beings inflict on themselves. They represent a hopeful face of the globalisation of culture and economics—perhaps even a new dimension of human consciousness turned in shared compassion and wisdom towards the needs of common humanity. These movements offer a common ground and a new way of understanding 'salvation'.

For many today salvation is a meaningful idea if it is connected not only to religion but to the environment and society. This suggests a salvation that is achieved through solidarity with others by collaboration rather than by having it delivered to us ready made. It is easier today to trust a democratised salvation. This is in fact echoed in the basic Christian idea of salvation that we are saved not in isolation but as part of humanity. 'No salvation outside the church', often used to exclude, can also have an inclusive meaning: we are damned by isolation. Modern individualism neglects the common human need for grace, that transcendent help without which the healing force cannot lift us to a new level of consciousness. But it is not all grace in a sense that would render us passive—and predestined. We are no less called, as St Paul put it, to 'work out our salvation with diligence' for ourselves. Buddhism's emphasis on self-reliance is one reason for its appeal to 'post-religious' Westerners. But both the individualism of Buddhism and the Body image of Christianity are complementary aspects of refined insights in both traditions into how the individual and the community relate to liberation and salvation. Buddhism insists on the need for *sangha*, or community and interdependence. The gospels contain a protest against the religious institutionalism that prevents people from coming to personal maturity and laying down their lives of their own free will. Any spiritual path asks for both individual psychological self-reliance as well as the inspiration, correction and consolation of others in the community of a living tradition.

Accepting that we do need to be saved—both *from* something and *for* something—frees us from extreme individualism. When others are seen only as threats to our individual freedom the necessary help of strangers is lost. With it is lost the wonder of finding the unexpected stranger become a timely friend. Seen in focus, salvation is about how interdependent humanity is. Even Sartre, who said that 'hell is other people', needed others to listen to him say so. To seek salvation alone—the danger of modern consumer spirituality—leads into the other and worse hell of total privacy.

An old Desert Father who had spent many years in solitude was upset because he could not penetrate the meaning of a particular passage of scripture. He prayed for the gift of understanding but however hard he tried no insight came. Finally admitting defeat and leaving his cell, he set off to ask one of his hermit neighbours for help. As he was on his way an angel appeared to him. It told the old man that admitting his need for help had brought him both salvation and wisdom. He could return to his cell now and he would soon find the meaning of the passage that was perplexing him.

Many grassroots social and spiritual movements today exemplify a new healing awareness of interdependence. But the role of the individual saviour working within the larger plan of salvation is not thereby negated. It is not only through collective movement that salvation is advanced but it is also found through relationship with a person who has health and can thus mediate healing. A saviour is not someone who extracts us up from the body of humanity and whisks us away to a world of make-believe. A saviour teaches realism. Relationship with a saviour is marked by compassion. A saviour acts with respect both for the way we are made and the way our wounds heal. A saviour's influence pervades rather than invades. It intervenes rather than interferes. It explores rather than exploits. It does not act destructively, but radically, against the disease. It initiates the healing process with an accurate and convincing diagnosis. Of course a saviour does more. He or she is more than a diagnostician or source of consolation. Saviours have something within them which works as a catalyst and changes things. This is possible because the saviour has learned the meaning of sacrifice.

Like us Jesus has suffered and been wounded and so is 'able to sympathise with our weakness'.[4] He made his suffering sacrificial by virtue of his love, his insight into the meaning of his life. The sacrificial love of Jesus highlights the moral meaning of the universe, the gift of unconditional love that awaits us at the heart of reality. In contrast to the mechanistic view of sin and punishment based on *karma*, love transcends the dichotomy of reward and punishment. This is the 'scandal of the Cross', its affront to the rational mind. We cannot perceive its moral meaning without also seeing how all-pervading is the activity of sacrifice throughout the universe. Even matter obeys the law of sacrifice. No physical or psychological, chemical or electrical transaction takes place without the sacrificial offering or yielding of one to another, the giving up of separateness to a greater whole. This unconscious law of sacrifice reaches plenitude when human consciousness becomes capable of, indeed longs for, the sacrifice we call love: the laying down of one's life for one's friends. This is the mystery of the divine sacrifice at the heart of the world which the question of Jesus unveils.

The pagan face of sacrifice, on the other hand, terrifies. It demands the appeasement of the anger of some omnipotent majesty. It is threatening, diminishing and destructive to human beings. This face of sacrifice greedily, meaninglessly strips us of what is precious to us without transforming it. It offends humanity rather than ennobling it. Yet the earliest human symbols also articulate the conviction that love transforms blind fate into destiny. Even what is inevitable can be freely embraced as a sacrifice. Seeing this gives salvific power even to death. Transformed as sacrifice by love even death can save.

In many ways today we are reverting to a paganism that views personal sacrifice as destructive, the enemy of self-fulfilment. That fear of laying down our life, which the early Christian martyrs seemed to have triumphed over, blocks the vision of the Friend for whom we can lay down our life willingly. Self-fixated on self-fulfilment we cannot see the Other we need in order to love. The saviour restores this vision by his sacrifice. He helps us see the freedom of other-centredness, the friendliness of the other. Courage comes when the ego's desires and fears are dispelled and the unclouded mind sees clearly. Until then, failing to see that there are two sides to individ-

[4] Heb 4:15.

uality, we fear sacrifice because it threatens our individual existence. If, from fear, we run away from sacrifice, we disturb the harmony and order of the universe. In the chaos that builds up, the ego's rejection of love and its denial of death deflect the demands of sacrifice from ourselves onto others. Those who refuse to sacrifice themselves usually sacrifice others. They seek scapegoats. Or they install others in positions of power to sacrifice on their behalf. Or, in a still more perverse disorder, they make sacrifice into self-mutilation and self-destruction.

It is in some such view of sacrifice that we must learn to see Jesus as a saviour whose sacrifice restores order to humanity. His laying down of his life in love for his friends, for humanity, is a great example. But his truth was so absolute that his sacrifice changes the way we see and experience ourselves. His death touches us by the power of love: the truth that sets us free. By his sacrifice of himself a universal healing is enacted in which, beyond our imagining or desire, we experience ourselves loved.

Learning to see the life and death of Jesus in this way is ultimately dependent on the light shed upon it by his Resurrection. Until we see that that is the light in which we see him, the sacred truth of sacrifice will be misinterpreted. It will seem destructive rather than creative, as bloody rather than healing, as horrid rather than beautiful, as sadistic rather than altruistic. In listening to Jesus' question, however, a light is seen that illumines how the loss of self, true sacrifice, is the *gift* of one's self to another. The sacrifice of redemptive suffering is a universal spiritual intuition. Each religion reveres it and expresses different aspects of its truth. The Hebrew prophet:

> And yet ours were the sufferings he bore, ours the sorrows he carried. But we thought of him as someone punished, struck by God and brought low. Yet he was pierced through for our faults, crushed for our sins. On him lies a punishment that brings us peace and through his wounds we are healed.[5]

And the Buddhist sage:

> If the suffering of many disappears because of the suffering of one, then a compassionate person should induce that suffering for his own sake and for the sake of others.[6]

[5] Is 53:4-5.
[6] Santideva, A Guide to the Bodhistava Way of Life, trans. Wallace (Snow Lion Publications: Ithaca, NY, 1997), 8.105, p. 103.

The saviour *knows* this. His example turns attention away from the fearful, external aspects of sacrifice and subdues the ego's resistance. His silent witness is of himself transformed by what he has let be done to him. This silence teaches the essential nature of sacrifice is *attention*. When we give ourselves faithfully in love to another or heroically for a noble cause, just as when we meditate, we turn the searchlight of consciousness off ourselves. This is the bloodless sacrifice of pure prayer:

> Therefore, my friends, I implore you by God's mercy to offer your very selves to him, a living sacrifice, dedicated and fit for his acceptance, the worship offered by mind and heart. Adapt yourselves no longer to the pattern of this present world but let your minds be remade and your whole nature thus transformed.[7]

It is only when we *feel loved* that the true meaning of sacrifice and transformation can be grasped. By love we are reintegrated into the community of the universe where we belong. Then we are naturally obedient to its laws. But we have first to feel, to believe, that someone has sacrificed himself, unconditionally and in pure attention to us in order to convince us that we are loved. Then we, in turn, become saviours capable of loving others. The saviour has given us the sacred gift of self-knowledge through love that releases the precious healing oil and anoints us. All sacrifice, all self-giving, bestows the Holy Spirit.

> Six days before the Passover Festival Jesus came to Bethany, the home of Lazarus whom he had raised from the dead. They gave a supper in his honour at which Martha served and Lazarus was among the guests with Jesus. Then Mary brought a pound of very costly perfume, pure oil of nard, and anointed Jesus' feet and wiped them with her hair till the house was filled with the fragrance.[8]

In Luke's account of this scene the expensive jar containing the precious oil is smashed open to release its contents. Judas, representing everyone's ego, misses the meaning of the sacrifice and sees only the cost and waste. Jesus' sacrifice applies the healing oil to a humanity that, in its ego, rejects the very notion of salvation. He fulfils in his individual humanity the cosmic law of the unconditional gift. The gift needs simply to be accepted by those it is offered to if the sacrifice

[7] Rom 12:1-2.
[8] Jn 12:1-4.

is to be fully accomplished. The offer stays on the table indefinitely: this is the significance of the salvation that comes into the world, into the range of the humanly possible, through Jesus. And it in no way diminishes what the other teachers of humanity have also, each in their turn, uniquely offered us for our journey—including all the wisdom traditions leading to enlightenment.

Completing the ritual cycle of the giving and receiving of a gift is the work that satisfies humanity and God. There are many gifts of love, however, that are not accepted. Fear, desire, anger or wounded-ness can wreak such isolation that it makes it impossible to receive what is offered. No human life escapes some experience of this terrible wreckage. But the healing gift of sacrifice does not fail even in the worst cases of failure, betrayal and disappointment. Love *cannot* be ineffective if it is patient, as long as its self-offering remains uncon-ditionally open. If love is indeed stronger than death, then hope does spring eternal. And despair is shown then to be the attempt of the ego to immortalise its suffering.

The gift of love has an objective potential reality while it waits with divine patience for a response. Saving love must be unconditional. The saviour unconditionally shares a universal love that he has un-covered in himself on behalf of others to whom he offers it. He does not withdraw the offer when he is ignored or rejected. In the Bodhi-sattva tradition of Tibetan wisdom love runs through innumerable aeons. Because of the unconditional nature of his sacrifice (the divine agape) the saviour saves us by love since eventually that offer *must* be accepted. No one can cling to the isolated side of the wall for ever. There is always a point, if only the point of physical death, at which the ego will yield and say yes. Were the saviour, the one offering love, to punish our rejection or withdraw his gift he would be shown to be a false messiah. He would become just another hurt and judgemental ego. The saviour knows he will not immediately succeed but that his sacrifice will eventually be justified.

I have not come to judge the world but to save the world.[9]

꙳O꙳O꙳O꙳

Salvation means being loved patiently *into* the freedom to love. The Cross on which Jesus died is a supreme and efficient symbol of love.

[9] Jn 12: 47.

It teaches that we are saved both from the fear which is the negation of love and from the foolish impatience which so often ruins it.

When you look at the Cross you may see only horrible suffering and injustice. If you were told without explanation that the person hanging on the Cross died in this awful way 'for you' how can you respond to that? You might even feel emotionally assaulted. For a child to be taught that this bloody death was undergone on your behalf is bewildering. It can make you wonder what you personally did wrong to make this necessary, if it was your fault. Then begin the feelings of guilt and anger that so many Westerners harbour towards the people behind this incompetent teaching of salvation. You are told to feel grateful but end up feeling shame. Seeing the way that people often first get introduced to Jesus as saviour it is hardly surprising they just want to look away from the Cross and look for something more positive.

The Cross however should be contemplated. Because it is unavoidably present in every dimension of human experience. Even when badly explained it is a necessary symbol. Perhaps this is why so may non-believers wear it around their necks! Its image of human dismemberment is accurate and cathartic. The Cross of Jesus plays this role for humanity because it expresses what has always and will always be most painfully true about being human. We are broken beings and we tend towards death. But it also teaches that what has been broken apart needs to be re-membered. The Cross is a saving symbol of what is undergone in the deepest part of each person. It proves that *we are understood*, even in those depths which are most mysterious and painful to accept in ourselves. And we are understood by that source of the universe that we often fear is cold, unfeeling, as horribly indifferent to us as the weather. The Cross starkly confronts us with the reality of innocent suffering and death. It also triumphs over them with a mysterious humility and asserts the essential goodness and beauty of life and the true, unfailing power of healing love and joy.

Rather than telling us that we must suffer in order to please God, the Cross of Jesus is a sign of the love which repairs us. As Jesus was led to the Cross the love in his heart had reached the fully individuated, *truly individual* state. He could forgive his enemies because he understood them from within and knew that they were within him. He had already considered them his friends. This inclusive love and even his physical body were thus consciously indivisible from the whole of humanity, past and future. He was one with the cosmos before time began. His love was God: who is the love which is simultaneously creative and redemptive and who flows through every open, broken heart. Like prophets before and since, Jesus had been ignored, misrepresented, mistreated. The exhausting truthfulness of his love, then as now, was too painful to accept, too good to believe. If his sacrificial love had to find expression in the Cross rather than in a more pleasant way it is only because its offer had been rejected. So Man, not God made the blood of the Cross necessary to show us that the sacrifice which saves us is always love. We demanded it because we cannot believe that we are as good, as loveable, as valuable to the universe, as close to the Kingdom as Jesus tells us we are.

We re-enact the Cross, as victims or as crucifiers, many times each day. When we gossip, spread rumours, slander or lie we are crucifiers. When we mock cruelly, strip others of their dignity, denigrate, humiliate or marginalise others on the basis of race or creed we are the soldiers who cast lots for the robe of the Crucified at the foot of his cross. When we sacrifice others in our stead, when we run away from ourselves, we are the soldiers piercing the sacred side. Every divorce court, every family or community, institution or multi-national corporation where dignity is denied is a Golgotha. For every human being there is a crucifier. And every human being can become a crucifier. The Cross shows how painful it is for human beings, individually and collectively to accept the offer of love and to hear the truth about themselves. Resistance to love turns the heart to stone and dams up the river of compassion that heals humanity. In refusing to be pierced open the heart is frozen by the fear of dying and rising again. Such deep self-evasion in humanity is what makes sacrifice so painful.

Theologically it can be said that the Incarnation would have happened even if there had been no sin in the world. Sacrifice could have been painless and joyful. The self-pouring of the Creative love of the cosmos into one individual would still have happened. God *needed* to sacrifice Himself in this way: *word made flesh* is simply the natural endgame of the evolutionary process. The creative force must express itself in a singular point in creation just as all consciousness seeks unity and simplicity. The creating intelligence *must* become what it creates if it is to fully express its own nonduality. Word hungers in love to become flesh.

But there was sin, old age, suffering and death, everything that the Buddha knew as *dukkha*, incompleteness and unsatisfactoriness. In its endless, manifold suffering humanity struggles with its desperate addiction to consoling falsehoods. It masters the art of denying what it finds unpleasant. Because of the agelong human habit of denial, of preferring fantasy to reality, when the moment of Incarnation came the divine self-sacrifice expressed itself as a salvation through suffering. But the same word that creates also heals. Its mission became the healing of humanity's greatest cause of suffering, the wound of the rejection of love and the laceration of self-hatred. A human healer who was himself wounded unto death would effect an all-embracing salvation. A messenger who was not to be recognised until his sacrifice was complete. The meaning and efficiency of his Cross is not limited by time or space. The humanity of Jesus is a singular historical point. But it extends backwards and forwards in time revealing, to those who see this perspective, his divinity. The wholeness of Jesus (his whole life, teaching, death and resurrection) touches every human being and insentient creation too. The Cross is thus also a cosmic reality translating the divine self-sacrifice into human terms through the tragedy of Golgotha. It is echoed in every human act of love and witness to the truth. The Cross is more than the logo of a religion. It is a symbol of humanity.

⟨०⟩⟨०⟩⟨०⟩

According to both Freud and Sri Ramana, the source of suffering is the ego.

Salvation unfolds as a shock to the whole ego system of perception. The shock stimulates awareness. This is accompanied by a profound sense of disorientation as the ego's way of seeing everything revolving around itself is overturned. The new way of seeing changes the way we behave. Vision not brute will is the means of salvation: a change of heart comes before a change of deeds. We cannot separate the way we see from what we do. The work of salvation heals the split in ourselves by making the inner and the outer dimensions of self one and the same. Not only do we *do* what we see but, according to St John, we even *become* what we see:

> What we shall be has not yet been disclosed, but we know that when it is disclosed we shall be like him, because we shall see him as he is. Everyone who has this hope before him purifies himself as Christ is pure.[10]

[10] I Jn 3:2-3.

Salvation is in a sense a trick of the light, a change of perception. And the saviour is something of a magician. We are not being fooled; it is *real* magic. But he makes something disappear from one place and reappear in another. This confounds our expectations, changes the pattern of the mind and releases the laughter of joy, discovery and relief. Jesus disappeared from the sight of his disciples after the Resurrection at the breaking of the bread, at the very moment when their eyes were opened to recognise him. 'He comes to us hidden and salvation consists in our recognising him,' as Simone Weil said. 'Where is he that we can we see him?' is the sceptic's question. 'Everywhere, where do we not see him, why are we failing to recognise him?' is the believer's response.

The cheap trick of the magician's sleight of hand is not a bad image for the expensive mystery of salvation. The gasp of the bewildered audience becomes a sigh of relief when we realise that a new way of seeing is not less than a new way of being. What has disappeared has not been lost. Sacrifice did not destroy individuality but transformed it beyond the boundaries of egotism. This is only understood when we *experience* our uniqueness and discover in its deepest solitude that we are saved *from* the hell of loveless fear and isolation. Saved for what? For divinisation, for a joyful homecoming, for being fearlessly ourselves, for loving divinely and creating the world anew. Turning from separateness to indivisibility is ecstatic. Ecstasy means to *stand outside* the normal parameters of time and space and to rise above the limitations of all psychological and material conditioning.

Salvation is a taste of the Kingdom. Like the Kingdom it is everywhere. It cannot be objectified and analysed but it can be known by love in faith. Two sayings from the Gospel of Thomas illustrate how the Kingdom is omnipresent:

> The disciples said to him, 'When will the kingdom come?' Jesus said, 'It will not come if you look for it. Nor can you say "it is here" or "it is there." For the kingdom of the Father is already spread out over the earth, but people don't see it.[11]

> The disciples said to him, 'When will the repose of the dead happen, and when will the new world come?' Jesus said, 'What you are waiting for has already come, but you don't recognise it.'[12]

[11] *Gospel of Thomas*, 113.
[12] Ibid., 51.

To recognise, it is first necessary to look. To listen, it is first necessary to hear. To feel, it is first necessary to be touched. We move to the second level of knowing Jesus as we sense that the healing that is happening in us is integral to our relationship with him. However superficial that relationship may have been up to this point it is now acquiring depth as the meaning of our own experience, self-knowledge, becomes more conscious. The faith that heals us has matured. We have still far to go—in wholeness and in our ability to say who we think he is. But the knowledge that we are following the way is inescapably reassuring. The self-transcendence that is the condition of self-knowledge also becomes more conscious and we see beyond ourselves. When we are ready we also see the greater world we find we are part of. We are now ready for the next stage of knowing him. In this new perspective the form in which we have to date known Jesus also changes.

We are beginning to see reality *with* him, in his Mind, as he knows it.

⟨∘⟨∘⟨∘⟩

We speak of the 'Cosmic Christ' not the cosmic Jesus. Yet the gospel asserts continuity between those two aspects of the one person: the historical Jesus and the Risen Christ. The Cosmic Christ is not a universal archetype projected onto the historical Jesus but the core of Jesus' identity revealed in the way history and geography were transcended in the Resurrection. Jesus the individual is *indivisible* from the whole of humanity (so are we all) but also (and in a way I could not say of myself or you of yourself) as the Word made flesh he is one with the creative source of humanity.

> In the beginning the Word already was. The Word was in God's presence and what God was the Word was. He was with God at the beginning and through him all things came to be; without him no created thing came into being. In him was life and that life was the light of mankind... So the Word became flesh; he made his home among us and we saw his glory, such glory as befits the Father's only Son, full of grace and truth... No one has ever seen God: God's only Son who is nearest to the Father's heart has made him known.[13]

[13] Jn 1:1ff.

St John wrote these mysterious words less than seventy years after Jesus' death. Already reflection on his question had led those listening to it to his cosmic dimension. Here we can see him as a concentration, a recapitulation of the cosmos. The bodiliness of Jesus was not regarded as a denial of this dimension. Quite the reverse, the Cosmic Christ bestowed a new dignity on the body and its capacity to unite the individual to the universe and the creator. For St Irenaeus human beings are the image of God because our bodies have been 'shaped after the pattern of the body of the incarnate God'. Incarnation does not diminish God but shows that 'flesh is capable of God'.

In a poignant episode in the *Bhagavad Gita*, composed about 500 years before the birth of Jesus, Krishna, an avatar of the god Vishnu, reveals the full extension of his cosmic body to his human friend Arjuna:

> If the light of a thousand suns suddenly arose in the sky, that splendour might be compared to the radiance of the Supreme Spirit.

> And Arjuna saw in that radiance the whole universe in its variety, standing in a vast unity in the body of the God of gods.

> Trembling with awe and wonder, Arjuna bowed his head and joining his hands in adoration he thus spoke to his God. I see in thee all gods, O my God; and the infinity of the beings of thy creation . . . Nowhere I see a beginning, a middle or end of thee, O God of all, Form infinite.[14]

Having seen what none had seen before Arjuna thrilled with joy, yet his heart trembled in fear. He longed and asked to see again the gentle, human face of Krishna his friend. When this prayer was granted he 'returned to his own self and his heart knew peace'.[15]

What was expressed mythically in the friendship between Arjuna and Krishna became historical in the friendship between Jesus with his disciples and—in the Resurrection—with all humanity. In fact his cosmic dimension as the incarnate Logos had already begun to dawn on the first Christians even before they stopped counting the days to his Second Coming. Gradually they realised that the time of the Spirit is not measurable on the calendar and that the 'Day of Christ' is the

---

[14] *Bhagavad Gita*, 11:12-16.
[15] Ibid., 11:45, 51.

present moment. His incarnation continues after his death and Resurrection, in them, in us and in the world. His presence grows stronger
as time extends his historical absence. They came to sense that 'on
the cross he had discarded the cosmic powers and authorities like a
garment' and that

> He is the image of the invisible God; his is the primacy over all
> created things. In him everything in heaven and on earth was
> created, not only things visible but also the invisible orders ...
> the whole universe has been created through him and for him.
> And he exists before everything, and all things hold together in
> him ... Through him God chose to reconcile the whole universe
> to himself, making peace through the shedding of his blood upon
> the cross—to reconcile all things, whether on earth or in heaven,
> through him.

> ... it is in Christ that the complete being of the Godhead dwells
> embodied and in him you have been brought to completion.
> Every power and authority in the universe is subject to him as
> Head.[16]

Paul's audience in Colossae, to which he wrote these words, was a
small group of Christians in what is now a small town in the west of
Turkey. They were a mixture of Jews and Gentiles influenced by prevailing beliefs in the 'elements' and 'spirits' that control the universe.
Taking these beliefs as his starting point Paul (or another author) drew
one of the first great descriptions of Jesus as the Cosmic Christ. After
the triumphalism of a millennium and a half of established Churches
and Constantinian Christianity we need to remember how very modest
was the crucible in which this vision of the Cosmic Christ was first
formed. For the early Christians Jesus the Christ was not a symbol of
political or religious authority. If anything he was seen in opposition
to worldly power precisely because he transcended it in the spiritual
realm. At first, if they took him seriously at all, magistrates, high
priests and emperors saw him as a threat not a support. Paul was
writing his vision of the Cosmic Christ from a prison cell. Christianity
was a marginal and ridiculed sect among many cults sweeping the
Roman Mediterranean. All this shows that the Cosmic Christ should
not be confused with the triumphalist Christ of later Western culture.

[16] Col 1:15-20; 2:9-10.

The Cosmic Christ *precedes* the political triumph of Christianity and its meaning was blurred when Jesus became identified with the kingdoms of this world.

Where in our *personal* relationship with Jesus does his cosmic meaning become felt? When we find him within ourselves. When we meet him in the cell of self-knowledge. The cosmic dimension of Jesus as the Christ is understood through the experience of the *indwelling* Christ. Paul, who sees Christ's personal identity as co-extensive with the universe and as its unifying principle, speaks of the 'secret being this: Christ within you the hope of a glory to come'. The Cosmic Christ and the indwelling Christ are two sides of the nonduality of Jesus. His cosmic dimension can be perceived only in relation to his personal, intimate presence. In the energy of his Resurrection he at the same time touches the depths of every human person and the outermost reaches of the universe.

A full experience of this third stage of relationship with Jesus is Christian faith at its most fully realised. It is probably very rare. It is not necessarily those who say 'Lord, Lord' most loudly or who force their faith onto others most confidently who have realised it. The test of faith is not the strength of the institution but personal authentic-ity—although the authenticity of the institution depends upon the strength of the faith of its members. The most complete and confident expression of knowing who Jesus is derives from the personal rela-tionship with Jesus—which is rooted in silence. It will not be afraid to declare itself, despite the inadequacy of words, but the genuine experience of Christ would never force itself on others or try to compel others to believe.

Our sense of the Cosmic Christ develops continually and in new ways by recognising the Risen Jesus who returns to our world of duality in the nonduality of the Spirit. Faith grows by being experi-enced, tested and practice. It is experienced when it is celebrated in the perception of how Christ 'dances in a thousand places'. His follow-ers recognise him unexpectedly and freshly in more and more people and places because through the Resurrection Jesus has been univer-salised without the loss of his recognisable individuality. Those who have found him in their own deepest centre also sense how he must be present in the universal centre: among the two hundred billion galaxies we can presently count in the universe, in the street-person huddled in a cold storefront, in the compassion of the passer-by who stops and cares, in the atoms and corpuscles by which they are known to each other.

·◠·◠·◠·

What does Resurrection mean? Our way of listening to the question of Jesus eventually turns on this question. At the end of the 1994 John Main Seminar, The Good Heart, the Dalai Lama, who had spent three days commenting on and discussing the gospels, turned the attention of his remarkable mind to a gospel account of the Resurrection. After sharing further insights he remarked that the Resurrection was a unique feature of Christianity with no specific parallel in Buddhism. The Resurrection does not fully translate into concepts such as reincarnation or the Boddhisattva. The Dalai Lama then paused and looking up from the page of the gospel he was reading, surprised a Christian sitting beside him by asking him what the Resurrection meant. It was a moment of stillness. A meeting-point was created through an inno cent question between two great traditions that serve and seek the truth. Once again the appropriate question asked in the right way at the right time prepared the way for truth. It was another instance of the redemptive question. It contained its own answer at a level deeper than the words it used. This was the level of friendship. In the Dalai Lama's love and trust, his reverence for the Christian mystery, his humorous acceptance of differences, his question expressed the simple human friendship in which the meaning of the Resurrection is most likely to be glimpsed.

Everything in this book that has reflected on the meaning of Jesus' redemptive question is highlighted by the Dalai Lama's question about the Resurrection. To read the gospels, to pray in word and sacrament, to meditate, to live within a Christian community, to study the traditions of orthodoxy, to alleviate the suffering of others—these are all ways of experiencing the Resurrection. We only discover its meaning by experiencing it, by *recognising* him. The answer to the Dalai Lama's question resides in an experience which can be known and be named. It can also be known and remain unnamed. Not all churchgoers have listened to the question and many who do not call themselves Christians listen to it deeply and have felt its fruits. Jesus said that many would see and serve him without recognising him.

The Resurrection is an epiphany of reality. A manifestation of the nature and meaning of the cosmos. Whatever is conscious will experience the Resurrection because what happened in Jesus is going to happen to each of us. Jesus did not rise because 'he was God' but because he was fully human. As in everything else in his life Jesus shows in the Resurrection what the real meaning of being human is. And only in the fullness of humanity can we see God. In Jesus we can find both our personal destiny and the end goal of the universe.

‹ᴏⷮᴏⷮᴏ›

Perhaps after all, as spiritual practitioners, it does not matter a great deal what we *say* we believe about Jesus. How we judge him is less important than how he loves us.

Relationship with him unfolds simultaneously at different levels of consciousness. We become aware of these levels with varying degrees of clarity. At times we may be more conscious of meeting him as the living Word of the gospels. At others we may feel his influence on our own process of healing and integration. We will often be better able to recognise him present in responding to the needs of others. Sometimes he will emerge in the context of other religions. He will be recognised in the holiness of individuals whatever their faith. He may be present in the rose that captivates our senses or in the holy mysteries of our bodies. No one dimension of his presence excludes another. Meditation opens the dimension in which he is known and recognised in the present moment in the power of silence.

Friendship, every form of love, compassionate service of others, meditation and devotional prayer, birth and death, loss and gain, beauty, and suffering, commitment, faith and betrayal: all these human experiences awaken the eye of the heart whereby he may be seen. A love of the scriptures and the Eucharist are precious ways in the Christian life of purifying spiritual vision.

‹ᴏⷮᴏⷮᴏ›

'But who do *you* say I am?' His redemptive question has a perennial power to open the eye of the heart and restore us to the true Self. Each generation hears it differently. We can only listen to it as members of our generation. Today we listen to it within the symphony of all the world religions. Some Christians fear that the music of Jesus will be drowned out if it is played alongside that of other faiths. Some prefer to play the Christian tune in an exclusive sound-proofed room. Harmony to them sounds like absorption.

To love your own religion loyally is a great and precious love. But just as to love one person is to grow in love of all humanity, so to love your own religion opens you to the challenge of its universality. We must be prepared for the ebb and flow of the relationship, the coming closer and the withdrawing, the appearances and the disappearances. We cannot see Jesus without also being prepared to lose him from sight because he draws us deeper into that mystery of the Father which is pure light.

I remember my first visit to a Buddhist monastery. I was attracted and impressed by its silence and its concentration on the meditative practice it taught. Many of the Christian monasteries of my acquaintance seemed (in my arrogant judgement) to fall short of this spiritual depth and seriousness. I was aware I had much to learn from Buddhism. For a moment however I felt sheer panic: I would lose my faith, my roots, my God, my identity. I was tempted to run but the monastery was remote and I didn't have a return ticket! The panic passed and my faith, more than ever focused in a sense of relationship to Jesus, seemed to enter a new phase. As I have grown more familiar with other faiths, through friendship and study, my relationship to Jesus has simplified and deepened. As it becomes more open it seems more mysterious. The traditional words of the Creed have grown more lovely and meaningful. I realise that on the other side of the separate Christian ego there is another kind of Christian identity waiting to be discovered. It is discipleship in which we can be more true to Christ and so also to our own journey of self-knowledge.

The question at the heart of this book remains one I can best respond to by listening more attentively to it. Like a secret waiting for us in the bosom of the Father and the mystery of the Mother, the question of Jesus sounds an immeasurable depth of being. Like Bere Island I could not imagine it *not* being there. Calling us always deeper into the mystery of God it plays the beautiful, sad music of humanity with joy and hope. It leads us deeper than humanity's own music into the silence of God which is the simplest and fullest answer of all.

That is why we have to learn to listen more deeply before we answer. Firstly, perhaps, we need to listen to the way Jesus puts his question.

But who do you say I am?

The answer to a question is the way it is asked. We can hardly not be moved, beyond words, by its gentleness, its innocence, the peaceful humility of self-knowledge it carries; by its being addressed directly to *me*. If the answer could be put into words I would suggest here that we might respond to his question by saying, '*You* must help me to know who you are. But *I* say that you, Jesus, are the humility, the humanity, of God.'

Further Reading
A General Bibliography

Abhishiktananda (Henri le Saux), *Prayer* (Delhi: ISPCK, 1967)

Abhishiktananda (Henri le Saux), *Saccidananda* (Delhi: ISPCK, 1974)

Aelred of Rievaulx, *On Spiritual Friendship* (Kalamazoo: Cistercian Publications, 1974)

Bhagavad Gita, trans. Mascaro (London: Penguin, 1962)

Bloom, Metropolitan Anthony, *School for Prayer* (London: Darton, Longman & Todd, 1970)

Borg, Marcus J., *Meeting Jesus again for the First Time* (San Francisco: Harper, 1994)

Brock, Sebastian, ed., *The Syriac Fathers on Prayer and the Spiritual Life* (Kalamazoo: Cistercian Publications, 1970)

Brown, Raymond, E., *An Introduction to the New Testament* (New York: Doubleday, 1997)

Brown, Raymond, et al., *The New Jerome Biblical Commentary* (London: Chapman, 1990)

Carrus, Paul, *The Gospel of Buddha* (Tucson: Omen Press, 1972)

Cassian, John, *Conferences*, trans. Ramsey (New York: Paulist, 1997)

Catechism of the Catholic Church (Vatican City: Libreria Editoria Vaticana, 1994)

Chitty, Derwas J., *The Desert a City* (Oxford: Blackwell, 1966)

Clement of Alexandria, *Works* (Ante-Nicene Christian Library, Edinburgh 1867)

Clement, Olivier, *The Roots of Christian Mysticism* (New York: New York City Press, 1995)

The Cloud of Unknowing and Other Works, trans. Wolters (London: Penguin Classics, 1978)

Dalai Lama, The, *The Good Heart*, ed. Kiely (Boston: Wisdom Publications, 1996)

Dunn, James D.G., *Unity and Diversity in the New Testament*, 2nd ed. (London: SCM Press, 1990)

Eckhart, *Meister Eckhart, a Modern Translation*, trans. Blakney (New York: Harper & Row, 1984)

Evagrius Ponticus, *Chapters on Prayer*, trans. Bamberger (Kalamazoo: Cistercian Publications, 1970)

Freeman, Laurence, *Light Within* (London, New York: Darton, Longman & Todd, 1987)

Freeman, Laurence, *Selfless Self* (London, New York: Darton, Longman & Todd)

Grant, Michael, *Jesus* (London: Sphere, 1978)

Griffiths, Bede, *The New Creation in Christ* (London: Darton, Longman & Todd, 1992)

Hausherr, Irenee, *The Name of Jesus* (Kalamazoo: Cistercian Publications, 1978)

Johnson, Luke Timothy, *The Real Jesus* (San Francisco: Harper 1996)

Johnston, William, *The Wounded Stag*, 2nd ed. (New York: Fordham University Press, 1998)

Julian of Norwich, *Revelations of Divine Love*, trans. Wolters (London: Penguin Books, 1966)

Lossky, Vladimir, *In the Image and Likeness of God*, trans. A.M. Allchin (New York: St. Vladimir's Seminary Press, 1985)

Louth, Andrew, *The Origins of Christian Mystical Tradition from Plato to Denys* (Oxford: Oxford University Press, 1981)

Lyons, Enda, *Jesus: Self-Portrait by God* (New York: Paulist Press, 1994)

Maccoby, Hyam, *Paul and Hellenism* (London: SCM Press, 1991)

Main, John, *Word into Silence* (London: Darton, Longman & Todd, 1980)

Main, John, *The Present Christ* (London: Darton, Longman & Todd, 1985)

Main, John, *Silence and Stillness in Every Season: Daily Readings with John Main*, ed. Harris (London: Darton, Longman & Todd, 1997)

Matthew the Poor, *The Communion of Love* (Crestwood, NY: St. Vladimir's Seminary Press, 1984)

McGinn, Bernard, *The Foundations of Mysticism* (New York: Crossroad, 1991)

Nolan, Albert, *Jesus Before Christianity* (Maryknoll, NY: Orbis Books, 1992)

O'Collins, Gerald, *Christology* (Oxford: Oxford University Press, 1995)

O'Collins, Gerald, *Jesus Risen* (New York: Paulist Press, 1987)

Pakaluk, Michael, ed., *Other Selves: Philosophers on Friendship* (Indianopolis /Cambridge, 1991)

Panikkar, Raimon, *A Dwelling Place for Wisdom* (Louisville, KY: John Knox Press, 1993)

Pelikan, Jaroslav, *Jesus through the Centuries* (New Haven: Yale University Press, 1985)

Rahner, Karl, *The Teaching of Vatican II on the Church and the Future Reality of Christian Life*, 'Quaestiones Disputae' (Freiburg: 1967)

Ramana Maharshi, ed. D. Goodman, *The Spiritual Teaching of Ramana Maharshi* (Berkeley, London: Shambala, 1972)

Ravindra, Ravi, *The Yoga of the Christ in the Gospel according to St John* (Shaftesbury: Element, 1990)

Riches, John K., *A Century of New Testament Study* (Valley Forge, PA: Trinity Press, 1993)

St Basil the Great, *On the Holy Spirit* (Crestwood, NY: St. Vladimir's Seminary Press, 1980)

St John of the Cross, *Collected Works*, trans. Kavanaugh (Washington DC: ICS Publications, 1991)

Sanders, E.P., *Jesus and Judaism* (Philadelphia: Fortress Press, 1985)

The Sayings of the Desert Fathers, trans. B. Ward, (Kalamazoo: Cistercian Publications, 1975)

Schillebeeckx, E., *The Eucharist* (New York: Sheed and Ward, 1968)

Schillebeeckx, E., *On Christian Faith* (New York: Crossroad, 1987)

Sommerfeldt, John R., *The Spiritual Teachings of Bernard of Clairvaux* (Kalamazoo: Cistercian Publications, 1991)

Southern, R.W., *Western Society and the Church in the Middle Ages* (Harmondsworth: Penguin Books, 1970)

Taylor, Charles, *Sources of the Self* (Cambridge, MA: Harvard, 1989)

Underhill, E., *Mysticism* (Oxford: One World, 1993)

Ware, Kallistos, *The Orthodox Way* (Crestwood, NY: St. Vladimir's Seminary Press, 1995)

Weil, Simone, *Gravity and Grace* (New York, London: Ark Publications, 1987)

Weil, Simone, *Waiting on God*, trans. Emma Craufud (London: Routledge & Kegan Paul, 1979)

Wittgenstein, Ludwig, *Culture and Value* (Chicago: University of Chicago Press, 1980)

The World Community for Christian Meditation

Meditation creates community. Since the first Christian Meditation Centre was started by John Main in 1975, a steadily growing community of Christian meditators has spread around the world.

The International Centre in London to co-ordinates this world-wide community of meditators. A quarterly newsletter, giving spiritual teaching and reflection, is sent out from London and distributed from a number of national centres, together with local and international news of retreats and other events being held in the world-wide community. An annual John Main Seminar is held.

The International Centre is funded entirely by donations and especially through a Friends of the International Centre programme.

The World Community for Christian Meditation / International Centre / 23 Kensington Square / London W8 5HN / United Kingdom.
Tel: +44 20 7937 4679 Fax: +44 20 7937 6790
E-mail: wccm@compuserve.com

Web Page

Visit The World Community for Christian Meditation Web site for information, weekly meditation group readings, and discussion at: www.wccm.org

Christian Meditation Centre / 1080 West Irving Park Rd. / Roselle IL 60172.
Tel/Fax: + 1 630 351 2613

John Main Institute / 3727 Abbeywood / Pearland / TX 77584
Tel: +1 281 412 9803 E-Mail: wccmcmc@infohvwv.com

Christian Meditation Centre / 1619 Wight St. / Wall / NJ 07719.
Tel: +1 732 681 6238 Fax: +1 732 280 5999
E-mail: gjryan@aol.com

Christian Meditation Centre / 193 Wilton Road West / Ridgefield / CT 06877.
Tel: +1 203 438 2440 E-mail: pgulick@prodigy.net

The Cornerstone Center for Meditation / 1215 East Missouri Avenue / Suite A-100 / Phoenix, AZ 85014-2149
Tel: +1 602 279 3154 Fax: +1 602 957 3467
E-mail: ecrmjr@worldnet.att.net

Medio Media Ltd.

Medio Media Ltd. is the publishing arm of the World Community for Christian Meditation.

A catalogue of Medio Media's publications—books, audio sets, and videos—is available from:

Medio Media / 15930 N. Oracle Road # 196 / Tucson / AZ 85739.
Tel: +1 800 324 8305 Fax: +1 520 818 2539
Web page: www.mediomedia.com